INFORMATION
WARFARE

INFORMATION WARFARE

CHAOS ON THE ELECTRONIC SUPERHIGHWAY

WINN SCHWARTAU

THUNDER'S MOUTH PRESS
NEW YORK

First edition
First printing, 1994

Published by
Thunder's Mouth Press
632 Broadway, 7th Floor
New York, NY 10012

Library of Congress Cataloging-in-Publication Data

Schwartau, Winn.
Information warfare : chaos on the electronic superhighway /
Winn Schwartau.
    p.   cm.
Includes index.
ISBN 1-56025-080-1 : $22.95
1. Computer security. 2. Computer crimes. I. Title.
QA76.9.A25S354   1994
302.2—dc20   94-2412
                                                                 CIP

Printed in the United States of America

Distributed by
Publishers Group West
4065 Hollis Street
Emeryville, CA 94608
(800) 788-3123

To the future generation of cybernauts who will be born, live, breathe, and die in Cyberspace.

If we did our job right, it will be a most pleasant place to spend one's time.

ACKNOWLEDGMENTS

I REALIZED WHEN I wrote this book how incredibly lucky we are to be living in this country. There are a lot of people less fortunate than we—billions more—and nowhere is it more apparent than when it comes to hope.

I constantly found myself amazed when comparing the enormous wealth of our country, relative to the destitution of more than half the planet. It made me wonder about a lot of things other than just computers. I hope it does the same for you.

While this book is about many things—information, computer technology, systems, governments, and economies—it is really about people. Ultimately that's what it's *all* about.

This book would not have been possible without endless contributions made by thousands of people I have met, in both my physical and virtual worlds. I owe every one of them a debt of thanks for their consistently stimulating discussions.

Most notably, though, I have to thank my wife Sherra, who tolerates the clickety-click-keyboard on my side of the bed, the absurd hours I keep, and the endless travels we endure. Her support and understanding make it all possible.

My kids, Ashley and Adam, are still asking when I will write a book they can read. The next one, guys, is for kids—I promise.

Kristan Noakes-Frye, a dear friend and highly respected

industry observer, provided invaluable insights and commentary, as did Mich Kabay, PhD, the Director of Education at the National Computer Security Association. He ceaselessly forced me to defend and reevaluate my positions. I also want to thank my personal cyberguru Chris Goggans for keeping the ropes on the 'net from getting too tangled.

During the production of this work, I only knew my editor Stephanie Chernikowsi in Cyberspace and much credit to her is due for putting on the final touches.

Unfortunately not enough people "get it," but Neil Ortenberg and Lisa J. Edwards of Thunder's Mouth Press do. This book would not have been possible without their vision and support. They understand that *Information Warfare* needs to be read by more than just the security industry's small choir. It needs to be read, and the message heard, by a large and diversified congregation that is willing to get involved and make a difference.

My thanks to everyone involved and the powers that be for the opportunity to be that voice.

—WINN SCHWARTAU

Contents

An Introduction to Information Warfare

"What we have is technology, organization, and administration out of control, running for their own sake. . . . And we have turned over to this system the control and direction of everything—the natural environment, our minds, our lives."

—CHARLES REICH,
The Greening of America

AT ONE POINT, if not already, you will be the victim of Information Warfare. If not you, then a member of your family or a close friend.

Your company will become a designated target of Information Warfare. If not yesterday or today, then definitely tomorrow. You will be hit.

Why? Because the United States is at war, a war that few of us have bothered to notice. The twentieth century information skirmishes, which are the prelude to global Information Warfare, have begun. Information Warfare is coming. For some, it has already arrived.

This book is about how we as citizens of both the United States and Cyberspace must come to terms with our electronic destiny, leading the world into the twenty-first century and the Information Age. We have some tough choices to make. The information revolution will not be an easy transition and the proposed National Information Infrastructure illuminates the complexity of the third generation of American dreams. But the opportunities are too great and the alternatives too grave for us to ignore. This book provides an overview

11

defining where we are today, where we are going, and what issues we must directly confront if we wish to design our future, not be consumed by it.

As the specter of apocalyptic global warfare recedes into the history books (and stays there!), a collective sigh of complacency is replacing the bomb-shelter hysteria of the midcentury. Despite the fact that nearly 175 million people were killed in the twentieth century from the effects of war and war-related politics, Strangelovian predictions thankfully never came to pass. However, as equally dangerous international economic competition supplants megaton military intimidation, offensive pugnacity will be aimed at the informational and financial infrastructure upon which our Western economy depends.

The Cold War is over and has been replaced by economic warfare, a competition between what is shaping up to be three major trading blocks: North America, Europe, and the Asian Pacific Rim. Richard Nixon was fond of saying in the 1970s and 1980s that World War III had already begun and that it was an economic war; perhaps one that the United States was destined to lose. In retrospect, we might have been more attentive to his prescience.

These three huge economic forces account for about one quarter of the population and eighty percent of the GNP of planet Earth. The stakes are enormous and everyone wants a piece.

The foundation of modern society is based on the availability of an access to information that will drive a thriving economy upward on its course or propel a weak one into a position of power. In today's electronically interconnected world, information moves at the speed of light, is intangible, and is of immense value. Today's information is the equivalent of yesterday's factories, yet it is considerably more vulnerable.

Right now, the United States is leading the world into a globally networked society, a true Information Age where information and economic value become nearly synonymous.

With over 125 million computers inextricably tying us all together through complex land- and satellite-based communications systems, a major portion of our domestic $6 trillion economy depends upon their consistent and reliable operation. Information Warfare is an electronic conflict in which information is a strategic asset worthy of conquest or destruction. Computers and other communications and information systems become attractive first-strike targets.

As I told a Congressional Committee on June 27, 1991, "Government and commercial computer systems are so poorly protected today that they can essentially be considered defenseless—an electronic Pearl Harbor waiting to happen. As a result of inadequate security planning on the part of both the government and the private sector, the privacy of most Americans has virtually disappeared."[1]

Computers at Risk, a report published in October of 1990 by the National Research Council, clearly echoed my sentiments. The authors concluded, "The modern thief can steal more with a computer than with a gun. Tomorrow's terrorist may be able to do more damage with a keyboard than with a bomb."[2] In a recent study, two-thirds of Americans polled said that computer usage should be curtailed if their personal privacy was at risk. As a country, we are only now beginning to recognize and accept the fact that our personal and economic interests are indeed merging with our national security interests.

Information Warfare is an integral component of the new economic and political world order. Economic battles are being fought and will continue to be fought, ultimately affecting every American citizen and company as well as the national security of the United States. As terrorism now invades our shores, we can expect attacks upon not only airliners and water supplies, but upon the money supply, a sure way to strike terror into millions of people with a single keystroke.

Since World War II the United States has based its defensive position on our adversaries' capabilities, not their intentions. Voila! The arms race. However, we have not kept up with the Joneses. The world is moving into Cyberspace, but our nation's economically competitive defensive posture is still firmly landlocked.

Cyberspace is a brave new world that only luminaries such as Marshall McLuhan and Arthur C. Clarke glimpsed in their mind's eyes, but not even they could presage the uncertainties unleashed in the last two decades.

Imagine a world where information is the medium of exchange and cash is used only for pedestrian trade. A world where information, not English, German, Japanese, or Russian, is the common language. A world where the power of knowledge and information usurp the strength of military might. A world totally dependent upon new high-tech tools that make information available instantaneously to anyone, anywhere, at any time. A world where he who controls the information, controls the people. A world where electronic privacy no longer exists.

Now imagine a conflict between adversaries in which information is the prize, the spoils of war. A conflict with a winner and a loser. A conflict which turns computers into highly effective offensive weapons. A conflict which defines computers and communications systems as primary targets forced to defend themselves against deadly, invisible bullets and bombs.

Imagine rival economies battling for a widening sphere of global influence over the electronic financial highways, sparing no expense to ensure victory.

Then imagine a world made up of companies that compete and settle disputes by regularly blitzkrieging each other's information infrastructure. A world where electronic and competitive espionage are the expected manner of conducting business.

Or imagine a world in which personal revenge, retribution, getting even is only a keystroke away.

"What kind of world is this? This is the world of Information Warfare. And we, as individuals and as a country, are not prepared for the future we are creating.

In Information Warfare, Information Age weaponry will replace bombs and bullets. These weapons are no longer restricted to the Government or the CIA or KGB. Computer and communications weapons are available from catalogs, retail store fronts, and trade shows. Many can be built from hobbyist parts at home. And, of course, the military is developing its own arsenal of weapons with which to wage Information Warfare.

Information Warfare is about money. It's about the acquisition of wealth, and the denial of wealth to competitors. It breeds Information Warriors who battle across the Global Network in a game of cyberrisk.

Information Warfare is about power. He who controls the information controls the money.

Information Warfare is about fear. He who controls the information can instill fear in those who want to keep their secrets a secret. It's the fear that the Bank of New York felt when it found itself $23 billion short of cash in only one day.

Information Warfare is about arrogance, the arrogance that comes from the belief that one is committing the perfect crime.

Information Warfare is about politics. When the German government sponsors intelligence-agency hacking against U.S. computers, the concept of *ally* needs to be redefined. Or when Iran takes aim at the U.S. economy by state-sponsored counterfeiting, we should have a glimmer that conflict is not what it once was.

Information Warfare is about survival. France and Israel developed their respective economies and based entire industries on stealing American secrets. Japan and Korea purloin American technology as it comes off the drawing boards with the help of their governments.

Information Warfare is about defiance and disenfranchisement in both modern and Third World societies. From the inner cities of Cyberspace come fringe-element hackers with nothing to lose. Some will band together to form Cyberspace's gangs, Cyberspace's organized crime. They recognize the economic benefits of waging Information Warfare.

Information Warfare is about the control of information. As a society we maintain less and less control as Cyberspace expands and electronic anarchy reigns. Given global conditions of the late 1980s and 1990s, Information Warfare is inevitable. Today's planet offers ripe conditions for Information Warfare, conditions which could not have been foreseen even a few short years ago.

Information Warfare currently costs the United States an estimated $100–300 billion per year, and the financial impact on our economy increases every year. Almost 5% of our GNP slithers through the Global Network and out of our control, thereby hurting deficit reduction efforts and impacting our export base and the current trade imbalance. With billions less in commerce, lower taxable revenues and taxable assets deprive the government of its fair share of profits. As a country, more than our image is tarnished by our role as victim in the Information Wars. Our credit is less credit-worthy; our ability to buy and trade suffers; our political and diplomatic impact is reduced because our economic strength is no longer that of the unquestioned leader. We're not the only tough guy on the block anymore.

But an annual $200-plus billion loss is mainly about people, some three to eight million Americans who might otherwise be working. They, too, are the victims of Information Warfare. Information Warfare takes advantage of our reliance on, indeed our addiction to, automation and modern computerized niceties. Information Warfare attacks our very way of life.

The threat of a future computer Chernobyl is not an empty one. It is only a question of who and when. Information Warfare is available to anyone with an agenda and an attitude, and can be waged at three distinct levels of intensity, each with its own goals, methods, and targets.

Class 1: Personal Information Warfare

There is no such thing as electronic privacy. The essence of our very being is distributed across thousands of computers and data bases over which we have little or no control. From credit reports to health records, from Department of Motor Vehicles computers to court records to video rentals, from law enforcement computers to school transcripts to debit card purchases, from insurance profiles to travel histories to our personal bank finances, everything we do and have done is recorded somewhere in a digital repository.

The sad fact is that these very records which define us as an individual remain unprotected, subject to malicious modification, unauthorized disclosure, or out-and-out destruction. Social Security Administration employees have sold our innermost secrets for twenty-five dollars per name. Worse yet, as of today, there is nothing you can do to protect the digital you. You are not given the option or the opportunity to keep yourself and your family protected from electronic invasions of privacy.

Your life can be turned absolutely upside down if the digital you ceases to exist. Electronic murder in Cyberspace: You are just gone. Try proving you're alive; computers don't lie. Or if the picture of the digital you is electronically redrawn just the right way, a prince can become a pauper in microseconds. In Cyberspace, you are guilty until proven innocent.

Class 2: Corporate Information Warfare

Corporate management has little feel for just how weak and defenseless their corporate assets have become. Although the wealth of corporations is increasingly measured in the timeliness and value of their information, no company lists information assets on its balance sheet. Yet without that information, the economic stability of that company is called into question. Putting a company out of business by attacking its information systems may soon become a preferred method of economic and political competition and retribution. The weapons and techniques of Information Warfare are now as common as spreadsheets and calculators.

Corporate board rooms often take elaborate precautions to protect themselves against the statistical probability that a tornado will blow away their operations centers. The one-in-a-million chance that a flood will rage through downtown Denver prompts companies to dig into nearby mountains to build underground vaults, expected to survive a direct fifty megaton hit. What companies have not prepared themselves for, however, is a well organized offensive assault against their information systems—not by Mother Nature, but by man.

We shall discover that it is difficult to indict corporate America alone on all of these counts. The last fifteen years of spiraling growth in information processing has been and is a world-shaking revolution driven by heady technical successes and evangelical visions. Meanwhile, diligence in weighing the risks associated with placing our entire faith on a technical infrastructure remains in short supply.

As we shall see, the federal government must shoulder much of the blame for our current posture. In fact, it is often not in the government's best interest to assist us in protecting our computers and networks. Their noncommittal attitudes have even harmed efforts now under way to enhance personal privacy and commercial national economic security.

Nonetheless, inane antique policies continue unabated, and in some cases, overt attempts on the part of the federal government have further undermined the electronic privacy of every American citizen. Even President Clinton's proposal to address personal privacy and protect American businesses was met with nearly universal derision, suspicion, and doubt. No matter how hard they try, politicians just don't get it.

Class 3: Global Information Warfare

Collective Capitol Hill and White House wisdom has not yet realized that information is a vital national asset. Still thinking in terms of military throw-weight, oil reserves, Japanese cars, and illegal aliens, they miss the fundamental concepts behind the New World Order, the National Information Infrastructure, and our place in the econotechnical Global Network.

Outside of a forward-thinking few in the bowels of the Pentagon and related intelligence services, national security assets are viewed as those tangible items with a value that is concrete, quantifiable, and replaceable. Information, on the other hand, is intangible and does not have an immediately quantifiable monetary worth—unless you lose it. Then it costs a great deal more than you ever thought.

As we move into Cyberspace, we must not ignore the possibilities that an unknown future may bring. We must take off the blinders and accept—not deny—that the New World Order is full of bad guys as well as good guys. We must prepare ourselves for contingencies that we might prefer not to consider, but such planning will be necessary to our national well-being. We have to accept that as the wealth of our nation shifts from smokestack to cybercash, our once well-defined borders are now ethereal concepts with hazy delineations at best.

We will find that it is our job to prepare ourselves and future generations for a world filled with hope and possibilities we couldn't have envisioned only a decade ago, but equally fraught with dangers and obstacles also never considered. Both will be as commonplace and normal for our descendants as hot running water is for us.

In our explorations, we will unfortunately find that a well financed, dedicated adversary has the capability—and I emphasize the word capability—to wage war against nation-states and political or economic spheres of influence as never before. We will find that international conflict may well be waged on the world's information highways or on our own National Information Infrastructure. We must begin to defend ourselves now.

We must ask, then, why will information warfare be fought? Is it a foregone conclusion? A necessary component of our future? The answers are timely and unique to the Information Age and the promise of a National Information Infrastructure. We will see that Information Wars are inevitable for many reasons, given our place in history:

1. The incredibly rapid proliferation of high-quality, high-performance electronic information systems have created the Global Network—Cyberspace—thus redefining how we conduct business. Not only did business and government buy into technology, but tens of millions of individuals were, within less than a decade, suddenly empowered with tools and capabilities previously limited to a select few. The comparatively simple technology required for Information Warfare is universally available. Technological anarchy is the result.

The Global Network is a historically unprecedented highway system that defies nationalism and borders. It places the keys to the kingdom, to our wealth and our digital identity, within equal reach of everyone with a computer. *Capability* as distinct from motivation or intent is a key theme that will be repeated many times throughout this book.

2. While we as a planet withdraw from a bipolar militaristic stand off, we unexpectedly find ourselves joined by dozens of new nation-states filled with unique nation-state histories, each competing for its own identity. The failure of communism does not mean that our system of democratic capitalism automatically wins and that every newly created nation-state will adapt. There are other alternatives, and not all of them are compatible. Self-interest rides high in the early part of this decade.

The rules of the competition for global economic and political influence aren't the same for everyone. We as Americans play by an old rule book in which goodness, Mom, and apple pie define our competitive ethos. Others are less likely to stick to the outmoded Puritan ethic by which we won the Industrial Revolution. Some will willingly beg, borrow, or steal what they want, in any way that they can. Others will resort to physical violence in the pursuit of their agendas, but Americans just don't work that way. America and Americans are still often viewed as spoiled, self-indulgent brats demanding instant gratification. That image makes us inviting targets.

3. Only twenty-five percent of the planet can be considered developed, leaving several billion inhabitants in the unenviable position of being the Have Nots. The Haves are the comparatively rich countries in Western Europe, Japan, some of the Pacific Rim, and, of course, North America. The Have Nots are everyone else. With the Global Network pouring avalanches of information in the forms of text, sound, and especially visual images, across the borders to the Have Nots, the Have Nots very quickly want to become Haves. Through CNN and *Dynasty* and upscale sitcoms and global programming, the Have Nots see for themselves how we, the other half, live, and they want their share of the pie. When there's nothing to lose, there's nothing to fear. The only way is up; going after the King of the Hill—America—is an obvious route.

4. Greed is in no short supply, and few individuals, businesses, or countries are exempt. Business and governments constantly jockey for advantage over each other, often relying on less-than-legal techniques to gain an edge. With the Global Network in place, and the proliferation of technology for everyone, greed has found its way into the fingertips of people who might otherwise never commit a crime. Greed operates at all levels, and due to the vulnerability of most information systems, provides ample opportunity to exploit their weaknesses for stupendous profits. Information Warfare offers tremendous financial gain to the winner and devastation to the loser.

5. The effects of Information Warfare are unique in the annals of conflict. InfoWars can be fought by remote control,

the ringleaders comfortably invisible behind a keyboard ten thousand miles away. No longer is it necessary to intrude physically upon the intended victim's turf. The Global Network offers a million points of entry.

The computer terrorist can inflict indiscriminate damage on millions of people with a single keystroke, sowing fear, suspicion, and doubt. Information Warfare is a low-budget, high-tech vehicle for mass destruction.

6. Information Warfare is a low risk/high reward endeavor. The odds of getting caught are low, of being prosecuted lower still, and of being convicted almost nil. On the international front, countries cannot agree what to do with nuclear weapons, much less an Information Warrior sitting behind a keyboard.

7. Essentially, we don't trust computers. They process information far too fast for us to comprehend, hence we perceive them as being out of our control. Most of us don't have a clue what goes on inside of them. Yet we need computers to sustain our society. Information Warriors leverage our inherent fear and distrust of computers—Binary Schizophrenia, digital addiction, and approximation anxiety— to their advantage.

8. Last, and perhaps most important, Information Warfare will be waged because it can be. History clearly shows that any new technology, regardless of its original intentions, soon finds its way into the arsenals of the warriors; in this case, computer technology has fallen into the hands of the Information Warriors.

Information Warriors come in all shapes and colors. On the global front, the Japanese and their cameras represent the equivalent of the Army scout providing headquarters with valuable strategic information. Hackers and phone phreaks have been waging InfoWar skirmishes against corporate America and the telephone companies for years, but the recent generation of young cybernauts is more aggressive, patently echoing the ills of the society as a whole.

The Soviets, of course, were Information Warriors par excellence. Now, tens of thousands of ex-Iron Curtain intelligence agents seek to ply their trade for the highest bidder; some going as far as offering their services in the classified sections of daily newspapers.

Power-hungry dictators, radical fundamentalists, and a score of international political sects are candidates to use Cyberspace to effect their agendas. The narcoterrorists are well-financed, armed with a bevy of technical advisors, and have already taken aim at the Drug Enforcement Administration with Information Weapons.

Radical environmental groups have shown their willingness to be physically provocative and Information Warfare offers them the ability to strike out in a new, imaginative, and less personally dangerous way at oil companies, logging companies, and other groups unsympathetic to endangered species.

Information brokers and data bankers sell your name, your upper-middle-class zip code, and the date of your last underwear purchase to anyone with a floppy disk—all without your permission. Banks and credit bureaus allow computers to make decisions that affect our lives and our livelihoods based upon information that contains as much as thirty percent erroneous data—all with virtual impunity.

Anyone can be an Information Warrior. Publications such as *2600: The Hacker Quarterly* and *Phrack* provide the basic training for inductees. Cyberspace itself offers safe havens for Information Warriors to build their armies, develop their weapons, and deploy them. An unhappy worker can suddenly turn against his employer with little chance of prosecution. A government employee may moonlight as an Information Warrior, or a teenager may live in Cyberspace twenty hours a day, alighting on Earth only for Coke and pizza. A hundred million potential Information Warriors, some less friendly than others, are out there waiting, honing their skills.

Information Warfare is about capabilities, the potential

power of the individual and the potential power of an organized group. The capabilities of kids, the capabilities of
technological mercenaries, and the capabilities of nation-
states are all threats we must face. Their intentions are
secondary. If a group or an individual chooses to wreak havoc,
today they have the weapons to do exactly as they please.

What will Information Warfare look like? How will we
recognize it? How will it be waged? Who are the Information
Warriors? Where are they? What are the weapons used in
waging Information Warfare? What can they do? Where can
you buy them? What steps are the government and industry
taking to prepare for upcoming Information Wars? This book
presents disturbing answers to some very simple questions
about our personal, corporate, and national future in the
Global Network.

But *Information Warfare* also provides hope, a way out of
the technocratic quagmire in which we find ourselves. The
first step is the admission of the problem and a willingness to
apply available solutions. Personal electronic privacy can be
achieved, and national economic security is possible—if we
think these issues are important enough to address. Cyberspace is a new place to live, and one way or another, we're all
moving in. We might as well figure out how to get along, since
both our individual successes and our national strength depend upon it.

Yes, this book is about Information Warfare—how it's
waged and who will be waging it. It's also about why Information Warfare is a necessary part of our technical evolution,
especially in these troubled international times. And it is
about a proposed solution that allows us to take control of our
electronic destiny.

Outline of a National Information Policy

That solution is a National Information Policy. At present,
life in Cyberspace is subject to few rules or common sets of

accepted behavior delineating right from wrong, good from bad, or legal from illegal. We really don't even know what the definition of information is, yet our economy is based upon it. We futilely attempt to jury-rig existing old, even archaic guidelines which simply will not work in Cyberspace.

Most of us don't even know what questions need to be asked in order to create a national information policy, and that is especially true in Washington. Cyberspace is, at its purest, absolute technological anarchy, and anarchists traditionally reject government control, preferring self-restraint.

Unfortunately, self-restraint and moral responsibility are not hallmarks of the last twenty years, and as technology and information further intertwine with our existences, rules are required. But even before the rules must come the ethos and morals, and before the ethos must come the thesis.

The National Information Policy is not a specific legislative proposal for Congress to debate, but instead it is a series of substantive issues and questions that must be asked, considered, and answered satisfactorily before we can live in the Information Age with any sense of security, stability, or trust.

Who will own and operate Cyberspace and the National Information Infrastructure? How will government and industry coexist during its birth and growth? Will they or should they function as partners in the economic interest of the United States, or is that too socialistic for our taste? Is an attack against U.S. industry or economic interests the same as an attack against the country itself? On the international front, how isolationist a stance should we adapt as part of the global electronic village? And should we have the right to personal electronic privacy as we evolve in this country's third century?

The answers to these and other questions will determine how we live in the next ten to one hundred years. The answers will tell the world what kind of country we are and want to be. The answers may well define the long-term success of the U.S. economic system. Indeed, the answers will tell us who we are.

The National Information Policy provides an outline by

which to create a foundation for the future: A Constitution for Cyberspace.

Information Warfare is real; it's about time we learn what we're up against.

Let us design our future, not be its victim.

1

The Econo-Politics of Information Warfare

"Economics is a continuation of war by other means."

—DANIEL BELL,
PARAPHRASING CLAUSWITZ

LIKE ALL WAR, Information Warfare needs a stage, and the stage is being set as the world changes daily.

Since World War II, the United States has been the greatest military power in history, but that's just not good enough anymore. The New World Order, post August 1991, has changed all of that.

We are now the world's only superpower, having placed the former bipolar militaristic world into history. It just doesn't make sense for an enemy to assemble an assault on New York City or an air strike against Los Angeles. The stakes are too high and the rewards much too low. NORAD, our military detection system operating out of Cheyenne Mountain, Colorado, would know within seconds, and the Pentagon's response would be swift and deliberate. America would cheer loudly at the victory, again proving our invincibility. The Russians aren't coming . . . at least in the way we used to fear. We won the Cold War and now we have to help the former Evil Empire develop a healthy economy, much as we did with Germany and Japan a half century ago. The Russians no longer want to bury us. They need us too much.

China, often cited as Nostradamus's "Sleeping Giant", although a nuclear power and 1.3 billion citizens strong, is an unlikely military adversary. The Chinese just don't have the throw-weight to successfully take us on. And neither does anyone else. No person or country in their right mind—would take on the United States militarily. Nuclear annihilation or a global conflagration becomes more unlikely as each day passes. The Doomsday clock, the timepiece that measured our Cold War date with Armageddon, has all but wound down.

A military attack against France, England, or Germany would again unite forces greater than those pointed at Baghdad in 1991. NATO would then put aside political differences and crush the foolhardy opposing force. Potential global conflict between two superpowers has been replaced by regional conflicts between comparatively small ethnic and political groups. The constant upheavals in Latin America do not present a military danger to the U.S. Cuba's greatest threat is the exodus of its population to our shores. The potential exists for a nuclear exchange between Pakistan and India, indeed terrifying unto itself, but one that we could militarily handle. Similarly, any conflict with North Korea, while unthinkable to the Koreans, would be localized, nuclear weapons notwithstanding.

Even the most radical fundamentalists in the Middle East have to know that a direct assault on any of the Good Guys could mean national suicide. Saddam Hussein, with the world's fourth largest army, showed us all what the Mother of All Defeats looked like. According to historical observer David Halberstam, Winston Churchill predicted "a wizard war" for technology and the military, yet the Iraqis were stilled because they were buried in World War II mindsets. Halberstam observes, "We knew where they were, we knew who they were, and . . . we even knew how many times a day their commanders went to the bathroom."[1]

Now the U.S. has to prepare for a number of smaller wars, spread apart by oceans and continents. But the solution to regional conflicts is not a simple Bombs Away to victory. The civil war in Bosnia is a Pentagon planner's nightmare with no right answer, only the smell of another Vietnam. Washington will pick and choose our conventional conflicts and interventions very carefully. Essentially, we only go in when we know we can win quickly because America doesn't have the stomach for drawn-out wars any more. There's too much else to do.

The Pentagon faces the unenviable task of figuring out just how to successfully launch these miniwars all at the same time. A few years ago all we had to worry about was a major Soviet move; either through Europe, to the warm waters of the Arabian Gulf, or from over the North Pole with thousands of missiles. Today, while our soldiers support humanitarian efforts in Somalia, the Pentagon must worry about Cuba's civil war, Macedonia and Greece getting it on, or a dictator of the week from Latin America making a move on Mexico. All the while, we have to sustain the capability to participate in a huge desert war in the Middle East. Given the media's axiom, "If it bleeds, it leads," CNN would have trouble figuring out which war to choose for its lead story.

The Pentagon is not only redefining its role, but is thinking up new ones. The push for budget cuts in the supposedly peaceful post-Cold War era makes the military's nearly $300 billion per annum spending habits as an obvious place to slash waste.

While no one recommends closing the doors of the Pentagon, big changes are coming; it's their turn to reduce size. Spending tens of billions of dollars for B-2 bombers is of questionable value. Strategic smart bombs are in; one hundred megaton thermonuclear warheads are out. An evolution toward an interservice centralized military command is gaining momentum for good reason: it will cost less to maintain a hierarchal command structure than redundant, overlapping, and competing forces. A single command, its proponents argue, will also be more efficient when called up to take action. The military is having to adapt to the New World Order, and it will probably be the better for the change.

The New World Order, however, is not all it was cracked up

to be. In many ways, the world was a safer place when the United States and the Soviets had their differences. The lines were clearly drawn. We had our puppets, they had theirs, and we battled over which econo-political philosophy was better.

With dozens of new countries emerging, the battle lines are no longer as clear. With no more Soviet-sponsored client-states trading ideology for financial support, everyone is on his own. Marshall McLuhan predicted almost three decades ago that as the world became smaller and boundaries ceased to be clear-cut, ethnic identification would increase dramatically. The New World Order is full of nations that haven't existed in generations, many now pounding their drums of nationalism and cultural history, decrying years of enslavement, or making religious and historical claims to territory. Countries once glued together by political agreement, terror, and intimidation splinter before our eyes. The USSR alone spawned fifteen discrete nation-states, each of which is trying to recreate its heritage, develop its economy, and stand alone and proud in the world community. The break-ups of Czechoslovakia and Yugoslavia created still more separatist groups claiming sovereignty. Meanwhile African nations yo-yo between names and governments as coups mar the sub-Saharan landscape. Rand McNally must be running our of erasers.

The terrain of a country like Yugoslavia is ideal for guerrilla warfare, and our experiences in Vietnam sensitized us to the potential political fallout from embarking on a military mission where no-win scenarios abound. Occasional American military impotence is also a recognized part of the New World Order.

The New World Order is complicated, much more complicated than the world has ever been. Alliances are made and alliances are broken, with governments playing a real-life game of Risk in which the stakes are enormous. The game is less about who gets the most land than it is about pure and simple survival.

For the first time in almost two hundred years, the United States is defending its own soil. The recent spread of terrorism in the United States is causing the government to rethink dozens of policies instituted to fight the Cold War; we are, in fact, much better prepared to protect our interests overseas than on our own soil. Theodore Sorenson wrote, ". . . non-military developments can pose genuine threats to the long-term security and quality of life of American citizens as surely as armed aggression—but cannot be repelled militarily."[2]

Perhaps it is better from a public relations standpoint for the government not to talk about all of the terrorist activities occurring here, but the ones we know about are bad enough. For example, one cell of the terrorist group Abu Nidal operated in the Midwest until early 1993, when enough evidence was collected to make arrests.[3]

The World Trade Center bombing, despite early administration denials, was soon traced to Iranian-sponsored terrorism by Islamic fundamentalists. The planned bombings of the United Nations and New York City tunnels, and the assassinations of political leaders, were found to have similar religious connections. The FBI recently thwarted several little-publicized attacks by terrorists. One group was planning to shoot rocket launchers at planes coming in and out of Chicago's O'Hare airport. Another planned to poison the water supply of a major Northeastern city. Outside CIA headquarters in Langley, Virginia, a Muslim Pakistani went on a shooting spree, killing several people, in alleged retaliation for perceived American indifference to Bosnia.[4]

According to Bruce Hoffman of the Rand Corporation, terrorism "is going to join the omnipresence of crime as one of the things we have to worry about in American cities."[5] Unfortunately, he's probably right. Understanding terrorism is difficult for the Western mind. Barrages of bullets in Rome's airport, suicide missions, the murder of athletes—it just doesn't compute to us. That's why it is difficult to respond effectively without turning the United States into an armed military camp that requires identification papers to get on the subway.

In *The Anatomy of Terrorism*, David Long, a State Depart-

ment expert, writes, "politically motivated terrorism invari-
ably involves a deeply held sense of grievance over some form
of injustice. . . . The immediate objective of the terrorist
group is to create terror—not destruction—and then use the
unreasonable fear and the resulting political disaffection it has
generated among the public to intimidate governments into
making political concessions in line with its political goals."[6]
Most of us would agree that the World Trade Center bombing
created terror, as does the threat of more such events. Long
maintains that "terrorism is basically a psychological tactic,
with fear and publicity two of its most important elements."[7]
Killing is often merely an ancillary result, viewed by the
terrorist as a necessary, understandable, and acceptable side
effect. There's no arguing that had the perpetrators succeeded
in destroying the Holland or Lincoln Tunnels in New York,
these goals would have been met.

The motivation for domestic terrorism can be purely political. In some cases the motive is merely that the United
States is a strong ally of Israel. Iraq suffered another cruise
missile strike by the U.S. for plotting against the life of former
President George Bush. Libya is still mad because we took
them to task over their Line of Death in 1986, and we're mad
because of their involvement in the bombing of the Pan Am
plane downed over Lockerbee, Scotland.

International terrorism has finally landed on American
soil. It's not just a headline about a European city struck again
by the fanatic of the week, but about terrorists working in
Denver and Des Moines, New York and Nashville, Boston,
Atlanta, and San Francisco. It turns out that America's open-
door policy to immigrants is part of the problem, for terrorist
groups have established themselves throughout the country. In
addition, American universities are hosts to tens of thousands
of students, some of whom are here functioning as intelligence
operatives for their governments, who may regard the United
States with less than friendly intentions.

According to the FBI, two hundred former Afghan fighters

make the New York-New Jersey area home, and many of them may be doing the bidding of the anti-West Iranian government. A *New York Times* report states, "Hundreds of radical operatives live in the U.S., making up a possible loose terrorist network that includes highly trained Islamic mercenaries."[8]

Terrorists plan ahead. They move into their target-host country and establish a comprehensive network of resources, manpower, communications, and intelligence. The House Task Force on Terrorism and Unconventional Warfare has been investigating domestic terrorism for years, and their report *Terrorism in the USA* brings the subject sharply into focus. "Since the early 1980's," the report says, "there has been a concentrated effort by Iran and Syria, and to a lesser extent Libya, with extensive professional help from Cuba and North Korea, to consolidate the terrorist infrastructure in the U.S., namely, intelligence apparatus, logistical and operational support systems."[9]

The U.S. is considered a *Kufr*—a heretic infidel—and a crusading imperialist state in bed with Israel. In the *Jihad*, or Holy War, the radical Muslims view the battle with the West as one between "evil and falsehood, and truth and justice." Guess who is who.

In fact, dedicated and motivated groups of terrorists are now working within our borders. That they may strike at airports or power stations or bridges is a terrifying thought, but apparently one we will have to accept. The department of Immigration is reviewing policy that has permitted the likes of cleric Sheik Omar Abdel Rahman, the alleged link between the World Trade Center bombing and intended tunnel bombings, to enter the U.S. when his past was less than pristine. A computer error was the only Government defense.

As the specter of the Soviet Union fades, we have our work cut out for us. The FBI is reassigning its counterintelligence agents from former Iron Curtain countries to antiterrorist activities, and it's a damn good thing they are. As one Pentagon official said, "we need to improve our capabilities, to try to out-think them, to out-imagine them."[10] They are way ahead of us. David Long concurs, "The highly developed skills of many terrorist organizations in avoiding detection have made the task of carrying our criminal investigations of terrorists acts particularly difficult."[11]

According to Long, "terrorism, first and foremost, is a political problem,"[12] but upon analysis of the New World Order, it could be argued that financial considerations rank almost as high on the terrorist's list. Money fuels international terrorist activities, and has been the primary focus of some efforts. A *New York Post* headline reported "Iran's Plot to Bankrupt America."[13] According to the House Task Force on Terrorism and Unconventional Warfare, Iran and Syria printed billions of dollars in $100 bills in an attempt to bolster their own faltering economies and "to destabilize the United States's economy by undermining confidence in the dollar."[14] And the U.S. government taught them exactly how to do it. The task force noted, "The high quality $100 bills are printed in the Iranian official mint in Teheran, using equipment and know-how purchased from the United States during the reign of the Shah."[15] The task force concluded, "The governments of Iran and Syria are actively engaged in economic warfare against the United States."[16]

We find an even more unlikely partnership in the New World Order; another one aimed at the United States and the Western World. Drugs account for about forty percent of the gross national product of Lebanon, as well as a huge portion of Syria's and a significant part of Iran's. Members of the highest levels of the Syrian government are believed to have used the huge illicit drug industry in Lebanon to finance their own stability. Using their intelligence agencies and their military, these officials smuggle drugs, particularly to Europe, as a highly lucrative endeavor.

However, the Middle East is not an ideal place to grow coca leaves, which yield both cocaine and crack. Enter the Medellín drug cartel and Pablo Escobar. In 1989, at high level meetings in Cyprus, a deal was struck whereby the Colombians would provide raw materials and expertise to the Syrians and their representatives. In return, the Syrians would teach the drug cartels all about terrorism: provide the training, the tricks, and equipment so they could assume the nom-de-guerre of narcoterrorist. One of their first acts was to blow up an Avianca plane moments after it took off from Bogota Airport, killing all 107 passengers on board. The explosive used was SEMTEX, and the detonator was similar to the one used on Pan Am 103. The House task force said, "The United States has been given an ominous warning of what impact Syrian narcoterrorism may have on the West."[17]

So who or what is the target of narcoterrorism? According to Long, "Terrorism always has victims, if not physically, then through severe damage or threat to people's psychological, social, political, or economic well-being. In most instances the victims are not the real target of the terrorist attack—that is the governing authorities the terrorists are trying to intimidate—but rather symbolic targets or merely innocent bystanders who happened to be in the wrong place at the wrong time."[18]

The drug cartels are all about money. It takes billions of dollars yearly to feed America's and Europe's drug habits. In varying degrees, the DEA and the War on Drugs both threaten to interrupt the flow of cash south of the border, to which the cartels have responded angrily, instituting reigns of terror in Colombia. Even though drug dealers are summarily executed in the Muslim states, the Syrians and Iranis are happy to assist in the moral downfall of the West as part of the *Jihad,* and they can use the financial profits, too.

In this case, the two groups have found a workable synergy, a means to double their attack on the West. Their motivations and chosen methods may not necessarily be the same as other terrorists. Strategically, says Long, "each group must choose a mix of specific terrorist operations that collectively are deemed to be the most advantageous in terms of effectiveness and risk. The mix could be called the terrorist strategy of that particular group, and the operations seen as tactics in that strategy."[19]

The Economic Battlefield

The New World Order accentuates disparities in quality of life around the world, breeding two distinct and potentially adversarial groups, the Haves and the Have Nots. East-West military tensions are rapidly being replaced with Have/Have Not tensions.

In the period immediately after World War II, the U.S. economy represented fifty percent of the world's gross national product, and today it still commands a respectable twenty-five percent of same. With less than five percent of the world's population, the United States stands as both an economic and military superpower, and the West in general represents a high standard of living unattainable by seventy-five percent of the global population.[20] We are among the Haves. As a single country, we are still the world's most powerful economic force by a factor of two, but that situation is rapidly deteriorating.

Much of the New World Order is defined by the efforts by the Second and Third World countries to graduate to First World status. In the most broad terms, that means money, and of course, the money is controlled by a select few.

For true Third World countries in Africa, Asia, and Latin America, the vision of the imperialistic *yanqi* breeds envy and resentment. Global communications systems allow the poorest seventy-five percent of the world to see how America lives, and resentment runs deep. Immigrants come to us by slave boat, open dinghy, or the wheel compartment of a jumbo jet—generally at great personal risk. They want a piece of the pie that has been denied them by happenstance of birth. People who risk death to improve their station in life, and the countries they flee from, are not to be treated lightly or ignored. We cannot solve all of their problems, but they have the capacity to make their problems ours.

The planet's Have Nots feel they have little to lose, so an engagement with the West is a no-lose option. They don't want a military confrontation, but rather an economic one, and they play by their rules, not ours. The Have Nots want to become Haves at any cost. The people of South America care little about the cocaine and crack problems in American cities. Coca production is their only means of support. Offer them an alternative, and maybe they'll change their ways; but few businesses are as profitable as drugs. The late Pablo Escobar allegedly put hundreds of millions of dollars into Colombia's rural infrastructure as a means of maintaining popular support for his operations. It's about the money; it's about survival.

In *The Fourth World War*, Count de Marenches, former head of the French intelligence services, maintains that the Cold War was really World War III, and World War IV is now under way, full of new enemies. He predicts, "The Fourth World War will be a terrorist war."[21]

He views the Haves versus Have Nots from a more geo-graphical perspective and, as is his style, without minicing words. "In the starkest terms, it [the Fourth World War] is one of South against North, poor and disorganized nations against rich, organized ones. Soon, there will be more than four billion people in these Southern nations, one billion in Africa alone, against one billion in all of the North."[22] According to Count de Marenches, the current conflict will be less polite, more violent, and less comprehensible than the recently closed chapters on the Cold War; a conflict we may soon view with fond nostalgia, just as we look back on the 1950s.

The Cold War was about money as much as it was about weapons. The United States spent trillions of dollars to defeat an erstwhile ally, but at what cost? Did we merely outspend them? Perhaps we even forced the issue. Padgett Peterson, Information Integrity specialist at Martin Marietta, a defense contractor, believes that we may have forced the Soviets to spend their economy into ruin. For example, he thinks it possible that the U.S. may have instigated the Toshiba submarine propeller incident (Toshiba was internationally censured for selling the Soviets sophisticated computer-controlled equipment that allowed their submarine propellors to operate almost silently) to force the Soviets to spend more than they could. In response, of course, the Pentagon's budget needed to be adjusted upward to counter the threat.

"History is clear," writes Lester Thurow in *Head to Head.* "While military power can sometimes outlast economic power for centuries, eventually military power depends upon having a successful economic base. America's success in the Gulf War proves that it is, and will be, a military superpower in the century to come. But its success in the Gulf in no way guarantees that it will be an economic superpower in the twenty-first century."[23]

As the world evolves into the New World Order, we must expect entirely new challenges. According to Thurow, "Economic arrangements that work in a unipolar world simply do not work in a multipolar world." What he is referring to of course, is that the United States is no longer the singular force driving the world economy. While we won the Cold War, the rest of the world prepared itself for round two—economic warfare. Richard Nixon has been making such predictions for almost twenty years.

Japan lost World War II militarily. In 1950, the Japanese economy was one twentieth the size of the U.S. In 1991 it was more than one half as large! Japan is host to the world's second largest economy and eight of the world's ten largest banks.[24] Who really won that conflict?

Europe was militarily, economically, politically, and socially devastated at the end of World War II. The Marshall Plan, however, financed by a few billion U.S.-supplied dollars succeeded beyond its designers' wildest imagination. We created our own competition. The American way: Beat 'em and build 'em.

Since 1986 the original twelve members of the European Economic Community (EEC) have been designing a New Europe, one in which trade barriers are removed between all countries, one in which an eventual monetary union will tie independent currencies together, thus lessening the disparity of its members. Western Europe's $8 trillion GNP and its 340 million people, combined with those from Middle and Eastern

Europe, create a single market in excess of 850 million people and an estimated $12-14 trillion. On the economic front, America will be dwarfed.

The New Europe is a formidable force that will have profound effects on the U.S. economy, for the rules that the Europeans and the Japanese play by aren't the same ones we use. In France, Airbus has received $20 billion in government subsidies, an advantage that Boeing and other U.S. airplane manufacturers do not share.[25] The closest American parallel to a subsidy is Pentagon spending on new military aeronautical and electronics technology. The difference is that European companies spend their government subsidies on civilian projects that benefit their people and improve their lives. We don't.

No one doubts that the emergence of three dominant economic competitors—the Far East, Europe, and the United States (with Canada and Mexico)—is a giant leap forward for mankind. Thurow writes,

"From everyone's perspective, replacing military confrontation with an economic contest is a step forward. No one gets killed; vast resources don't have to be devoted to negative-sum activities. The winner builds the world's best product and enjoys the world's highest standard of living. The loser gets to buy some of those best products—but not as many as the winner. Relative to the military confrontations of the past century, both the winners and the losers are winners in the economic game ahead."[26]

Indeed the rules are changing.

Analyst and writer Peter Drucker says that the economic realities of the New World Order require a substantial shift in our concepts of trade and value. He refers to this as postcapitalist society which "is more likely to resemble a liquid"[27] than its crystalline forebearers such as central planning and rigid Western capitalism. The global nature of business will require a new interdependency, where alliances and panoceanic ventures become the norm. Drucker's vision for the future implies vast and almost total shifts in attitudes and perceptions. "That the new society will be both nonsocialist and a postcapitalist society is practically certain. And it is certain that its primary resource will be knowledge."[28]

NATO's presence and necessity in Europe gave the U.S. immense influence over European political and economic affairs. The Soviet threat resulting from the Warsaw Pact indirectly helped U.S. interests. Now the role historically played by NATO is not so clear. Nixon writes, "Without a military presence in Europe, we will have no voice in Europe."[29] Experts and planners have been exploring alternate NATO missions for the twenty-first century to keep America's foot in the door and our influence intact. Drucker suggests that "under conditions of modern technology, defense means a permanent wartime society and a permanent wartime economy. It means the Cold War State."[30]

On the Pacific front, the United States effectively defended Japan after World War II. According to Japan's U.S.-approved constitution the nation's $30 billion defense budget and 250 thousand-man army isn't permitted to leave Japanese soil, leaving it an impotent show of pomp without muscle. Thus, they begrudgingly paid $11 billion for the privilege of not sending troops to Desert Storm. Outside of similar regional events with United Nations or U.S. involvement, such as a conflict with North Korea, Japan doesn't need much military protection.

But bonds and alliances are formed from fear. Once the threat is gone, the alliance tends to weaken, the friendly bonds become less cohesive, perhaps more curt, less congenial. Japan and the United States have been exchanging particularly undiplomatic barbs regarding trade imbalances. We say they employ unfair trade practices; they say we haven't learned how to play the economic game where we don't have a monopoly.

Sintaro Ishihara, author of *The Japan That Can Say No*, predicts that military warfare will be replaced by economic wars in which Japan will, of course, be the winner.[31] An old Japanese adage succinctly sums up the attitude of their economically pugilistic society: **Business is War.**

German Chancellor Helmut Kohl threw down the gauntlet and essentially declared economic war against the Japanese in a televised speech in which he maintained, "The 1990's will be the decade of the Europeans and not that of the Japanese."[32]

The three schools of capitalism will also be competing in style as much as in form. The Japanese business style is monopolistic in nature. Interlocking and mutually supporting business relationships controlled by a few megacorporations are known as *keiretsu*. A handful of companies, in concert with MITI, the Japanese government's trade organization, run the industrial sector of the country with market domination and economic control as a highly focused aim. Recent downturns in the Japanese economy, though, have shown their wealth is as much a function of world economic health as ours. Time will tell.

In Europe, banks own businesses and defend their industries from undesirable foreign ownership. In the United States, both of these activities are illegal. They are violations of both antitrust and banking laws. Foreign governments invest heavily in their domestic industries, whereas the U.S. is weak in such direct investment. Our system is more of a free-for-all, a Wild West competition until it gets too wild and the federal government steps in. However, it tends to do so very selectively. It will only get involved when the going gets real rough, as it did when it came to the aid of the nearly-bankrupt Chrysler in the early 1980s, when it broke up AT&T, or when it investigated possible antitrust action against Microsoft. Otherwise, the concept of a centrally managed economy or centralized national policies have not been part of Washington's lexicon since the Great Depression. How Bill Clinton fares with his centrist views on federal economic stimuli has yet to be seen. In the meantime, the three systems of practicing healthy capitalism are vastly different, the rules of the game are not consistent, the playing field is not level, and the outcome is suddenly not so sure as we would like to pretend.

Not only are the published rules of the economic game skewed against the United States (the European and the Japanese systems are philosophically closer to each others than to ours), but the not often discussed rules of engagement are different. The morals and ethics of business vary widely from country to country, company to company, and from individual to individual. As we will see, industrial espionage is real. Just because you wear a white hat doesn't mean that you can't cheat. And in the global economy, cheating is more widespread than crib sheets in high school.

Lester Thurow quotes France's Edith Cresson as saying, "Japan is an adversary that doesn't play by the rules and has an absolute desire to conquer the world. You have to be naive or blind not to recognize that."[33] What she doesn't say is that the French break quite a few rules themselves. We have been blind, as Cresson suggests. We have been so preoccupied with immediate military invincibility that, with relatively few exceptions, we have allowed our economy to erode without noticing until it has reached a critical point. Outspending the Soviets may be viewed as a very stupid move by future historians.

Nonetheless, the United States needs to make a fundamental decision; a decision which will set the tone for the next century. We need to decide if the American economy is a strategic asset of the United States. We must decide if domestic economic concerns are an issue of national security. Do we have the political flexibility, the acute foresightedness, to realize and act upon the premise that a defensive economic posture is as critical to this country as is our military defensive posture? If not, our two formidable competitors will likely have a field day buying up America, just as Japan bought Rockefeller Center and Michael Jackson.

Occasionally, Congress will get involved and question the sale of Fairchild to Fujitsu or Loral to the French. But a thorough and complete laissez-faire regard—or disregard—for the importance of the economy to our national security bodes ill for the future. Our style of individualistic capitalism, largely free from socialistic-smelling government intervention, may be inadequate for the challenge.

The economic battlefield, as we will learn, is unique. Gun-toting armies will not sail into San Francisco Bay and announce victory. We know how to deal with that contingency. Rather, business-suited visitors invade with better products at cheaper prices. The guy who can build the best mousetrap at the best price sells the most mousetraps, yet now we're importing the mousetraps that we originally invented. We discover that we have indiscriminately given away industry after industry to foreign interests; from steel to electronics to home entertainment to automobiles, we have lost countless trillions of dollars due to political and fiscal mismanagement.

Any domestic business that has been hard hit by imported products has learned this lesson well, yet it seems to have escaped the notice of Washington. Extreme political positions such as those espoused by presidential also-ran Pat Buchanan reek of the fiascoes caused by historically damned protectionism. According to former President Nixon, "Had we engaged in Europe, rather than sulking in isolation after World War I, we could have tipped the balance of power against the aggressors, possibly deterring rather than fighting World War II."[34] We face similar questions today that require better answers than those provided in the past. We must be aggressive players on the global economic field if we are to maintain power and influence on the world scene in the future.

So which is right? Are we going to be constantly battling in regional military conflicts, thereby justifying large expenditures to maintain America's national security? Or should we realign our priorities and concentrate on economic competition instead? I believe that you will find, as I have, that the two are synonymous and, if we are to be successful, we have to address both as part of a more comprehensive world view. We need to identify and maintain that delicate balance which reflects the realities of the New World Order and the economic dynamics that will increasingly drive successes and failures across all national, cultural, or ideological boundaries.

That new reality should certainly include the obvious but by no means trivial observation that we can expect a lot of cheating by everyone involved. Generally speaking both Japanese and European organizations have admitted that they cheat for economic survival. The Soviets have admitted extensive cheating. Their space shuttle, for example, bears striking resemblance to ours. And well it should, considering they acquired (both legally and illegally) the results of billions of dollars of U.S. taxpayer-sponsored space research. The Russians, when asked if they are still cheating, offer circumspect and suspect answers. Of course they are; it's in their economic interest to do so.

And what is the goal of all of this cheating?

Information.

Information is what makes both the Old and the New World Order go around. Information is what gives one player an advantage over the others. In military-speak, information about the enemy's capabilities, positions, strengths, and weaknesses is crucial in determining political stances and military responses.

On a global scale, knowing what the other guy is planning gives you a leg up; you are better prepared to respond or react or subvert. With KH-series spy satellites that can read a license plate from high in orbit, the U.S. knows which training camp in the Sahara Desert is preparing terrorists for which organization. Our satellite surveillance is second to none.

For decades, spies from the CIA, the KGB, MI6, and from other groups who don't "officially" exist have lived in the pursuit of a single commodity: information. Information is a commodity to be bartered for a comrade's freedom or exchanged for other information. We're in a giant game of Monopoly, in which information is the medium of exchange.

The Cold War generated war stories and tall tales of cloak and dagger adventures that spawned an industry of spy thrillers from the likes of John LeCarre, Ian Fleming, and Robert Ludlam. Yet again, the key was information, as readers of *Mad* magazine, which regularly satired the antics of government espionage in its comic department "Spy Vs. Spy" may recall.

Spies have been around forever, gathering information for the other side. During the Revolutionary War, Benedict Arnold sold out West Point for twenty thousand British pounds. Two hundred years later, John Walker sold priceless military information to the Soviets over a period of seventeen years for mere thousands of dollars. Russian spying once maintained an active entourage of 900,000 for the KGB and GRU, both of which were tasked with stealing different types of information. Almost a million people were keeping tabs on anything and everything they deemed valuable.

Writer Ronald Kessler said in *Spy Versus Spy*, "Unlike the KGB, which seeks economic, political, military, and scientific information, the GRU or Chief Intelligence Directorate of the Soviet General Staff . . . focuses only on military secrets."[35] The Soviets were dead serious in their aim to get hold of sensitive U.S. information.

The U.S. spying machine is anemic in comparison. Richard Nixon ought to know. "The entire U.S. intelligence community—which includes not only the CIA but also the Defense Intelligence Agency, the National Security Agency, parts of the Federal Bureau of Investigation, and other agencies—employs approximately 35,000 people."[36]

So what does this say about our preparedness for an economic competition where spying is the dominant form of cheating? It suggests that we are sadly ill-prepared. Perhaps the Lone Ranger syndrome is at fault. As a people, we want to win, but we want to do it honestly. We want to see ourselves as the good guys, the white hats, the cavalry to the rescue. We can't resort to the same dastardly techniques that the bad guys use. It's not sporting; it's not next to Godliness. Such outmoded and self-denying attitudes invite failure in the economic battleground of the New World Order.

Despite secret intelligence operatives and so-called "black" budgets, our intelligence services are vastly outnumbered and outspent by not only the Russians, but by intelligence services from every major country from Israel to Korea. No wonder U.S.-developed technology shows up in every corner of the planet. Nixon comments, "In the 1930's, the Kremlin sought to boost the Soviet economy by stealing scientific knowledge and technologies—from basic research to blueprints for turnkey factories—through spies."[37] It seems that whatever we build, someone else wants—and gets—for free. That's where it all begins.

In the truest sense of the word, the CIA and other domestic and international alphabet soup intelligence agencies wage a distinct form of Information Warfare. Spies are the original Information Warriors, and membership in their club is indeed exclusive. The Soviets were obviously less picky but more motivated; they recruited twenty-five times as many active participants as we did.

The Soviet spying machine was well-financed, and was clear and concise in its mission. "The CIA reported that in the early 1980s, Soviet intelligence services targeted 3,500 items annually. The KGB Directorate T orchestrated efforts that secured about one-third of these items every year."[38]

On the espionage front, a transition was and is still occurring. The information being sought now focuses less on the military than in the confrontational past. Nonmilitary, civilian technologies, products, and processes are now the targets. And it seems like everyone wants to play.

But herein is a difficult conundrum to resolve.

Since World War II, the Pentagon has based the U.S. defensive posture on a single overriding premise, a potential adversary's capabilities, not their presumed intention. National Security Advisor Brent Scowcroft, former-President Nixon, and a host of others may use slightly different words to describe that thinking, but essentially the U.S. continues to structure its defense policies upon that premise. While we have successfully implemented that dogma militarily, our obviously fatal flaw is in failing to expand that strategy to include our national economic interests. We can contend with a madman in the desert (sort of) and build invisible aircraft (sort of), but we have done precious little to aggressively protect the economic well-being of this country.

We tend to think in either military or economic terms instead of recognizing the synergy of the two, and treating them as a single concept as our adversaries have. William Sessions, former director of the FBI, addressed the need to do so when he said to a House Justice subcommittee, "Now and in the future, the collection strategies of adversaries and allies alike will not only focus on defense-related information, but also include scientific, technological, political, and economic information. [Soviet and Russian] defectors . . . predicted that the new independent states will escalate industrial espionage activities in the years ahead to bolster their economies and foster increased technological progress."[39]

If we apply military thinking to economic competition, cheating covers a much wider scope than industrial espionage. Information, disinformation, extortion, blackmail, destruction, or other means of overt economic disruption must be anticipated. The weapons that will be used to effect a national or corporate economic advantage are ideally tailored to their purpose and we again find ourselves on the short end of the stick. Simply put, the United States is not ready to defend itself or its economic interests against a dedicated Information Warrior or economic aggressor. From a military perspective, our economic vulnerability is patently unacceptable.

As we meander through the world of Information Warfare, we shall see that the government and its nonelected guardians of information have been entirely too protective of their turfs. Under the guise of national security, they have kept critical basic information out of the hands of the American public. This information can be used to defend a business or a technology or to provide the means by which a U.S. company can level the playing field with a few dirty tricks of its own.

But first, we need to understand just how dependent we are upon computers, just how incredibly and invisibly prevalent they are in our everyday lives. Only then can we appreciate the attractiveness of information systems as targets and the magnitude of our personal, corporate, and national vulnerability to Information Warfare.

2

Computers Everywhere and the Global Network

"I see a world wide market for about three computers."

—JAMES T. WATSON, 1947, CHAIRMAN OF IBM

"There is no reason for any individual to have a computer in their home."

—KEN OLSEN, FORMER PRESIDENT OF DIGITAL EQUIPMENT CORP.
AT THE WORLD FUTURE SOCIETY IN 1977.[1]

DESPITE THE PREDICTIONS ABOVE, there are 125 million computers out there and more coming.

With the world's econo-political situation neatly providing the required ingredients for Information Warfare, what we need now is a battlefield, the place where rivals wage the skirmishes and full-scale attacks.

That battlefield is call Cyberspace.

Cyberspace is that intangible place between computers where information momentarily exists on its route from one end of the global network to the other. When little Ashley calls Grandmother, they are speaking in Cyberspace, the place between the phones. Cyberspace is the ethereal reality, an infinity of electrons speeding down copper or glass fibers at the speed of light from one point to another. Cyberspace includes the air waves vibrating with cellular, microwave, and satellite communications. We are all wired together in dozens of ways on the Global Network and are thus an integral part of Cyberspace. According to John Perry Barlow, cofounder of Electronic Frontier Foundation, Cyberspace is where all of our money is, except for the cash in our pocket.

Putting aside for a moment the business, government, and econotechnical infrastructure, let's see just how computerized our life has become.

An estimated three billion computers run every aspect of our lives. These computers aren't quite so obvious to us because they tend to be invisibly enmeshed into the fabric of daily chores. These billions of computers, plus the hundred million-plus business-oriented computer systems, are what we call Computers Everywhere. They are indeed everywhere. You can't ride an elevator, microwave food, or watch Vanna White flip letters without interacting with a computer. There's a little computer running nearly everything we touch these days. How many tens of millions of VCRs have been made? TV sets aren't just a couple of knobs and an antenna anymore. Programming your viewing habits is crucial to their operation and your mental well-being. Specialized computers run them as well as their companion video cameras and their brethren, the automatic no-need-to-focus-just-press-the-button point-and-shoot still cameras. Washers and dryers are programmed by Mr. or Mrs. or Ms. Mom at an exact temperature to the microsecond, and the appliances' internal computers respond on command. Mortgages, utility bills, Home Shopping Network—it's all done by computer. Computers run the Department of Motor Vehicles, Social Security, hospitals, doctors. Even our family vet is fully networked. Book an airline, reserve a hotel room, or go to Disneyland, and you talk to a computer. We can no longer ignore the impact of Computers Everywhere on Everyman and Everywoman.

Wherever we go, there's a computer somewhere inside. Have you ridden in a taxi and asked for a receipt lately? The computerized meters have calculators with tiny little printers and are so simple to use that they don't require an instruction manual. Even cash registers are driven by a powerful computer chip. Credit cards are read for authorization by a digital reader, just like bank cards are read by the ATM machine.

Here is an interesting exercise to try. Sit back and think about how much in your life is computerized. How often do you interact with a computer? Fax machines? Electronic car ignitions? High-end digital cassette machines? What about hand held calculators? Home security systems? God knows how many of the kids' toys are computerized. I count nineteen computers in my family and we don't even have Nintendo. (Nintendo alone accounts for almost ten percent of Japan's chip production.) How many hundreds of millions of computers does that make? If you add clock radios, Mr. Coffees, digital watches, sprinkler timers, oven timers, and street lights, you add a billion or so additional computers to your list.

My mother has three VCRs, each run by its own internal computer. Her new five-disc CD player can do a random search and is programmable for hours of customized listening pleasure. She has two programmable clock radios, an answering machine, a digital microwave, two remote control televisions, an automatic 35mm camera, a digital water-softening system, "smart" hot water heater cycling, a programmable sprinkler system, and her own 286-class computer. Let's see, that's fifteen computer-controlled devices in her two-bedroom condo and that doesn't even include her assortment of calculators.

Her interaction with Computers Everywhere doesn't stop there. Mom had to learn how to use an ATM machine. In retirement communities, the ATMs actually speak in English to help customers find their way through all of the options. Weights and measures at the grocery store are measured to the nearest 1/1000 of a pound on digital scales, and bar codes tell the cash register how much to charge for Charmin. When she purchases an item from the Home Shopping Network, she interacts with "Tootie," the order-taking computer, instead of a live person. Billions of computers are invisibly embedded in almost everything we do.

Computers Everywhere

On the other hand, some pretty humongous computers live in Cyberspace, ones with which we communicate every day.

Our telephone system—The Phone Company, henceforth TPC for short—is just a huge computer-controlled electronic switch, albeit a fancy one, with hundreds of millions of terminals (phones) worldwide. The telephone gives you incredible power. You can tell this immense computer to make anybody's phone ring, anywhere in the whole world. And how many people do you know who went to school to learn how to use a phone? The biggest computer system in the world is also the easiest to use.

The telephone is not marketed as a computer. It is sold as a tool, a necessity of life. There is no computer phobia to overcome. Telephones just work, most of the time. Just plug it in and dial away. Nonetheless, at the heart of it all lie super powerful computers. (Of course transitions, such as to touch-tone dialing in the 1960s, were not entirely painless for everybody. Touchtones didn't have the same weight and feel as the older phones, creating some generational resistance.)

Is there a major company in the world that doesn't force you to talk to its computer before you can speak with a real live human being? The miracle of voice mail has produced more disgusted hang-ups than all of the telephone answering machines ever built, which, we must remember, were also originally met with horror due to their impersonality. Making airline reservations can be a frustrating exercise for those of us with fewer brain cells than we were born with: "Thank you for calling Honest-We'll-Be-Here-Tomorrow Airlines. To speed your request, please use this automated attendant. Press 1 for international flight arrival times; Press 2 for international flight departures, Press 3 for domestic flight arrival times, Press 4 for domestic . . ." and by the time 9 comes around, you have forgotten what 1 was, and you either have to call back or figure out which button will start the whole list over again. So what do you do the next time? Write it all down on paper. With a pencil. Rather ironic, isn't it? Once that gauntlet is traversed, selecting flight information is a breeze if you know the flight number, the date, and the airline city codes. Just type them into your phone. . . .

I still prefer a polite voice which, in three seconds or less, can tell me how late the eight o'clock flight from New York is going to be. Call me old fashioned.

Customer service organizations are the worst. They never give you the option you want. It never fails: "Thank you for calling Appliance Conglomerate of America. This is your automated information attendant. Please wait until you have heard all of the options before making your selection. Press 1 for toasters, Press 2 for microwave ovens, Press 3 for convection ovens, Press 4 for popcorn poppers . . . Press 64 for refrigerator condensers. . . ."

Then they put you on hold.

And what about "smart cards"? A smart card is about the size and shape of your favorite American Express card with a little tiny computer built into each one. Our wallets will soon be filled with half-a-dozen or more of these little computers that will allow us, as humans, to interact with the computers that run the companies and organizations with whom we deal: Go to the grocery store and whip out a Computerized Winn Dixie Debit Card that will immediately debit the correct amount from your bank account. (Better keep track of that sucker!) A Nynex Computer Phone Card will soon be required, as both a cost-saving measure and a deterrent to crime, to make a call from a pay phone.

Smart cards will become the electronic equivalent of a social security number, which by the way, will be emblazoned in the silicon guts of your personal smart cards. The memory circuits will know all about you, perhaps including a medical history, personal and family information, driving records, identification for all of the financial institutions with which you deal, and an emergency savings account.

At the heart of President Clinton's health plan is a smart card that has privacy advocates up in arms fearing even further erosion of what little remains of our personal electronic privacy.

Computers Everywhere will only increase.

The Global Network

Sometime in the last few years—we have no exact date—the Global Network was born.

The Global Network is the offspring of Computers Everywhere. Some cybernauts maintain that the existence of Computers Everywhere begat the union of information systems to each other, that the Global Network was a foregone evolutionary conclusion. Others might argue that the Global Network is an interspecies offspring: one parent is the do-nothing-without-being-told silicon life form of digital electronics and the other is the highly evolved, cognizant, carbon-based cybernaut. Others hold a purely technocratic view and think that attributing personality to information systems is the mark of a madman. In any event, at one point, the Global Network started to take on a form, a shape, a texture—a look and a feel, if you will. The exact date of birth is immaterial, for today the Global Network, still in its formative infancy, is a living, breathing entity on planet Earth as much as we are.

Our reliance on the Global Network has become so immense that if the entire Network were turned off, we would literally die. From that perspective, we and the Global Network have become symbiotic. We need it to survive and it wants to grow.

The Global Network is the interconnecting tissue of Computers Everywhere. The Global Network is a form of Cyberspace, a place where one can travel electronically, projecting one's being to any place on the planet. The Global Network is the ability to connect any computer to any other computer or connect any person to any other person. The Global Network is instantaneous communications anywhere—by voice, video, or data. The Global Network is The Phone Company. It is satellites, modems, faxes, cable television, interactive television, dial-a-poll politics, home shopping, cellular phones and Wrist-Man television. The Global Network is instant feedback and instant gratification.

The concept of "life" for computers and software was first

conceived in automaton theory, which was pioneered by the early computer genius John Von Neumann. Its simple, albeit controversial, premise is that software and computing machines are really life forms with whom we cohabit on planet Earth.

Artificial life (or "a-life") researchers have been trying for years to come up with schemes to create a workable silicon-based imitation of the human brain, thus the intense work today on brainlike neural networks that have the ability to learn. But, is that life?

One argument maintains it is only human prejudice that insists life forms must be carbon-based, breathing creations. A more liberal view would include crystals, which do indeed meet a broader definition of life. Software programs definitely exhibit attributes of life. A self-running graphics program can be instructed to behave in certain ways. It can be told to move one inch to the left, then one to the right, add an arm or leg to the image, or whatever the programmer dreams up. When left to run on its own, the antics on the screen do in fact echo many of nature's life forms, such as reef growth.

To most a-life researchers, life can be based on mathematical formulas and software programs, as well as on carbon or silicon. What matters is the activity, not the materials involved.[2] Although images of Frankensteinian software running amok down Main Street are the products of over-active imaginations, a-life certainly does conjure up some possibilities for the Information Warrior.

Robotics will most assuredly contain arguable degrees of a-life, and perhaps that is where the Mary Shelley parallel is most likely to arise. No one can tell where a-life is going, but groups such as the Santa Fe Institute in New Mexico spend a great deal of time thinking about such things.

A clear distinction between artificial life and artificial intelligence must be made. True AI, Artificial Intelligence, can be considered a form of artificial life, but artificial life would not necessarily be considered artificial intelligence. Douglas

Hofstadter condenses the salient requirements for life to exist quite admirably.

No one knows where the borderline between non-intelligent and intelligent behavior lies; in fact, to suggest that a sharp borderline exists is probably silly. But essential abilities for intelligence are certain:
to respond to situations with flexibility;
to take advantage of fortuitous circumstances;
to make sense out of ambiguous or contradictory messages;
to recognize the relative importance of different elements of a situation;
to find similarities between situations despite differences which might separate them;
to draw distinctions between situations despite similarities which may link them;
to synthesize new concepts by taking old concepts and putting them together in new ways;
to come up with ideas which are novel.[3]

No one classes an amoeba with a Mensa member (there's a joke there somewhere), but no one would deny that an amoeba is a life form. One must then look at the Global Network for a moment and ask: are any of these capabilities applicable to a computer network? Those cybernauts who assign the attributes of living beings to the Global Network would say yes, the Global Network is in its infancy and it is still learning.

The biological parallels are quite evident. Each individual element of a network can perform certain tasks alone without the help of its neighbors. Each tentacle of the Global Network, after all, is a computer in its own right, each designed to execute specific tasks in specific ways. In addition, much like its biological counterpart, when vast numbers of computers are interconnected, Buckminster Fuller's concept of synergy applies:

Synergy means behavior of whole systems unpredicted by the behavior of their parts taken separately. Synergy means behavior of integral, aggregate, whole systems unpredicted by behaviors of any of their components or subassemblies of their components taken separately from the whole.[4]

Two heads are better than one. Brainstorming, think tanks, free association—all are forms of mental synergy. In a synergistic world, 2 plus 2 could equal 5 or 6 or 300 or 3.14159 or whatever. Synergy plays a vital part in the development of Information Warfare.

When the personal computer was invented, there was no way to predict that the world would be transformed as dramatically as it has in a mere decade. A very few academics and futurists certainly had a glimmer of the possibilities, but even today, mainstreamers have trouble realizing that new technologies and the continued expansion of the Global Network will have even more profound effects on modern society, in ways we cannot begin to fathom.

Thus, the Network-is-a-Lifeform cybernauts maintain it was impossible a decade ago to predict that Cyberspace would be populated with millions of people spanning the globe. It was impossible to predict that various new subcultures would arise, many of which are distinctly at odds with the establishment's way of thinking. Chaos at work.

Today's Global Network is like a baby's brain, an evolving neural network in which the connections grow and multiply. Indeed, a neural network that grows connections is said to "learn," and the same argument can be made for the Global Network.

In the novel *Terminal Compromise,* a Dutch hacker makes the point:

"Ya," Dutchman laughed. "So as the millions of neural connections are made, some people learn skills that others don't and some computers are better suited to certain tasks than others. And now there's a global neural network growing across the face of the planet. Millions more computers are added and we connect them together, until any computer can talk to any other computer. Ya, the Spook is very much right. The Network is alive, and it is still learning.[5]

A first-time mother soon finds out that her new baby doesn't come with a user manual. She has to figure it out herself—determine what's right, what's wrong, what's best for the child—but she can get help by asking others and learning from their experiences.

The same goes for the Global Network.

No one knows what the infant Global Network will look like when it grows up, but we can hypothesize for a moment.

An Apple II cost $3,000 in 1980. The first IBM personal computer with no hard disk and a mere 64K of memory also cost $3,000. The first 286 class machines cost $3,000. Computers double in power roughly every eighteen months. So, eighteen months from now, a computer costing $1,000 will be twice as powerful as a similarly priced machine today. In a decade, the same $1,000 will likely buy a computer 128 times as powerful as you can buy today.

What can we expect? Virtual reality piped into every home computer. Cyberpsych, an electronic noningestible drug that rings of Woody Allen's orgasmatron in *Sleeper*. "Reach out and touch someone" morphs into the twenty-first century. Meanwhile Marshall McLuhan's adage, "The medium is the message" is the cybernauts' motto. The medium, of course, is Cyberspace and most of us haven't gotten the message yet.

On the downside, all of this computerization can cause a severe headache, Carpal Tunnel Syndrome, the need for bifocals, or a number of other maladies that are only now being associated with the incredible proliferation of computers and the number of people who sit at their terminals for hours and weeks and years on end.

The psychological impact of Computers Everywhere and the Global Network on society and individuals is not quite so obvious. We have to learn to live with the new life forms that the cybernauts proclaim exist. Or at least, we must learn to coexist with information systems that are impossible to avoid.

Welcome to the Information Age

It is easy to make a strong case that the Information Age is here and it is also easy to argue that the best is yet to come. "Wait till you see what we come up with next!" the silicon saviors accurately promise. But we have to admit we have already arrived in the Information Age, that magically mysterious era that provides our daily amenities, our pleasures, and our livelihoods at the push of a button, and that it is no longer a distant goal. The first day of the Information Age was that day when our dependence upon computers and communications systems and high-tech gadgetry exceeded our ability to live without them.

Our graduation into the Information Age, whenever that was, spawned complex reactions. For a society whose very existence requires the reliable and continued operation of countless millions of interconnected computers, communications systems, networks, and satellites, we have been derelict in technointrospection.

The technological evangelists of the 1980s promised fabulous futures, with smaller and friendlier and ever more powerful calculating machines, machines which would enrich our lives beyond the wildest dreams of the previous generation. So we bought in, we plunged enthusiastically into the uncharted realms of Cyberspace. We invested hundreds of billions of dollars in a twenty-first century utopian vision shaped by Apple Computers founder Steve Jobs, Microsoft's Bill Gates, and a handful of others—the rightful heirs of English computer patriarch Charles Babbage. The American captivation with successful entrepreneurship and sexy-high-tech toys, as well as Baby Boomer desire for self-indulgence and instant gratification, permitted virtually unbridled growth of systems which we handed control of our day-to-day lives. We didn't see what was happening because the evangelists neglected the downside of their vision. What we didn't hear then, and still don't hear today, is that omnipresent automation may not be all it's cracked up to be.

Since the fifties, automated systems have crept into big business, causing a very subtle shift to occur, one that we still do not fully understand. Value used to be based exclusively upon tangible assets. The company had desks and inventory and buildings and a factory, and those established its worth. Wealth was based upon the gold standard and could be established internationally with little division.

But a mere forty years later, the value of a company is now in its information. The formula for Coca-Cola is worth a whole lot more than one hundred Coke bottling plants. The plants can be replaced. The formula cannot. Think about it: Coke's formula and countless company secrets are kept in Cyberspace, a place we still don't fully comprehend.

American business is as much in the information business as it was in the industrialization business a century ago. Dr. George A. Keyworth, II, science advisor to President Reagan and now a distinguished fellow at the Hudson Institute, wrote in a 1992 briefing paper, "We're moving increasingly toward a business environment in which information itself is the product, and in which the strategies by which businesses use information become critical elements of their success or failure."[6]

As we learn more about Information Warfare, business's reliance upon unprotected Computers Everywhere represents the largest potential threat to the economy of the United States in our history.

Computers Everywhere and the Global Network have taken their place alongside homo sapiens as residents of Planet Earth but along the way, we also transformed the essence of value, what we think of as money, into a new commodity which no one even fifty years ago would recognize.

Cybercash

Individual wealth and worth is now determined by endless zeros and ones entered into, stored upon, analyzed within, and retrieved from hundreds of computers. Virtual money, or as Joel Kurtzman calls it in his book *The Death of Money,* "megabyte money," has replaced real hard cash as the valued medium of exchange. According to Kurtzman, "Money is the network that comprises hundreds of thousands of computers of every type, wired together in places as lofty as the Federal Reserve . . . and as mundane as the thousands of gas pumps around the world outfitted to take credit and debit cards."[7] Money is stored on disk drives and tape drives where the proper combination of 1s and 0s determines one's degree of wealth.

The world's gross national product is about $27 trillion with the New World Order's tripolar economic superpowers controlling the vast amount of the planet's wealth. The United States generates about twenty-five percent of it, Japan and the Far East between seventeen and twenty-three percent, and Europe about forty percent, depending upon whom you include. A disproportionately low twenty-five percent of the population controls nearly ninety percent of the world's goods, services, and money.

One trillion dollars is a lot of money. One thousand billionaires or one million millionaires. A trillion dollars could just about build a brand new New York City, buy two thousand B2 bombers, or provide every American with $4,000. Iran's war with Iraq cost it nearly $600 billion, not quite a trillion, but an incredible amount of money nonetheless. A trillion dollars would pay off twenty-five percent of the national deficit—a start—or get Chrysler out of trouble nine hundred more times.

The $27 trillion planetary output, though, is dwarfed by a parallel economic system that is only two decades old. Behind the $27 trillion "real" economy of goods and services is a hidden, mysterious "financial" economy that rewards speculation, legalized international hedging and fudging for hundredths of a percentage point gain or loss. The financial economy is between twenty and fifty times as large as the real economy: one quadrillion dollars.

The financial economy was created on August 15, 1971, when President Richard Nixon altered the structure of global commerce to such an extent that it "represented the greatest challenge to the world economy since the Great Depression."[8] Nixon, in one swift, bold, and almost unnoticed stroke, removed the American greenback from the gold standard to which it had adhered for decades, permitting the dollar to fluctuate along with the rest of the world's currencies.

The post-World War II monetary system was based upon the July 22, 1944, Bretton Woods Agreement at which the world's major currencies were locked to the dollar, which in turn was locked to the price of gold. This historic agreement stabilized the world's financial systems for almost thirty years. At the time of Bretton Woods, the U.S. necessarily assumed the role of global policeman and the world's financial manager. Nixon changed all of that.

Thus the financial economy was born, and, as it turns out, it could never have grown up without Computers Everywhere and the Global Network. The financial economy consists of the stock options and futures markets. Its global nature is emphasized by the incessant, twenty-four-hour trading of the world's major currencies as they fluctuate by the microsecond. Financial speculators gamble on whether the dollar will go up or down when a hurricane strikes Florida or when we whip Iraq. Floods in the Midwest affect the price of corn and thus soy beans and beef in Texas. A freeze in Southern California drives orange prices higher, and thus the speculator who gambled correctly lands a windfall for his accurate predictions. During September of 1992, one investor alone made an estimated $1 billion by correctly gambling in the financial economy. Good guess or good information? Political events in the U.S., Europe, and the Far East drive the markets wild while Wall Street prognosticators base their careers and fortunes on their analyses. There are winners, and there are losers.

Megabyte money in the financial economy exists primarily in Cyberspace. Computers do the trading, the guessing, and the analysis based upon never-ending volumes of information that must be collected, sorted, analyzed, and evaluated. Computers which are part of the Global Network instruct other computers to buy, sell, trade, or hold to investments and positions based upon instantaneous decisions made often without the intervention of a human mind or a live finger on the keyboard.

The hidden financial world of options, futures, and global hedges is a legal and erudite form of gambling. The world's financial economy, in excess of $1 quadrillion ($1,000 trillion), dwarfs the power of any single country or sphere of influence, and, with the proper incentives, could bankrupt any nation on Earth. Speculation breeds volatility. For every real dollar, speculators manipulate the markets with twenty to fifty financial dollars. Writes Kurtzman, "As a consequence, speculation holds far more sway over each nation's economic livelihood than we generally give it credit for."[9]

Behind the financial economy is a dizzying array of technology designed specifically to keep track of the 1s and the 0s, the dollars and the cents. There has been massive investment in the technology to manage thousands of trillions of dollars. Wall Street firms spent between $30 to 40 billion in the 1980s on Computers Everywhere, with $7.5 billion spent in 1991 alone.[10]

The trading rooms on Wall Street are as complex as a NASA facility. Thousands of computer terminals spread across acres of high-rise floor space offer on-line, real-time, dynamic sources of easy-to-interpret information presented in graphs, charts, three-dimensional models, and just about any other conceivable format. These systems all have a single goal: give the trader or stockbroker or currency rooms enough information to make a decent bet.

Wall Street in many ways is even more demanding than the

military for advances in computer and communications technology. The first Stock Exchange computer was installed by Burroughs (now part of Unisys) in 1964. Prior to that all transactions were done by hand. The financial economy's investment in technology is a relatively small amount compared with the value of the transactions that occur daily. The New York brokerage and trading houses alone pass $1.9 trillion over their computer networks every single day. That's almost $800 trillion per year, which doesn't include Tokyo, London, Frankfurt, Hong Kong, or other international trading centers. One New York brokerage house, Solomon Brothers, trades $2 trillion every year. The Federal Reserve System transfers $1 trillion every day over the Fed Wire. The world's other networks move another $2 trillion-plus every day.[11]

Incredibly vast sums of money, most of it real only in Cyberspace, offer the owners control and power over the destiny of companies, countries, and people. I think it becomes terribly obvious at this point that the Information Warrior has a terrific interest in the financial economy and its underlying technical infrastructure.

So far we have identified four of the components necessary to wage high-level Information Warfare:

- The New World Order
- Computers Everywhere
- The Global Network
- Megabyte Money in a Financial Economy

The last ingredient that the Information Warrior needs to achieve his goals is to understand the psychology of his potential victims. Given the state of technology versus man, the Information Warrior finds a fertile breeding ground to fully exploit and leverage his activities.

Binary Schizophrenia

JUST LIKE THE TERRORIST, the Information Warrior wants to mess with our minds.

As a society, we pretend that we are sophisticated enough to deal with just about any situation that life offers. We tend to project a cavalier nonchalance when incredible technological achievements leave the lab and arrive at the mall. Who watches space shuttle launches or is impressed by Dick Tracy watches anymore? What technology and Computers Everywhere have precipitated is a complex set of psychological ills which permeates our culture. The bottom line is, we really aren't comfortable with what the technical wizards and gurus have wrought and what their evangelists have sold to us.

The same argument could have been made over a half millennium ago when the first of four stunning social and technological achievements cracked open the door which would eventually lead us into the Information Age. In 1450, German inventor Johann Gutenberg invented the printing press. For the first time in history, the human race had the ability to mass produce and distribute information. Gutenberg was a visionary who believed he would change the world with his one invention. According to historian Daniel Boorstein, "He was a prophet of newer worlds where machines would do the work of scribes, where the printing press would displace the scriptorium, and knowledge would be diffused to countless unseen communities."[1] I seem to remember Steve Jobs being described in similar terms a mere five hundred years later.

Prior to the printing press, the literate few controlled what was read and written. The Bible, during the fifteen hundred years prior to Gutenberg, was meticulously and arduously copied and translated one page at a time. The political implications are inescapable. Indeed, some historians maintain that the Bible was translated according to the religious-political mores of the day; the high priests would meet with the Charlemagnes or the Vatican and decide how best to alter the contents and wording of the Bible to keep the masses in line. Few people checked the Bible for information integrity, and fewer still were willing to be burned at the stake (or worse) for announcing any errors in translation.

As it is today, those in control of the information were in control of society. The Soviet Union, for all of its impressive technological achievements, had strict bans on copy machines and typewriters—not to mention computers of any sort. Stalin's paranoiac preoccupation with restricted information flow— "only tell them what we want them to know"—continued until *perestroika*, and ultimately until the collapse of the Soviet Union. It wasn't that Russian and Ukrainian citizens didn't want access to information, or want to distribute their ideas to others. It was just that they could go to a labor camp for that sort of thing. Giving voice to free thought was treated as a criminal act of sedition against the state. Maybe we can credit Xerox and CNN for the final downfall of the Soviet Union.

After Gutenberg turned the world upside down, the great Venetian scholar Aldus Manutius (1450–1515) pioneered portable books, to the chagrin of many in the church. "We can't have them reading the Bible on their own," Church officials objected. "They might start thinking and come up with different interpretations than those we tell them about." Right. That's the whole idea.

The pen is mightier than the sword. Maybe, maybe not. But without doubt, the availability of information to the masses would evolve over the centuries into a formidable political and economic weapon. The Magna Carta, the Declaration of Independence, the Bill of Rights, the Emancipation Proclamation—they all set the tone for this nation's beliefs and tenets before there was a fax machine in sight.

The second technological development destined to change the way in which information was exchanged was the telephone, invented and first used by Alexander Graham Bell on March 10, 1876. Originally conceived as a mere ancillary tool for businesses, telephones proliferated in the homes of the more well-to-do within little more than a decade. According to author Bruce Sterling, "The telephone was not managed from any centralized broadcast center. It was to be a personal, intimate technology."[2] Eventually anyone with a few pennies could traipse down to their local corner drug store and use a pay phone. All they had to do was ask the operator to dial the number for them.

In 1876, the U.S. was wired with 214,000 miles of telegraph wire connecting 8,500 telegraph offices. Despite the opportunity before them, Western Union dismissed the telephone as a parlor toy, failing to purchase the rights to the invention.[3] Big mistake.

By 1904, the emerging telephone system crisscrossed the American continent, offering the general populace an easier means of communication than the telegraph. In a parallel to today's technology, Western Union attempted to centralize control over their communications systems. The Bell Company and its holding company, AT&T, gave the power to the people—the consumer—to do with the telephone service as they pleased, when they pleased, and from wherever they pleased. AT&T wanted to control the network, the wires that connected businesses, governments, and people in a century-old manifestation of Cyberspace.

The third explosion for information exchange was the radio, which sent electromagnetic communications through the air. Portable information exchange—without wires—set the tone for the century's opening decades and indeed, the entire century. Nikolai Tesla invented the technology, but because his poor business skills and personal idiosyncrasies distanced him from contemporary industrial giants such as George Westinghouse, Marconi has received history's credit for the invention of the radio.

Satellite communications, accurately predicted years earlier by science pundit and author Arthur C. Clarke, changed the face of information exchange when the expensive, time consuming, and occasionally dangerous laying of transatlantic telephone cables was replaced with an orbiting satellite, launched from Cape Canaveral, Florida. Telstar expanded the concept of the network, the phone system, and primitive Cyberspace.

In under thirty years, satellite communications became an absolute necessity for international transactions. Today, the demand is such that hundreds of new satellite launches are being planned. Motorola's Iridium Project, for example, will ring the planet with sixty-six satellites, permitting portable phone users to talk to anyone, anywhere, at any time.[4] A true multinational effort is under way, including Japanese money and manufacturing and Russian orbital launch capabilities. Two competing consortiums have also begun staging their own satellite-based competitive global communications efforts.

The fourth major revolution in information technology was the personal computer. The power of information was further shifted from those in centralized position of power to everyman and everywoman. Prior to the personal computer (circa 1950–1970) early cyberpriests hunched over paper-tape readers, punch cards, and massive clunky disk drives, changing vacuum tubes to keep their behemoth systems crunching.

Only the largest companies—and the government of course— could afford to keep a computer running, and the entire computer industry was basically owned and operated by IBM. It wasn't well until the 1970s, when pioneering companies like Intel and Apple made computers small and affordable enough for any home or office, that the makings for the personal computer revolution were complete. And now we have Computers Everywhere and the Global Network. The Information Age is here—but we've been saying that since the fifteenth century.

In 1964, the French philosopher Jacques Ellul contended that technology had reduced man, its inventor, to a mere cog serving a global megamachine. Politics and the state have been surpassed by the importance of technology, he argued. Economics, whether capitalistic or socialist, no longer matter in the grander scheme of machine over man. Man had little will left, and even the political system which promulgated the machine was a scripted component of the inevitable bureaucracy required to support the machine.[5] All of this thirty years ago. What would he say today?

Seven years later, in *The Greening of America*, Charles Reich also noticed that technology and society were at odds. "What we have is technology, organization, and administration out of control, running for their own sake. . . . And we have turned over to this system the control and direction of everything—the natural environment, our minds, our lives."[6] This was a decade before the personal computer.

Americans, perhaps more so than our better educated technological planetary neighbors, are distinctly schizophrenic about Computers Everywhere. Now, I have no desire to enter into a foray about clinical terminology with the American Psychiatric Association; I am using the term schizophrenia, and more specifically Binary Schizophrenia, only to make a point. By and large, as a culture, we suffer from the pressure caused by two opposing and very strong forces pressing for our attention. Very few of us indeed would disagree strongly with these simple statements:

I Need Computers
I Don't Trust Computers

When these two conditions are forced to coexist, an internal conflict arises. I refer to this technologically-created conflict between preference and cultural necessity as Binary Schizophrenia.

Let's see how this condition manifests itself.

You are a very important person with important things to do (should be easy to imagine). Your importance requires that you travel a lot to see other important people, so you can do important things together. A meeting in Las Vegas requires that you be there, rarin' to go, at 9:00 AM PST. It is absolutely essential that you be there—this will be the most important thing you will have ever done.

No problem. Your secretary talks to the travel agency, takes care of all of your travel needs, and presents you with a neat, prepackaged itinerary with everything covered down to the last detail. In order to fulfill your needs as quickly as possible, your secretary and the travel agent need to use computers: computerized airline, car rental, and hotel reservations; fax machines to confirm those reservations; credit card authorization for immediate payment. You need to be in Vegas. To do this you need computers. Condition one of Binary Schizophrenia is met.

You arrive at the gate ten minutes before departure—as is your usual habit—carrying a bulging briefcase and an expensive leather garment bag. First class is the only way to go: a big seat and a drink in hand before take off. But wait; your seat is occupied. Two clone airline tickets with duplicate seat assignments. Damn computers.

The gate manager can't figure it out. "Oops. But since the other gentleman was here first, he should have the seat. Terribly sorry." They try to negotiate with other passengers, but the flight is full and there are standbys. No one will trade seats with you, not even in coach and not even with the added incentive of compensation. You *have* to be in Vegas.

"Sorry, there's nothing we can do . . . but we will pay for your ticket. . . ." The only way to Las Vegas tonight routes you from La Guardia to O'Hare Chicago for a two-hour layover and then into McCarran Vegas at 1:00 AM instead of 8:30 PM. You needed to get to Las Vegas early so you will be in shape for your meeting. Worst of all? No first class available. Ecch. Damn computers.

So you arrive in Vegas at 1:00 AM, but the good news is that the car rental firm is open all night—as is everything else in the desert mecca of indulgence. You are tired, but looking forward to the drive to your hotel in a Jaguar convertible to give you a much needed buzz.

"What do you mean you never got the reservation . . . ?" You are staggered.

"Our computers were down for a while . . . and I guess the records got a little screwed up . . . but don't worry, we still have cars." Maybe there is a God, you think, only He's having a bad hair day and taking it out on you. "We still have a couple of Volkswagen Vanagons and a selection of Yugos," the young lady says pertly.

A Yugo? For an important meeting? "Never mind. I'll call for a limo." One long, embarrassing, limoless hour later, you begrudgingly choose the bright yellow Yugo because it was the only one without red and orange flames painted on its side and hood. Damn computers. You don't trust 'em. Condition two for Binary Schizophrenia has been met.

At least Caesar's will treat you right.

"I'm sorry, sir, there must have been some mistake. We just don't have any record of your reservation and we just don't have any rooms, none at all. No suites either. You see, there's a computer convention in town."

Damn computer convention.

By 3:30 AM, Caesar's is kind enough (they really are sorry about your problem) to have found you a room. It's only a few blocks down the strip. The rates are $17 for every three hours. Cash only.

Damn computers.

Now I don't know about your level of tolerance, but if you haven't blown your cork by now, only one more thing could completely ruin your year.

Phew! You made it. Tired, but you made it. 9 AM. Your important meeting with important people. On the twenty-third floor with a big view. The secretary is very pretty and very congenial, but you sense something amiss in her kindness.

"I'm sorry, sir, I guess you didn't get the message. That meeting was moved to Tuesday, next week."

Shock. Rage. Denial. Disbelief. Fury. Heavy sigh.

"Why wasn't I called?" you ask, pulling out your combination Skypager and "Star Trek" cellular phone. Unfortunately, the back-lit LCD display on your three-and-a-half-ounce personal communicator is flashing a message:

ERROR 21 NO SERVICE AVAILABLE

Damn Phones. Damn Computers.

Such a chain of crises is thankfully very rare, but most of us have been encumbered by similar detours and they are frustrating to say the least. We can readily appreciate the increasing level of internal panic that comes from being out of control. (Prozac fans can relate.) The unpredictable next-steps taken by those who are out of control after exceeding their tolerance levels to constant roadblocks is entirely up to the reader's imagination. But I don't believe I've yet heard of a court case where the defense is based on the premise that "The computer made me do it." But the computer gets blamed for just about everything, doesn't it?

We have an inherent need for computers, yet at the slightest sign of error, they instantly become the target of our vehemence. The computer is wrong. The computer must have goofed.

The airline captain tells his captive passengers after sitting on the tarmac for five hours, "We're waiting for maintenance to put in a new backup computer. For safety's sake."

Your stockbroker: "The sell order never made it through. The computers were overloaded."

Your bank manager: "I'm sure if you bring in your canceled checks we can find the error in a couple of days and reopen your account. Maybe that's why the ATM ate your card, too."

News magazine subscription clerk: "I'm sorry, but I can't find you anywhere in the computer. Do you spell your name any other way?"

Grocery checkout line after the ice cream already melted: "The scanners aren't working. Give us a few minutes more."

A computerized letter from the IRS: "Tax Lien: Please send $145,376.00 to this office within five days or . . ."

"The number you have dialed is experiencing difficulty, please try again later."

"Sorry, you entered your password with the wrong finger. Please re-enter."

Arguing with a computer is about as useless as teaching Congress how to spell "balanced budget." We've all tried. Even worse are the clerks whose voices merely echo what their computers tell them. The words "But the computer says . . ." really mean, "Read my lips. The computer says so. If you continue to yell in my face, I'll call the police. Next."

Our Binary Schizophrenia is not limited to the business world; it creeps into our psyches everyday. It's what I call "approximation anxiety."

How do you tell time? Are you one of those who respond to the simple inquiry, "Got the time?" with "It's two thirty-seven, seventeen seconds," or do you prefer, "Quarter of three?"

Computers have forced us to speak digital instead of human. Digital interfaces have been subconsciously training us to program our VCRs to the nearest half-minute, prevent us from ruining the dinner in the microwave by an extra ten seconds on high, or drive at exactly sixty-six MPH. You used to buy a pound of meat, and now you receive 1.03 pounds. I don't mean to imply that accuracy is bad—it certainly is a boon. However, as a result of heavy reliance upon digital information, we are losing our ability to discriminate. Can you recognize that if you enter 20 x 26 into your calculator and get an answer of 620, the answer is wrong? You trust your calculator for an extra answer and you can't even approximate an answer in your head, on your own?

For most of us, saying the moon is a quarter million miles away is close enough for discussion but not for science. What about spreadsheets? At one time or another, we have all spent the night working on a long complex budget, or financial analysis, or projections. We hand them in and, to our horror, someone else finds a single column addition error that throws off every other number in all 2,048 rows and XXIV columns. All of that work gone . . . all because most of us don't have the ability to scan a spreadsheet and quickly identify an absurd answer. Far too many of us rely exclusively on what the computer says.

Damn computers.

Humans are essentially fuzzy in their logic. Our eyes don't tell us that the tree is 376.5 yards away. We might say it's ¼ mile or a thousand feet away: both are wrong but useful approximations. Our ears don't tell us that the piano note is 1760 cycles; we hear an A, which we would also hear at 1750 cycles or at 1770 cycles. The computer is exact.

On the other hand, some of us are outwardly pugilistic when computer answers don't match our expectations. Have you ever disagreed with the calculation made by a computer? Of course you have. We all have. "That can't be right," we say. And then we bring out the pocket calculator to double check the results. So what do you trust more in that case? The computer or the calculator. Intriguing dilemma. Enter, enter. If the calculator agrees with the computer you might go, "Oh well, I guess it is right," and shrug off your accusation. On the other hand, if the answer differs what do you do? Accuse the computer of being in error, yet enter the numbers again into the calculator to double check. What confidence! Not many of us can honestly say we bring out a pencil and rely upon our own brains to solve the problem. We have the need to trust computers. If we didn't trust them, at least to a certain extent, we couldn't get much done.

Binary Schizophrenia extends into corporate America's public relations as well. Few companies admit that they have had a computer break-in or were the victims of computer crime. The potential public relations fall-out is just too radical to consider.

Imagine that the Big Bank of Los Angeles (BBLA) has been living a charmed life. Bank of America was hit by hackers, fraudulent ATM cards, and millions of dollars of bad software. Security Pacific supposedly almost lost it all to Information Warriors trying to wire $5 billion overseas via the SWIFT satellite network. But so far, for mythical Big Bank of LA, nothing.

Until, one day, customers receive their monthly statements and their balances are off by varying amounts. Tens of thousands of confused and angry customers find themselves short substantial amounts of money, while others try to figure out how to capitalize on a bank error in their favor. Quick, write checks before the mistake is caught. The bank is inundated with customer calls. Teller lines at the hundred-odd branches snake into the streets. The media gets wind of what's happening and, as the eyes and ears of public concern, start asking questions. Questions the bank doesn't want asked because there are no answers yet. BBLA management has commandeered every computer expert they can find. "What happened? No, don't tell me, just fix it."

By the end of the day, there are still no answers, just problems. A few calls to the right federal agencies and Washington moles descend on the bank within hours. All of the bank's records have been corrupted, going back at least a week. Restoring the computer's memory will require thousands of man-hours to manually recreate accurate records. What will they tell their customers until then? Then, the worst imaginable scenario that any bank can imagine. Customers are demanding their money. In droves. It is a run on the bank, a bank's worst nightmare.

No bank, and no business for that matter, can stomach the

idea of admitting their problems outside of their cozy little boardrooms. Yet, if a bank experienced such problems, you can bet it won't be a well-kept secret for long. It's the equivalent of an electronic meltdown. A private computer Chernobyl. All systems No-Go.

The Information Warrior will count on corporate America's Binary Schizophrenia as a weapon as much as he will use and abuse the technology itself. The Information Warrior knows that stability is an illusion, a perception of reality that may or may not have any true substance. He can take a bank or business or small government that is not shaky in the least, and manipulate its information to his advantage. He can create the perception of instability by using the Global Network and the news services that control the information we see at home on one of our five hundred channels to leak, spread, or alter information garnished from the target. The Information Warrior will massage the new perception into a new reality. Once people hear that a bank just might be shaky, they will take out their money to avoid being victimized. The bank then will actually be shaky, which is exactly what the Information Warrior wanted to achieve.

Digital Addiction

As Thomas Hughes observed, "The price we pay for a cornucopia of goods and services is slavery."[7] That slavery is no more evident than in our addiction to technology.

Nintendo, for example, has addicted an entire generation to interactive video game playing, with riots occurring when insufficient supplies are made available to anxious consumers.[8] Billions of dollars are spent every year so that addicts from preteens to octogenarians can spend endless hours in front of a fourteen-inch computer monitor, trying to find Carmen San Diego, playing with Mario's joystick, or attempting to fit oddly-shaped geometric pieces into compact spaces. Our children spend an average of thirty-five hours per week glued to the television screen inhaling incredible quantities of information of dubious value. Addiction to be sure; Nintendo and Sega are the drugs.

Hackers are similarly addicted to computers. Many live solely for their keyboards and screens, and their meanderings through Cyberspace, across the Global Network into computer systems where they don't belong. In May 1993, a nineteen-year-old British computer hacker, who had admitted breaking into computers and causing hundreds of thousands of dollars in damage, was found not guilty by reason of addiction to computers.[9]

Virtual Reality machines offer an all-immersing plunge into Cyberspace, activating most of our senses with excitement. When body suits offer cybersexual encounters for the price of an arcade ticket, an entirely new addiction—AIDS free—will permeate society. Technology makes it all so easy, and we eat it up with every new gadget and toy that the silicon gurus can muster.

But our addiction far surpasses the entertainment value of Computers Everywhere, transcending age group, ethnicity, and vocation. Once a society gets used to high-speed computers, instant communications, and recreational or professional gratification at the push of a button, it's impossible to wean them of the habit. In 1968, Marshall McLuhan said that emerging information networks are "direct extensions" of our own nervous systems. Losing an ATM machine, according to that reasoning, is the equivalent of a leg or an arm. People panic when their computer goes down.

The financial markets, which make instantaneous decisions on how to handle their trillions, lose millions of dollars an hour if their computers fail. According to Kurtzman, "Today's world is very different from the world of the past. Economic success in this world—especially in the financial sector but increasingly in other sectors as well—is dependent on assimilating large quantities of information very rapidly."[10] We have come to expect computers to work all of the time, exactly when we want; if they fail to perform, our addiction to them forces a virtual shutdown of business—such is the psyche of the modern businessman. The government is probably more addicted to Computers Everywhere than any other segment of society. Who can fight a war without computers? When is the last time you saw a handwritten check from Social Security or the IRS? It won't ever happen, ever again.

The Information Warrior knows and understands our cultural and personal addiction to the tools and toys we have allowed into our homes and businesses. He understands that by causing a computer system or network to malfunction, he will certainly create problems. But he also counts upon the corollary digital addiction to help him in his aims. As we shall see, the Information Warrior will tailor his battle plans to maximize the synergy between the machines and the people who run them. He will count upon our addictive frailties and the resulting human reactions—fear, distrust, and confusion—to exacerbate any crisis he intends.

Information Overload

"Cyberspace, like the earth itself, is becoming polluted. Too much information is filling it. And our brains are just too tiny to sort through it all. Information overload threatens to bring further catastrophe, no matter how well the trading rooms are designed."[11] Kurtzman refers to the overload of technology itself, but the human element faces the same crisis.

We are pushing the systems and networks harder than they were designed to be pushed. The Internet, a major part of the Global Network, moves billions of messages. It's approaching capacity; nonetheless, we demand more from it. Companies are closing their networks, their personal pieces of Cyberspace, to further growth until they can handle the additional overhead. The digital superhighway proposed by then-Senator Albert Gore is an attempt to overcome that limitation, but technical information overload will occur again at some future date as we continue to push the limits of data capacity.

The superhighway descendant, the National Information Infrastructure, will virtually guarantee conflicts between man and machine in the coming years.

Information overload is an invitation to disaster for us personally, corporately, and nationally. With five hundred television channels to choose from, what do you watch? You just can't watch the diet channel and the sci-fi channel and "Married With Children" and "I Love Lucy" reruns and the boating channel—and still have a life. Couch potatoes morph into cyberspuds. How do we decide what information we want? That is an unanswered question. Can we make rational, well-informed decisions about which information is truly valuable, or will we inundate ourselves with the inanities of the infomercials and supermarket tabloids, to the exclusion of quality news and information? The Global Network offers literally tens of thousands of choices—seemingly overwhelming freedom of choice—for our edification and growth. How do we make those choices?

Many of us find that TV is our sole source of information about the world around us. Are our politics shaped by Bernard Shaw or Dan Rather? Do our cultural assumptions and beliefs come exclusively from Wile E. Coyote and the Fox Network, or do we allow ourselves a smattering of PBS shows as well? Is Rush Limbaugh the staple diet for the political right, or do John Metzger's anti-black, anti-Semitic white power local cable shows feed our already divided, hate-filled society with more distortions and lies?

More and more, the media has become the central filter by which we view our world, and thus make judgements and decisions about what we will do, how we will respond, and what we will teach our children. The media are filled with people just like you and me, whose personal biases, beliefs, and interests act as the filter for our perceptions. Those of us who read and view only what we already believe, to the exclusion of all else—particularly that which we may find disturbing—do ourselves and our culture a terrible disservice. We allow the media to control our thoughts by feeding us sound bites and quick, tidy synopses of what are in fact world shattering events. Condensing events in Bosnia or China into a three-minute segment to be ingested over salad and dessert is a ratings necessity for the big networks, but we miss out on opposing viewpoints, crucial facts, and in-depth analyses that must be considered before we ourselves can make an informed decision or hold a defensible position. The news—as attractive multimedia stimulation—informs America of highly interconnected global events by reducing them to a form of personal entertainment—an addiction similar to Nintendo—instead of events worthy of thought, interpersonal discussion, and reflection.

The print media offers far better alternatives but *Newsweek* and *US News and World Report*, as do all magazines, have their own editorial slants, opinions, and biases. No reporter, unless he or she is totally devoid of human emotions, can be completely objective. He, by definition, acts as the filter to the news information we receive. The print media has the format to provide in-depth coverage of major issues that face us today. Yet someone who only reads *Time* magazine will get their information filtered through their slant to the exclusion of Bill Buckley's *National Review* or the plethora of left-wing publications.

The New York Times, the *Los Angeles Times*, the *Washington Post*, and the *Wall Street Journal* offer in-depth reporting and intensive editorials, but we cannot be blind to their necessarily human biases. And we have to keep in mind that the likes of the *New York Post* and similar newspapers across the country appeal to sensationalism and headline news with little or no substance. The readers of such news media, who do not partake of more substantial reporting, find themselves at the bottom end of the information filtration process, where the body of their worldly knowledge arrives in 72-point headlines which reduce events to bumper-sticker slogans.

The average American cannot read five newspapers daily as well as a selection of magazines representing the spectrum of political views. Yet, increasingly, we as citizens need more and more information just to keep even. Corporate America faces the same dilemma, as it throws more and more technology at more and more information in hopes that it will be able to make the decisions necessary to survive and compete. Estimations are that the data storage requirements of a large corporation will soon exceed one petabyte or one billion gigabytes. Artificial intelligence systems will have to decide which information is relevant and which is irrelevant: more computers to decide which other computers are worth listening to. Human intervention, even in the decision making process, will no longer be possible. We will have to trust that the cyberpriests develop artificial intelligence machines smart enough—human enough—to make decisions with which we are comfortable.

The talented Information Warrior with a Dale Carnegie course under his belt now has a whole new approach. He no longer needs to go after the underling computers used to sift through the primary sources of information upon which modern society depends. He can talk to the computer that makes the decisions and convince it to see things his way, just as any salesman would do. Who or what can you believe? Is the computer really right, or does the information manager at the World Bank need to question every decision made by the computer itself? Binary Schizophrenia at the highest level.

And so we come full circle. We need to trust the computer that trusts the computer that trusts the computer that trusts the computer. . . .

4

On The Nature
of Insidious

"Information is the only asset that can be in two places at the same time."

—CHARLES ROBERTELLO
INFORMATION SECURITY EXPERT.

THE INFORMATION WARRIOR is a clever fellow. He knows that out-and-out destruction of buildings or bridges or airplanes will not meet his real goals. The lack of subtlety of the terrorist attacks and attempts in New York City in 1993 make him cringe. "What amateurs," he thinks. The Information Warrior knows there's a better way.

But first, let's take a quick look at what the high-level goals of the Information Warrior really are: Not the details of a particular operation, like which company or trade secret is under attack, but a generalized set of strategic goals for any purpose.

1. Theft of Information

As Robertello states above, information is that unique asset that can be in two places at the same time, and if that information has been purloined competently, only the thief—the Information Warrior—will know that it is in two places. The victim won't have a clue. Regardless of motivation, theft of information is a primary goal for the personal, the corporate, and global Information Warrior.

Stealing corporate secrets can provide competitive advantage. The legal pilfering of our patent offices on a daily basis by organized cadres of Japanese Information Warriors threatens the global competitiveness of American industry. The theft of military secrets and communications codes are relegated to the world of espionage, with many amateur Information Warriors paying the ultimate price for their troubles and receiving only minimal rewards. The nation-state that sponsors such activities still benefits with little or no risk or retaliation on our part.

The theft of credit card numbers, telephone calling card access codes, and other modern "electronic money" devices has a direct pecuniary effect upon the victims. Such purloined information has inherent value that is immediately translatable into goods and services. Stolen access codes for telephone credit cards are sold to dozens of co-conspiring Information Warriors all across the country within minutes of the illegal acquisition. Valuable information will exist in many different locations at the same time, unbeknownst to its legitimate owner, until it comes time to pay the bill.

Then we have blackmail. We all have secrets, skeletons, or even thoughts and ideas that are better kept to ourselves. If they become public, such information can destroy a company, a career, or a life. The Information Warrior, exploiting such techniques as are described in this book, will keep blackmail as one of his options. And you can't have information returned to you and be sure all other copies are gone—ever.

2. Modification of Information

Instead of out-and-out stealing information, the Information Warrior may find that merely altering the information itself suits his particular goals. In the security business, we use the term *integrity* to describe whether or not information has been modified.

The integrity of information is essential in the financial community. We'd all like to be sure that the check for $17.98 we wrote to the drug store doesn't subtract $1,798.00 from our checking account. Banks want to ensure that the wire transfer is for $1,000,000,000.00 and not for $10,000,000,000.00.

But integrity of information—or the lack thereof—can hit home, too. At the personal level, an Information Warrior could make your life miserable if your credit files are mangled beyond recognition, full of falsehoods and distortions. Your mortgage won't be approved, the lease on your new car will be denied, and depending upon your occupation, your future employment opportunities will suffer.

Or if your medical profiles or health records are maliciously modified (in distinction to the ever present accidental errors), you may be denied health insurance or a job. Your status as a medical deadbeat would be easily confirmed to anyone with $50 and the desire to look. The Information Warrior can turn the picture of health into electronic genocide.

Alteration of data is an ideal method for the Information Warrior to instill fear, inflict damage, or embarrass victims with no warning. Imagine a corporate report so filled with errors that SEC investigations and stockholder lawsuits are triggered. Long, complex legal documents with endless minutiae can be intentionally filled with subtle errors that invert the meaning or intent. Errors in spreadsheets are difficult to detect, but compounded faulty calculations can render results meaningless or worse yet, indicting.

3. Destruction of Information

If the Information Warrior has the ability to alter and manipulate information, he also has the ability to destroy it. There have been countless cases of the accidental destruction of information when a computer system simply runs out of steam, or is hit by lightening, by a bomb, or by a flood. But, as we will see, some first-generation Information Warriors have, either out of frustration or pure hostility, simply denied legitimate users or owners access to their own information resources. Phone phreaks have effectively blackmailed some companies by threatening to destroy their PBX systems unless given voice mail boxes for their own use. Companies who don't succumb have lost the use of their entire phone system.

The old adage, "If I can't have it, no one else can, either," is a sophomoric dating game easily applied to Information Warfare. If the goal is to steal information, then an excellent means of covering up the crime is to destroy the access to the very information that was stolen—further complicating the investigative and restorative process. The Information Warrior may destroy data and information as a cover-up. Where have we heard that before . . . uh . . . Watergate, maybe? The courts ruled in 1993 that Government employees may not erase or destroy their own electronic messages, or E-mail, since they are part of the public record of democracy at work. We will see how the Information Warrior will use the destruction of data and information to his advantage when fighting an Information War.

4. Destruction of the Information Infrastructure

We know how critical information networks and communications systems are to the sustenance of companies and to the national economic security of this country. The Information Warrior may well decide that it is within his strategic goals to totally shut down his adversary's ability to process information at all. Inexpensive weapons are available to potential Information Warriors that will accomplish just this. Weapons heretofore exclusively under the domain of governments and military organizations have hit the streets and, properly used, will put any information-processing-based business or entity out of commission.

Insidious Weapons for the Information Warrior

We now need to understand the nature of the weapons used to effect these goals. The Information Warrior has a unique set of needs and his weapons are tailored to the task at hand, just as the military uses task-specific weapons when it wages conventional conflicts. The military may design a fighter plane that provides high speed performance with a small payload. A low altitude bomber has different tasks, thus different requirements from a B-52. Some bombs are designed to explode at a predetermined altitude, others are set to explode only after penetrating a structure or digging themselves into the ground. Some explosive projectiles are designed to be armor piercing; others used for antipersonnel application throw concentrations of skin-piercing shrapnel. They all have a purpose. The Navy patrols the seas armed with a wide range of military options that suit a variety of potential situations: Aircraft carriers, frogmen, big guns, F-15s, depth charges, cruise missiles, ASW. The Army, Air Force, and Marines also deploy a complex mixture of weapon systems each of which is apropos to the circumstances.

In the business world, a company can gain competitive commercial advantage with impressive audio-visual and multimedia demonstrations, better research, and hundreds of other strategies affecting the market. To the "Business Is War" mentality, each of these elements can be thought of as a weapon, to be used judiciously as part of the master plan.

The Information Warrior, however, is less interested in weapons of physical destruction. If all else fails, or as a consequential effect of another act, the Information Warrior might resort to the physical destruction of information systems by conventional explosive means. But such means lack the qualities that the Information Warrior so cherishes. The Information Warrior prefers the elegant approach; he seeks to leverage his advantage of surprise and strengthen it with qualities and characteristics that will synergistically increase the effectiveness of the attack. Familiar criteria are important to the Information Warrior; they correspond to military equivalents.

1. How much damage can be done when the weapon is used? The strength and power of information weaponry can be equated to conventional explosive weapons.
2. From what distance is the weapon effective? The military wants to know and control how far it can shoot its weapons. U.S. battleships stationed off the coast of Beirut can hurl explosive shells over twenty miles into the city. Cruise missiles are effective for several hundred miles regardless of the warhead used. ICBMs can cross the globe and hit their targets within a couple hundred yards. Similarly, the Information Warrior has to gauge the distance versus effectiveness of his weapons, whether they are going to be used against a faraway target in Cyberspace or against a business on the third floor of his office building.
3. Sensitivity is a measure of how weak a signal can be detected by the radio or satellite or other type of listening device. Much of the Information Warrior's arsenal is based upon the ability to eavesdrop invisibly on one's adversary, thereby stealing information.

INVISIBILITY

A secondary set of criteria upon which the Information Warrior evaluates the abilities of his weapons arsenal provides a clearer picture of the nature of Information Warfare. When applied against defenseless businesses and organizations, these criteria will appear to be almost magical. It is these characteristics that make Information Warfare techniques so potentially dangerous to our econotechnical information infrastructure, and ultimately the national security of the United States as a whole.

If the Pentagon could buy invisible tanks, they could park them anywhere they wanted, from the outskirts of Los Angeles in preparation for a riot to the desert fringes of Baghdad. At the first sign of trouble, they would launch a quick surgical strike and then get the heck out of Dodge before anyone knew what hit them. In fact this rationale is the argument for the development of the Stealth bomber. Fly a huge plane carrying a few nukes into enemy territory, drop 'em, and go home. Stealths aren't really invisible, but the enemy's radar systems won't see a reflective signature any larger than that of a basketball— good enough for "spook 'em and nuke 'em."

To the Information Warrior, invisibility is an absolutely crucial quality of his armaments. He does not want to be seen or be in any way identified with his activities, which undoubtedly sit on the wrong side of the law. If you can't be seen, the reasoning goes, then you can't be caught. The first and obvious intent is that he remain physically invisible. However, there is a second and equally important intent: electronic invisibility.

The Information Warrior fights many of his battles in Cyberspace on the digital highways that hold our society together. While physically he may be lounging in a wicker chair by the beach, his terminal is connected to the rest of the Global Network. His power stretches as far as his modem can dial. The Information Warrior needs to insure that his electronic being, the part of him that is projected across networks everywhere, cannot be traced back to the physical him.

Most of the tools that the Information Warrior has at his disposal will provide him with a high degree of invisibility. Of course he has to use his weapons properly, and as time goes by, the Information Warrior will improve his skills. He will get more creative, bolder with his efforts. We could conceptually say that convicted computer hackers forgot one of the Information Warrior's first edicts: Stay Invisible. They didn't. They got caught.

PASSIVITY

The Information Warrior loves passive weapons. They are stunningly elegant, and unless he really screws up, he won't get caught. One of the best examples of passive Information Warfare is the debacle at the U.S. Embassy in Moscow. During the early 1980s, we used Soviet workers to pour concrete and nail sheetrock in the construction process of the new embassy building, a political decision reflecting attempts at brotherly detente. So what did the Soviets do? Out of the kindness of their hearts, they fed thousands upon thousands of electronic diodes into the concrete soup that was poured into columns and floors to support the structure. Using a couple thousand dollars worth of diodes, which cost a penny or two each in quantity, the Soviets confounded our ability to determine if the Embassy was bugged or not, since a diode and a bug look the same to countersurveillance and sweeping equipment. A pretty neat trick, brilliant in its simplicity, to disguise the fact that they might have placed hundreds of real bugs amidst the ersatz ones. The upshot is that over $100 million later, the U.S. is preparing another embassy site. But the elegance of the Soviet trick makes an intelligence agent on either side wink in appreciation, and the Information Warrior nod knowingly.

The Information Warrior places great faith in his passive weapons, the weapons that when used against his victims will leave no scars, no damage, and no one the wiser . . . until the Information Warrior decides that such a course is propitious.

The U.S. government's ability to use passive weaponry against its uninformed citizens causes great concern for constitutional scholars. The passive tools of the Information Warrior have rendered personal and corporate electronic privacy virtually nonexistent. One encouraging thought, though, is that the same passive techniques are available to you, the potential victims.

DRONING

Smart Information Warriors do everything they can to ensure that they don't get caught. Once you're caught, the game's over. So, in order to avoid detection or have his real or electronic face seen, the Information Warrior will use remote control methods when at all possible to effect his strategies.

The most modern and illuminating example of a drone weapon is the Cruise Missile. Guided by computers and sophisticated internal mapping, it can fly hundreds of miles and find its target with pinpoint accuracy. Reminiscent of Hitler's early attempts at technology with the V-1 and V-2 rockets aimed at England, the cruise missile is relatively inexpensive, coming in at less than $1 million each. But more important to the folks here at home, the expendable cruise missile saves American lives: They don't have to be piloted by native sons from Kansas. These remote controlled mechanisms are called drones.

The Information Warrior wants to create deniability—the government loves that word, too. It is amazingly simple to "drone" oneself and one's goals in Cyberspace, and thus droning is a favorite tool of the well-honed Information Warrior. If he can have another person indicted for his deeds by the use of electronic drones, all the better.

FALLOUT

To most of us, the word *fallout* connotes dread, bringing up visions of long-term aftereffects from a nuclear blast. To the Information Warrior, though, fallout is a very desirable characteristic of his weapon. Typically, fallout is the mass effect that a single event caused by an Information Warrior can have on people and organizations other than the primary target. For example, if a computer network, the primary target, is disabled, a large number of people are immediately affected, and then other people who depend upon that network are also affected. The biggest single network is the phone company. In the past few years we have seen just how widespread the effects of a phone computer failure can be. The Information Warrior wants to get the most bang for his buck, and may elect to use weapons which provide plenty of fallout after the initial strike. But he must also keep in mind that the fallout may be indiscriminate, and affect groups it was not intended to, or have little impact upon the intended victims.

A typical bomb goes off once, does its damage, and that's that. But imagine a bomb that goes off, then marches down the street, and goes off again, then moves on to another target, on and on until the bomb is finally disarmed or destroyed. That kind of "bomb" is popular with and available to the Information Warrior. The Information Warrior must design and pick his methods carefully, for too much fallout, too early, might send future plans awry.

INSIDIOUSNESS

When a bomb goes off in an airport terminal, there is no question that an extreme act of violence has occurred. While the placement of the bomb might be insidious, the act itself is overt and will be reported on CNN within minutes. Often the responsible parties will take credit for the act in the furtherance of their own agenda. A bombing at an airport or at a London office building, or a massacre with machine guns, has immediate and usually predictable effects: panic, terror, destabilization, personal trauma, and a military or paramilitary response.

The Information Warrior, though, is not always in search of immediate gratification and headline-grabbing national attention. In many cases he prefers to wait, staging his attack when conditions are optimum. His goals and means are not always as obvious as in the case above. Time is on his side. His victims may not even know that they have been targeted, and the results of his efforts may have unpredictable long-term effects.

We need to remember that the Information Warrior does not want to capture and occupy territory; maintaining financial control or political influence are more likely aims. Being an occupying landlord no longer has the same attractiveness that it once did. The Information Warrior does not want to be bloodied by killing off opponents. Disabling them financially or destabilizing their powerbase is often sufficient. The vengeful Information Warrior will derive greater pleasure from watching his prey wriggle rather than from watching him die. If the target is a well-known company or organization, reading the *Wall Street Journal*'s accounts of its troubles might well bring glee as the tottering company suffers public indignity and its information systems collapse.

In a competitive economic war, the battles are tedious, lengthy, costly, and subject to fluctuating outcomes. Compaq and Apple became powerful economic forces over a period of years, not weeks or months. It took Japan twenty years to gain a thirty-percent share of the U.S. auto market; their early imports were a disaster. Economies tend to move slowly, thus permitting the Information Warrior the luxury of time.

But insidiousness is more than just clever. Investigators found enough pieces of the cassette-player bomb that downed flight Pan Am 103 over Lockerbie, Scotland, to enable them to trace the bomb to its makers and ultimately to the plot's sponsors. Even though the bomb explodes, it leaves traces that, when retrieved, are put to the most rigorous analysis money can buy. The FBI operates the finest criminal forensic laboratories in the world. Their tools are second to none and when applied with vigor, otherwise insignificant evidence can be transformed into case-breaking and courtroom case-making arguments. Microscopic evidence provides the investigator with unique opportunities such as DNA identification, nuclear magnetic resonance, and spectrum analysis. In short, a conventional explosive weapon is traceable.

The Information Warrior would like to eliminate that word from his vocabulary. "Traceable" is just not part of his modus operandi. He wishes to stay deep in the background, plan and plot, quickly and quietly deploy his weapons, and make sure he is a safe, undetectable distance away.

Insidiousness is further exploited by the Information Warrior due to general ignorance on the parts of "computer experts," management, and government policy makers. Most people, unless properly trained, rarely consider that someone may be out to get them; that data errors and systems malfunctions may be intentional; that they may be purposely attacked by an Information Warrior whom they have never met.

Thus far we have taken a high-level strategic view of what qualities the Information Warrior desires in his weapons and what broad-stroke concepts and philosophies he would consider when choosing a weapon appropriate for a particular type of strike.

- Theft of Information
- Modification of Information
- Destruction of Information
- Destruction of Information Processing Capability
- Invisibility
- Passivity
- Droning
- Fallout
- Insidiousness

So far we have looked at the big picture, something all too often not done by those in need of developing a strong defensive posture. The private sector is nearly blind to the capabilities of the Information Warrior, and the government is in much the same sorry state.

In December of 1992, I was invited to speak to about five hundred U.S. intelligence agents from the CIA, the FBI, Army Intelligence, the NSA, and every other alphabet soup agency Washington, D.C., could muster. I asked the promoter of the Open Source Solutions conference, Robert Steele, "What am I going to say up there? These guys are on the front lines. They already understand what this is all about." I was terrified of boring a highly sophisticated audience.

Robert merely smiled and said, "Do your thing."

The CIA was in the rear, filming the presentation, and I was flabbergasted to see that the audience followed my descriptions of Information Weaponry with more than merely polite attention. Afterwards, I was pleasantly surprised to have a crowd of intelligence agents come forward and ask for more information about Information Warfare. Perplexed but pleased I asked them, "Hey, aren't you guys the ones who are supposed to know about these weapons? Aren't you supposed to know how to fight these battles?"

One voice interrupted my questions with, "We can't talk to each other about what each of us is doing or knows. It's considered classified. We're not supposed to see the big picture. You've put it all together." The government, especially the spooks, spies, and goblins, compartmentalize and restrict information flow so thoroughly that most of what I spoke about was a complete surprise to them. From the government's viewpoint most of it was, and still is, classified.

In the next few pages, you—and they—will begin to see the pieces that make up the big picture.

5

Influenza, Malicious Software, and OOPS!

"Software makes the world go around, the world go around. . . ."

—NOT FROM *CABARET*

"There's always one more bug."

—MURPHY'S SOFTWARE PROGRAMMING LAW

COMPUTERS EVERYWHERE and the Global Network are run by software. When a computer screws up, the problem can only be one of two things: either the hardware or the software, and odds are it's the software. Software tends to fail, especially the complex kind.

When the first F-16 was undergoing flight tests years ago, the computers and backup systems were being shaken-down for accuracy and endurance as much as were the wings and fuselage for stress and life with aerodynamic realities. But when that F-16 crossed the equator and flipped upside down at 750 miles-per-hour, it was software that was at fault.

Software is the brains behind Computers Everywhere. It is the stuff that permits the Global Network to live and breathe throughout Cyberspace. And, software, that intangible stream of 0s and 1s, is a strange beast. Software is less than perfect and thus is one of the most sensitive pieces of a computer system, making it most vulnerable to attack by the Information Warrior.

Software tells the microwave oven to heat the frozen pizza at 450 degrees for six minutes. If the software goes awry, the pizza either remains a pepperoni iceberg or becomes shrunken nuclear waste. Software tells the ATM machine to spit out two twenties when you ask for $40.00 in cash. Not one or ten. Just two.

We think of computers as benign desktop work horses, personal companions, or behemoth disk drives and tapes spinning in climate-controlled rooms processing tens of millions of credit card statements every month. But behind the metal cases, the keyboards, and the photographic-quality screens lie the smarts, the rules by which the computer operates.

Software is a set of human-programmed instructions that tell the computer what to do when it is asked to perform a given task. And what if the software malfunctions? The computer will do something totally unexpected; perhaps innocuous, perhaps life-threatening.

If a computer didn't have software, it would make an excellent reef. It's useless. Software is that necessary invisible companion to you and your computer. Software is what makes your computer behave and look smarter than it is.

A word processor is a software program that tells the computer to accept your keystrokes, display them on the screen, and then save them to disk. Spreadsheet software adds and subtracts and analyzes numbers according to rules you tell the software to execute. A database program sorts information according to your requests. Software can also be a game on floppy disk or a CD-ROM.

A fax machine has built-in software to accept the numbers you dial and it might have a memory for cheap-hours transmission. Your VCR is chock full of software so the kids can tape Barney the dinosaur.

Throughout the growth of the Global Network, we have come to expect software to work correctly, although it all too often does not. We don't even need to consider the Information Warrior to see just how much damage can be caused by software that makes mistakes. On November 21, 1985, the Bank of New York almost crashed and nearly brought down much of the financial system along with it. A faulty software program kept their computers from receiving incoming electronic money, yet was paying all of their bills. At the end of the day, the Bank of New York was short a staggering $23 billion. The only place to raise that kind of cash in a hurry was from the Federal Reserve Bank. Software engineers spent a long sleepless night to find the errors that ultimately cost the Bank of New York $3.1 million in overnight interest.[1]

In August of 1991, an AT&T telephone switch in Manhattan failed. This software- and computer-controlled phone switch not only managed regular telephone services but provided the communication links for air-traffic controllers. That single software failure forced major East Coast airports to shut down, disrupted hundreds of thousands of travelers, and caused worldwide airport chaos for nearly a day.

The Audi 5000 was the target of national news and Department of Transportation investigations for allegedly accelerating when the brake pedal was pushed. The debate is still on, but some experts have suggested that software errors in the computer controlled car were at fault.[2] The Mariner 18 space probe was lost due to a one-line error in its vast coding. Hundreds of millions of dollars and years of work went down the tubes in an instant.[3] The Genini V capsule splashed down one hundred miles off target upon its return to Earth because the NASA programmers forgot to factor the Earth's rotation around the sun into their calculations.[4] During testing of an early F/A-18 jet fighter, it was discovered that its computers were programmed to reject pilot commands deemed too dangerous by the computers. The planes crashed until the software was corrected. A less fatal software error in 1988 cost American Airlines $50 million. It seemed that seats on their normally busy routes were bare because their new whiz-bang Sabre reservations system and its software program had a tendency to say seats were booked when they weren't.

Countless medical devices with errant software have caused death or medical trauma.[5] A software-controlled pacemaker was accidentally reprogrammed by a microwave therapy device, killing the patient. In the mid 1980s, the Canadian-made Therac-25 X-ray machine was found to be overdosing patients with radiation, killing at lease one person and maiming others. A subtle programming error delivered radiation at twenty-five times the lethal dosage. "The tiny error in the software had laid dormant for years, waiting for the particular set of circumstances that would cause it to go berserk."[6]

In 1983, the Bank of America began a design for a huge computer system called MasterNet, a secret project that would have given them an edge over their competitors. When the system was first deployed in 1987 the results were disastrous. Nothing worked properly, causing Bank of America an estimated of $1.5 billion in losses.[7] They gave up the MasterNet experiment in January 1988 after spending over $20 million in development costs alone.

Making software work is expensive. Costs go up like the national debt. One of allstate's software programs for its operations was originally budgeted at $8 million. The final estimates were in the $100 million range.[8]

The examples go on and on, and in most cases, are kept as quiet as possible. No major company is going to willingly announce that they just wasted $50 to $100 million on developing a software program that didn't work.

Software has become incredibly complex, and the likelihood of making it completely reliable is a distant goal. Software for desktop applications like Lotus 1-2-3, Windows, and hundreds of other popular programs has grown to hundreds of thousands of lines of software code, or instructions. Mainframe and large applications run into the millions of lines of codes—entirely too large for any one person to thoroughly understand or make work. It is no surprise that early releases of even the most rigorously tested software are historically "buggy" (containing flaws), often to the point of being unusable. Version 1.0 of any new software is full of problems. Microsoft's DOS 6.0, generally panned by customers, was soon succeeded by DOS 6.2, which corrected the previous version's problems.

Software can be so unreliable that one software company used the following disclaimer to legally protect itself against lawsuits in case their software glitched:

The Honest We Tested It Thoroughly Software Company does not warrant that the functions contained in the program will meet your requirements or that the operation of the program will be uninterrupted or error-free.

However, Honest We Tested It Thoroughly Software Company warrants the diskettes on which the program is furnished to be of black color and square shape under normal use for a period of ninety (90) days from date of purchase.

We don't claim our Program You Paid For is good for anything—if you think it is, great, but it's up to you to decide. If the Program You Paid For doesn't work: tough. If you lose a million because the Program You Paid For messes up, it's you that's out of the million, not us. If you don't like this disclaimer: tough. We reserve the right to do the absolute minimum provided by law, up to and including nothing.

We didn't really want to include this disclaimer at all, but our lawyers insisted. We tried to ignore them, but they threatened us with the shark attack at which point we relented.

This is a rough translation of a real disclaimer, normally written in intergalactic legalese, that comes with most software. At least this company had the guts to say it so we'd all understand what they were saying.

Future software systems are so complex, and we expect so much of them, that a National Academy of Sciences report says, "Confirmation of software performance in all network modes and conditions may prove unattainable."[10]

Then there's Star Wars. In its heyday, the space-based defense system was estimated to need 100 million lines of code,[11] yet there would be no way to test it except for actual use in a world war.

To get an appreciation of how hard it is to make software work, assume that within the New York City telephone directories, there is one error. Only one. Either a phone number with one wrong digit, an address off by one number, or one name misspelled.

Go find it.

And while you're at it, until that error is found and corrected, the rest of the phone book is no good either. That's what happened to Mariner 18. One error. Assume the possibility, indeed rest assured, that software will have errors: It only requires some simple math. Let's say that a software program is required to make decisions based upon one hundred sets of conditions. That's not a lot in complex systems these days. But the number of possible combination is astronomical, 2^{100} in fact. It turns out that if we tried to test all of the possibilities that the software might encounter, it would require more time than the age of universe, or roughly twenty billion years.

The bottom line is that it's impossible to test software thoroughly enough to make sure it works all of the time. Sooner or later, the software, the computer, the system, will fail. According to a book on computer ethics published in the United Kingdom, "Honest programmers generally admit that for nontrivial software it is impossible to write a program that they guarantee to be bug-free. And this is even truer of sophisticated software such as compliers and operating systems."[12]

The complexity of software, with millions of lines of code, presents fundamental philosophical questions that underscore the problems we have with the reliability of computer systems, from both malicious software and unintentional programming errors. These questions offer us assistance in presaging what kinds of problems will come our way as even more complex systems are required.

At the heart of the matter is an inescapable mathematical theorem set forth by German philosopher Kurt Goedel in 1931. The formal treatment is incomprehensible to anyone but a PhD in mathematical gobbledy-gook. The succinct way of putting Goedel's Incompletness Theorem is as follows: "All consistent axiomatic formulations of number theory include undecidable propositions."[13] That means there's something wrong with our system of calculating. The problem is one of logic, and software is based upon logic. If we interpolate, Goedel implies that software, which is based upon mathematical logic, is inherently flawed because the underpinnings of our system of mathematics are faulty in one of two, if not both, places: consistency and completeness.

Software is a series of carefully crafted instructions, meant to carry out specified tasks in a certain, precise manner. In a short program, the logical flaw is not a problem. But when software is tens of thousands of lines long, the instructions often call up loops, nested loops, routines, subroutines, sub-subroutines: The possibilities are almost endless. It is these loops that are the problem because they tend to be conditional. In a simple conditional case, if the computer receives X signal, it should then perform task A. Or if the computer receives both an X and Y signal, it should then perform task B. But large programs have literally hundreds and thousands of conditions that affect every single decision the computer makes. There is no perfect fix. The Congressional Office of Technology Assessment agrees with Goedel by observation of the results. They say, "Errors in large computer programs are the rules rather than the exception. Errors in the code, and unforeseen and undesired situations, are inevitable."[14]

So what does this condition bode for our increasing reliance upon software and the computers that they control? This inconsistency offers the Information Warrior untold opportunities to ply his trade to the detriment of industry, health, the economy, and the defense of the United States. National Science Foundation scientist Dr. William Wulf said, "Software is a problem of major importance to the entire nation. I do not think that the general population appreciates how important software is to both our economic and military health."[15]

Indeed, most of us don't. The Binary Schizophrenic doesn't sit back and cogitate that an inevitable software error is at fault when his airline reservations send him to Nome instead of Bermuda. He doesn't think twice about reading the riot act to an underpaid Avis employee when the red Jaguar he ordered is nowhere to be found. And I didn't think twice about leaving Fortune Bank in Florida when the ATM machines left me cashless, consistently reporting a balance of zero despite having adequate funds available.

In contrast, the Information Warrior is well aware of the subtleties of software, and he also knows exactly how to exploit the weaknesses that software systems exhibit even without his help.

The most visible example of malicious software is the headline-grabbing computer virus that affects, by and large, IBM-style MS-DOS and Apple computers. The headlines scream, "COMPUTER VIRUS TO CLAIM 5,000,000 VICTIMS," or "MICHELANGELO VIRUS DUE ON HIS BIRTHDAY." Dan Rather, Bernard Shaw, and Tom Brokaw offer us a healthy fix of technonews every few months when the next computer-virus scare comes along: Columbus day, 1989; Michelangelo, March 1992; the 1988 Internet Worm; Friday the 13th; Stoned. Viruses are generally attributed to an untraceable and mythically brilliant virus writer in another country—or just to "the Bulgarians." Computer viruses have cost American industry and government billions of dollars and the end is nowhere in sight.

"Virus" is the one computer-security buzz word that has crept into the lexicon of the general public. Most people may not know exactly what a computer virus is, but they know it's not good. However, the offensive nature and resulting fear of computer viruses fuels Binary Schizophrenia and other tech-nomalaises of the Information Age, not to mention causing increased expenditures that reduce productivity. We see it manifested as viraphobia, the fear of losing a month's work to the effects of a computer virus on the loose. Software doesn't always work as we expect—that's bad enough—and viruses don't help in the least.

During the October 1989 Columbus Day Virus scare, an older family member called and asked me in all seriousness, "This virus I hear about, is it dangerous? Can I catch it? Should I be concerned?" She doesn't even own a computer.

The medical parallel is clear. When you catch the flu, your body has been invaded with a microorganism that makes you ill. The flu bug travels from person to person through personal contact. You can't see it. You can't smell it. You don't feel the effects until you are already infected, and by then it's too late. Similarly, the computer virus is designed to invade your computer. The virus software is carried into your computer when it "contacts" software or when two computers communicate in Cyberspace. Physical contact is not necessary. Viral software is meant to fool other software systems into behaving differently than planned.

A virus is simply a piece of software written like every other piece of software with one key distinction: it has the desire to propagate clones of itself. That is, virus software is designed to make copies of itself, spreading from one computer to another over time. But unlike its biological counterparts, viral software is hermaphroditic in that each generation has only one parent that spawned it. What makes the popularly-known viruses dangerous or virulent are the instructions that the virus writer puts into the program. Conceptually, a computer virus is designed to penetrate or enter a system without the computer user's knowledge. It is offensive in nature. What it does once inside the computer is impossible to predict, except by the person who wrote it. Some popular viruses are known to search out all of the files on your computer and then erase them, perhaps while displaying a message that says, "MEMORY TEST IN PROGRESS. DO NOT REBOOT COMPUTER UNTIL FINISHED." In actuality, that message is giving the virus enough time to finish its instructions and by then it's too late. A viral Trojan horse is a program that accidentally gets put onto your computer because you think it is supposed to do one function but, in Homeric tradition, it really has an ulterior purpose.

A "time bomb" is a computer program that is designed to go off when certain conditions are met. For example, a preset date, such as Friday the 13th, Columbus Day, or Michelangelo's birthday could trigger the logic-bomb component of a virus to detonate and perhaps erase your work over the entire last year. A "logic bomb," related to the time bomb, could be set to go off when a user types in the words "Mickey Mouse" on his keyboard, or the name of a company, or if he answers a question correctly. A Chinese virus, for example, queried the user's political beliefs. The correct answer allowed one to continue unharassed; a politically incorrect response trashed the hard disk and all of its contents.

Some viruses and their malicious codes are suicidal and destroy themselves in the process of activation; others hide themselves only to be reawakened at a later date, just like a Soviet mole from a LeCarré novel. The mutating or polymorphic viruses of 1992 sent chills throughout the computer field. This new batch of viruses are built with a mutation engine, or self-encrypting algorithm. Simply put, every copy that the virus makes of itself is unique. So if we start with one virus that then infects two floppy diskettes, we then have three different viruses to defeat. If each copy makes two copies of itself, we then have six strains of the original. And so it goes, with every virus having unique characteristics.

Advanced viruses look for antiviral software, and if they are detected, will initiate defensive mechanisms to keep themselves alive. Some viruses are hardware-oriented in their designs, but thankfully Information Warriors have had limited success with their distribution. These viruses are designed to physically chatter a hard disk until it dies, cause chips within the computer to overheat and burn, or force a monitor to go up in smoke.

Computer viruses are generally distributed by putting one infected diskette in a desktop computer or by acquiring a piece of software grabbed from somewhere in Cyberspace. Respectable hardware and software firms like Novell, Intel, Adobe Systems, Leading Edge, and others have all been victimized by viruses that invade their facilities, are duplicated by the thousands, and then distributed to their customers. In each case, an honest, proactive response by the company mitigated major damages in spite of causing major embarrassment in the press. These incidents forced manufacturers to take the problem of viruses more seriously than they had been, and an industry has been built around the medical equivalent of inoculating computer systems against viruses.

A few short years ago, there weren't any wild viruses, but that changed in 1985. For his PhD thesis, Dr. Fred Cohen wrote about the nascent concept of self-replication software. Viruses. The highly technical thesis sought to define what viruses are in mathematical terms, how they work, and how they bypass or trick other software. Today, tens of millions of dollars in antiviral software is sold every year by small companies and huge industry leaders such as Microsoft, IBM, and Intel. Virus-fighting has become a "chic" business, with some of the players becoming quite wealthy in the process.

Virus busters and the virus writers are first generation Information Warriors. A virus buster designs ways to protect against what the virus writers conjure up. The virus buster will write a piece of software that should be able to reliably detect the presence of a virus or other unwarranted software. Until, that is, the virus writers come up with another new virus meant to defeat the last defensive software put out by the virus busters. And then the virus busters come out with a new revision, an update that fixes that problem, but the virus writers are already onto the next one . . . and the cycle begins again, a game on the chessboard of the Global Network.

In 1987, there were only six viruses; by 1990, virus busters were combating one thousand viruses; and as of September, 1993, over three thousand computer viruses and strains had been cataloged.[16] If the current trend continues, some projections estimate that by the end of the decade as many as 100,000 distinct computer viruses may be actively circulating through Cyberspace.

Viruses capture the popular media's attention, to the chagrin of many virus busters and other computer professionals. The detractors say that media exposure only encourages the virus writers to write more viruses and see if theirs will make the 6 o'clock news. Others maintain that the media exposure creates self-fulfilling prophecies. Virus busters tend to say that the media exposure helps people protect themselves.

The Michelangelo virus has been dubbed the "John McAfee Virus" because of his media prominence during the event and his exaggerated warnings that as many as five million computers could be struck. His company's sales doubled to $6.3 million for the first six months of 1992, venture capital poured into the firm, and plans were made to go public.[17] Estimates suggest that fewer than 25,000 computers were hit by Michelangelo[18] and some virus busters claim that like early warning systems for a hurricane, they were responsible for the minimal damage of the impending virus attack.

Virus busters are susceptible to the same software errors that plague major systems. One of John McAfee's antivirus software products actually made it impossible to use the protected PC, prompting one user to say, "The product is worse than the virus itself."[19]

Antivirus groups look for and collect viruses, catalog them, dissect them, and write antidotes for them. Firms such as the National Computer Security Association bridge the gap between the virus busters who make the products and product claims, and the users who merely want to keep their computers healthy. Magazines and newsletters and on-line bulletin boards services, or BBSs, keep thousands of people informed about new viruses and new virus busting techniques. Indeed, it is a healthy and thriving industry.

Of the thousands of viruses out there, few have admitted authors, underground braggadocio aside. Some semibenevolent virus writers do not advocate the indiscriminate spread of virulent and malevolent viruses, and a small segment of the software programming population believes that virus writing is a good thing. They claim a higher purpose, asserting that their motives are pure science, and the only no-no is releasing viruses into Cyberspace. But one has to wonder. A free software program distributed across the Global Network and BBSs worldwide called the Virus Construction Laboratory is just what its name implies. It automates the process of writing computer viruses; thus, they can be cranked out by the gross. Just for education's sake, of course.

The Little Black Book of Computer Viruses, a how-to manual about writing viruses, contains heavy doses of philosophy. "I am convinced that computer viruses are not evil and that programmers have a right to create them, possess them, and experiment with them."[20] The author, Mark Ludwig, makes a case that viruses are legitimate life forms; an outgrowth from John Von Neumann's early research into automation theory. With references to Karl Marx, the IRS, and the First Amendment, Ludwig devotes considerable time to the defense of viral research as if it were a social service to the computer community.

Ludwig and virus researcher Dr. Fred Cohen both maintain that researching and learning about computer viral behavior will put us in a better position to defend against malicious viral strains in the future. The First Amendment is also thrown in, with virus defenders taking the position that software writing is a form of protected free speech.

"Computer viruses are inherently not dangerous," the book claims.[21] From a purely theoretical standpoint he may be correct, however, in practice I don't know many who agree. Ludwig warns the reader of his book, "This book contains complete source codes for live computer viruses that could be extremely dangerous in the hands of an incompetent person."[22] In pursuit of the perfect virus, the same company began publishing the *Computer Virus Developments Quarterly*, a magazine dedicated to the high art form of writing viruses. Virus busters are besides themselves.

David Stang, PhD, editor of the *Independent Journal of Virus News and Reviews* is virulent in his response to Ludwig and others. "Virus writers belong in jail."[23] He has zero tolerance for any sort of computer virus and he isn't alone. On

June 10, 1993, the National Computer Security Association held Virus Awareness Day on Capitol Hill, in Washington, D.C. Congressman Ed Markey from Massachusetts, along with representatives from Rockwell International and 3M, held hearings on viruses and related computer-crime issues.

Peter Tippitt, a respected virus buster, suggests that laws against viruses be introduced. Defining an illegal virus in an unambiguous way is an exercise in semantics, subject to interpretation. If we get too strict in our definition, we could see prosecutors go after software programmers who make an honest mistake, or the legitimate virus researcher who accidentally releases one into the Global Network could find himself in jail. It's a complex issue, with no immediate social, legal, or moral answers.

Is there such a thing as a good virus? Most professionals do not believe that a virus has any place within the computer field. Ever. The argument is simple: "I don't want anything on my computer that I didn't put there. It's my personal piece of Cyberspace. Stay out unless invited in." But arguments have been made that some good viruses are possible. Their uses are indeed arcane, stretching the imagination a little, but nonetheless intriguing. On January 6, 1994 General Magic, owned partially by AT&T and Apple Computer, announced an adaptable technology called Telescript, an "agent" which behaves like a microorganism. The user tells the agent which instructions to follow, and it meanders through the Global Network executing those commands. For example, the user might tell the agent to find the best rates and scheduling for an airline flight, book the seats, pay for them, and inform the user of any delays or problems. While AT&T and other firms see agents as key market growth items, critics see parallels to virus distribution and are uncomfortable.[24]

One question is often posed by advocates of the military applications of computer viruses: "If you could defeat an enemy by inserting viruses into his computers, would they be considered good viruses?" Dr. Stang immediately interjects an unequivocal "No," but others have to think twice and stammer about such apparently beneficial uses of malicious software. The Iraqi Virus Hoax, as you will read later, claimed that the U.S. used a computer virus to shut down the Iraqi air defense system during the Gulf War.

A common pro-virus argument suggests benign computer viruses could be used to update software revisions on thousands of computers in big companies, saving costly labor expense and valuable time. Technically it's possible, and maybe in the future a modified version of the concept will make sense. But today, people want control. Call it a manifestation of Binary Schizophrenia, but computer operators and business owners are not comfortable with software running around their networks looking for something to do, no matter how well-intentioned the effort.

Network maintenance is also suggested as a possible use for benevolent viruses. Such viruses could run around the company network, testing its computers and switches, and making sure everything is working properly. Should it find something amiss, the virus would call the maintenance man and suggest a timely fix. The same arguments against such use of viruses apply here as well.

Viruses are going to be here awhile. In *Star Trek, the Next Generation,* 400 years in the future, the Starship Enterprise is confounded by a computer virus. And this is where the Information Warrior enters. What can he do with software? Just about anything he wants to do. To the Information Warrior, the software virus is an excellent weapon.

Most virus writers today, those who purposely unleash their creations into the wilds of the Global Network, are young, amateur programmers with few skills. That's one of the reasons that only about three hundred computer viruses have had significant effects. There is a need among this group to feel immediate gratification, to see their names in headlines, and to brag to their compatriots on their private electronic bulletin boards. Virus writers run on ego.

Popular malicious software has largely been relegated to the underground, the province of younger hackers who write surreptitious software designed to steal passwords and shuttle rounded-off pennies to another bank account. The more sophisticated Information Warrior, without the need for notoriety or acknowledgement, uses viruses and malicious software to his advantage. He will exploit the malicious software in a more insidious manner, biding his time, maximizing the desired effect, and never, ever, claiming responsibility. Therein lies the value of malicious software to the Information Warrior and the skill with which he practices his art. He might be well-financed, and have a bevy of able virus writers in his stable. With that premise, the potential for damage is vast.

Consider, for example, that the Information Warrior owned or bought a small software company, perhaps a shareware company that makes quantities of second-tier software programs at super-cheap prices. And let's say that somewhere within the thousands of lines of those programs some malicious command are intentionally placed. Over an extended period of time, a year or two or more, this company's software is widely distributed and has a fine reputation. But because this Information Warrior is in no hurry, he can wait. For you see, his malicious software, a logic bomb maybe, is set to "explode" five years to the day after the fall of the Soviet Union, or perhaps on some arbitrary date years hence. Every computer that runs that program on or after that date would be affected. Maybe it will erase an entire hard disk, bring a computer to a grinding halt, or make the screen wiggle. The more widely distributed the software, the greater the effect. Worse yet would be a big legitimate software company distributing a hugely popular program which had been infected with a virus or other malicious software. If (purely for example's sake) Miscrosoft Windows contained a logic bomb or other malicious code set to go off in 1999, tens of millions of computers would suffer catastrophically and all at once.

The Information Warrior could find other applications for malicious software. At General Dynamics in San Diego, an employee planted malicious software, a logic bomb, into one of the company's weapons-development computers in the hopes he would be hired back to fix the problem he created. Michael Lauffenburger, 31, felt underpaid, so he wrote a program that would not detonate until he was long gone, hoping his involvement would go undetected. It was discovered. Through a plea-bargain, he received a fine of $5,000 and community service.[25]

On a larger scale, the introduction of intentionally defective or destructive software into huge software development projects would potentially have a greater and definitely targeted effect. With U.S. companies spending over $100 billion per year in software development, there is ample opportunity to get inside any number of potential targets.

Do software moles actually roam the hallways and digital highways of corporate America? Does a dedicated Greenpeace advocate work for a logging company as a programmer or in another technical capacity? Would a financial firm hire a mole-programmer to work for a competitor, instructing him to slow things down—software-wise? Would an immigrant or political adversary of the United States be able to work for the Internal Revenue Service or one of their contractors and make sure that appropriate amounts of malicious code was sprinkled through the software? Could a pro-lifer insert malicious software into the computer of an abortion clinic?

It's all a matter of intent and dedication.

Remember, the essential difference between malicious code and a software error is intent, and we know how many "honest" errors get through. So the Information Warrior will exploit this knowledge and situate himself or one of his soldiers to insert the malicious code to act when the time is right. The hit can come sooner or later. The malicious code might look like a legitimate error, or it might erase its own tracks, compounding the problem for the malicious-code police.

Joel Kurtzman addresses that very issue when speaking about the Bank of New York's small $23 billion problem. He suggests that the consequences might have been more dire. What if, he asks, "the problem had been caused deliberately by a virus, by a computer hacker, or a financial terrorist?" Or what if the bank's databases has been destroyed and records no longer existed? Or what if the problem was systemic to the entire FedWire and debts of $1 trillion or more had accumulated? "A disaster that large would take weeks, perhaps even months, to sort out. The costs would have been catastrophic."[26] The possibility exists, and the defensively-postured Information Warrior must guard his econotechnical information infrastructure against that capability.

Kurtzman's financial perspective also provides an insight into what kind of effect well-designed and strategically placed software weapons could have on the national economy. "If VISA's computer went down for just a few hours, it would be enough to show up on the Commerce Department's data on retail sales. If payments were disrupted or cash unavailable on Cirrus during the Christmas shopping season, it could cause riots."[27]

Software errors tend to be subtle, and the subtle Information Warrior can induce errors that, over time, can have significant ramifications. Banks and regulated financial institutions have to account for every penny to their government overseers. It must have caused Chemical Bank in New York great consternation that its ATMs had withdrawn an extra $15 million from over 100,000 checking accounts. The software error doubled every customer's withdrawal—an accident hopefully not to be seen repeated.[28] Malicious software could be written that would offset accounts by mere pennies over a period of months. The cumulative effects would be noticed only during audits, but tracing back the compounded minute errors is like finding the one wrong digit in the phone book. Leonard Lee, in his book, *The Day the Phones Stopped* says, "A University of Minnesota study found that if (a software manufacturer's) software were to completely fail, banks would have to close within two days, retail distributors would be backlogged within four days, and factories and other businesses would have to close by the end of the week."[29] The Information Warrior isn't stupid. He can come up with lot more malicious schemes in a day than you or I could in a year.

The military could easily argue that it has the most acute concern for software reliability—and rightfully so. The Patriot missiles used during the Gulf War are essentially software propelled by a rocket on an intercept-and-destroy mission. The accidental shooting down of an Iranian civilian airliner was partially blamed on the software of an incredibly complex array of electronic systems. To Lee, the sophistication of the new generation of computer controlled aircraft is such that "the major concern with fly-by-wire aircraft is that even if the systems do not fail completely, they could be vulnerable to software errors hidden somewhere in their programming."[30]

As we examine more of the weapons necessary to wage Information Warfare, we will see that many of them are software-based, or indeed use software to control the hardware.

Keep in mind, the difference between a legitimate software error and malicious code is intent.

The Information Warrior's intention isn't honorable.

Sniffers and the Switch

"No matter what you do, you can't trust the phone company."

—RAY KAPLAN TELECONFERENCE, NOVEMBER 24, 1992.

SNIFFING THE NETWORKS IS A FAVORITE TECHNIQUE of the Information Warrior. Networks are groups of computers that have been connected to each other with wires or, in some cases, talk to each other over radio signals. Put together enough networks and we end up with the Global Network, populated by Computers Everywhere. A LAN, or local area network, is the easiest to visualize and is found in almost every office. In a LAN, one computer can retrieve information from another computer on the same LAN, or several computers can use the same network-ready software that is shared by everyone. Printers or modems may be shared, and everyone can inundate everyone else on the network with boring E-mail messages, directions to the company picnic, or politically incorrect jokes.

Literally millions of small networks are tied together throughout corporate America, the Government, and small businesses, and it is this massive proliferation of communications connectivity that makes these networks such an inviting target for the Information Warrior. Why? Because during the 1980s, when networks were designed and built, and even

114

today, security has been an afterthought—if considered at all. Networks are essentially wide-open sieves to anyone with minor technical skills and the desire to retrieve other people's information.

The Information Warrior will want to break into a company's network for one of several reasons:

1. To listen to conversations between the computers on the network.
2. To gain illicit entry into the computers and look around for valuable data.
3. To gain illicit entry into the network for the purpose of shutting it down.
4. To learn passwords and access code that will give the Information Warrior unlimited access to the networks any time he chooses.
5. To listen to "private" electronic mail (E-mail) between users on the network.

Given the kinds of private, financially valuable, time-sensitive, and mission-critical information that traverses the Global Network at any given moment, is it any wonder that Information Warriors are constantly on the lookout for means of gaining entry? Of course not. Hundreds of technical articles have been written in the last couple of years describing in great depth just how the Information Warrior gets into networks.

If the Information Warrior is good at his job, his unwanted presence within a company's network will go unnoticed for days, weeks, or months. What can he do during that time period? Pretty much anything he wants, as long as it won't give his activities away.

The Information Warrior may merely be on a hunting expedition, looking for tidbits of value to himself or his superiors. Cliff Stoll's Hanover Hacker in *Cuckoo's Egg* searched around university- and government-sponsored research computers for anything to do with SDI, Star Wars, and a list of similar key words. Or the Information Warrior may have targeted a particular company for very specific information. During the summer of 1991, a U.S. automobile manufacturer estimated it lost $500 million because a hacking Information Warrior broke into their networks and stole designs for future cars. Those plans instantly ended up in the hands of their competitors.[1]

How the Information Warrior breaks into a network offers insight into just how hard it is to protect them. Perhaps the most insidious method is that of "sniffing."

Remember that networks are built with wires connecting the computers together. All of the data run down those wires. How can the Information Warrior get at it? Invisibly. One method is to use a network analyzer. The analyzer is a piece of test equipment meant to diagnose and assist in the repair of the network. It reports who is on the network; how much of the network is being used or is under-used; if the network is operating properly or where it needs fixing; and it divulges secret passwords and access codes. A powerful tool for the network administrator, it is also a fine weapon for the Information Warrior.

Software provides other means of sniffing a network. Commercially available sniffer programs that can run on small desktop or laptop computers are also able to get the information the Information Warrior wants. In some cases, the software is written so that the legitimate network administrator doesn't even know someone is snooping. The manufacturers of such LAN sniffing software aren't attempting to build an arsenal for the Information Warrior, but the capabilities are there nonetheless.

The Cyberspace underground stockpiles a number of software-driven sniffers that function the same way, except that many of them are designed specifically to meet the goals of the Information Warrior. One such program is called "IPX Permissive"; it allows the interloper to read and decipher Novell network packets.[2] According to those familiar with the development of underground software, dozens of similar software programs exist that allow users to listen in on data transmissions undetected.

The employee at a large company who wants to decode other users' passwords might only have to install the correct software on his own computer and let it listen to passwords for days at a time. Once the passwords are in his possession, what he does with them is ultimately at the expense of the company. He might sell them to other Information Warriors, or he might use them to get even more valuable information to which he is not normally given access.

One of the dangers facing a company's networks is the incredible maze of wires that connect the computers. They run down hallways, over doors, under carpets, and through dropped ceilings. The network wiring is functionally invisible and, once installed and working, is generally forgotten— except to the Information Warrior. He could, for example, connect a "sniffer" to the network wire, hiding it in the ceiling of the research and development department and capturing the latest great designs which can then be sold for millions to competitors.

The Information Warrior may elect to use a method known as passive sniffing. Instead of a hard-wired connection, a magnetic inductor, (also known as a current probe or transducer) is strapped around the network wire where it picks up the magnetic fluctuations caused by the electrical data flow, converts them back to an electrical signal, and into the sniffer. The advantages are clear:

1. There is no disruption to the network while the sniffer is installed.
2. Since there is no electrical connection with the network, there is no simple way to detect the sniffer's presence.

The Information Warrior would have little trouble installing a small passive sniffer in most companies. Often the most protection that the company provides the network, and thus their information, is the receptionist. Consider the following scenario:

At 4:20 PM on Friday, the Secrets for Big Shots Co., Inc., on the thirty-second floor of a Park Avenue high rise in New York, is celebrating the boss's birthday. Everyone is looking forward to the weekend. The elevator bell rings, the door opens, and into the reception area walks a telephone company man. He's dressed in jeans, a Nynex workshirt, a white and blue telephone company hard hat, and his belt is full of tools and phone gear. In his hand is yet another mysterious-looking piece of electronic gear. He says to the receptionist, "Jeeeez, what a day," as he wipes his sweaty forehead. The receptionist barely glances at him, more interested in the revelry behind the glass doors where the cake is being cut.

"Yeah, Thank God it's Friday," she agrees.

"I really hate these last minute emergencies. I was on my way out to the shore for the weekend. . . ."

"What's wrong?" the receptionist asks. If the phones go down, it makes her look bad.

The phone man smiles. "Nothing for you to worry about. Simplex Corp. on the seventeenth floor lost half of their lines, and I've got to fix them before I can get outta here. Where's the phone room?"

"Oh, yeah. Sure." She hands him the keys. "It's over there. And, do me a favor?"

"Sure," the phone man responds. "Whatever."

"If I'm gone when you're through, put the keys back in the top drawer? I'm kind of new and . . ." she hesitates.

"No problem. Most bosses are jerks anyway, and don't know what real work is all about."

"Gee, thanks," she says, smiling a big appreciative smile.

The "phone man" opens the closet, located next to elevators where it was easy to install long wires up and down the height of the building. But, in this phone closet, the Secrets for Big Shots Co., Inc. also put a lot of its network controls. It's a lot easier to run the phone and network wiring at the same time and thus put the control gear in the same place.

He walks into the small phone closet, turns on the lights and, just as expected, a dizzying maze of wires, boxes, power cords, blinking lights, and racks of equipment fill the room. He smiles. This is perfect.

He takes a small donut-shaped piece of metal from his belt, opens it and snaps it tightly around one of the wires. He then plugs a small wire from the metal clamp to the box he carried, and then plugs that into the wall. Power on. Lights on. Good, everything seems to work. He moves a few wires and proceeds to hide the box and the clamp behind a large rack that contains a seemingly endless array of electronic gear. He brings out a walkie-talkie.

"Well?" he asks.

The receiver crackles. "We got it. Not much traffic, but enough to show it works."

"Ten four."

The phone man slaps the walkie-talkie back in his belt, opens the door, turns out the light, and hands the keys back to the receptionist.

"Done already?" she asks.

"Yeah, I was lucky. It was just a dirty connection. Looks like I might beat the traffic yet! Have a great weekend."

"Thanks. You too."

Obviously this wasn't the case of a phone man fixing a faulty line. It was an Information Warrior installing a passive network sniffer which also contained a small radio transmitter. The radio broadcasts all of the data and passwords that the network processes to a remote receiver. Invisible. Passive. Insidious.

Networks are highly vulnerable to the Information Warrior, and he knows of at least fifteen specific Achilles' Heels in the average network. All he needs is the right software or hardware to take advantage of the weakness of the network. In the continuous search for passwords, for example, these vulnerable points are:

1. The user himself.
2. The memory inside the keyboard.
3. The terminal emulator.
4. The LAN, or network driver software.
5. The LAN connection card.
6. The network cabling itself.
7. The network server.
8. The peer, or other user's nodes.
9. The gateway, router, or bridge to other networks.
10. The WAN, or wide area network, interface.
11. The WAN itself.
12. The mainframe front-end processor.
13. The channel to the mainframe.
14. The mainframe itself.
15. The mainframe application.[3]

Many networks are much more complicated than this and have many more points of vulnerability, but the point is clear. To adequately protect the network, the defensive Information Warrior has to secure countless points of possible attack; the offensive Information Warrior only has to find and exploit one weakness. It just doesn't seem fair.

Destruction of the network, thus crippling the company, is another potential goal of the Information Warrior. The Internet WORM of 1988 was just such an event. Robert Morris, Jr., the son of a respected scientist who works for the National Security Agency, single-handedly brought thousands of computers across this country to a grinding halt. His method? He wrote a computer program known as a WORM, which eats up the memory and resources of computers, effectively rendering them useless.

Only when affected users talked to each other did they discover that they all had the same problem. The search was then on for the mysterious piece of software traveling around the Global Network which was turning high speed computers into crawling snails. Releasing a WORM on the Internet, accidental or not, was a major incident, but the same technique is available to any Information Warrior. He might merely choose to aim the WORM at a smaller target; perhaps just one company or one type of computer.

The Internet connects two million host computers and allows access by millions more. Almost every country has at least one Internet connection, and over 100,000 million bytes of data travel across its wires every day.[4] With the volume increasing at fifteen percent per month and doubling every six months, the Internet is getting full. According to David Clark, a researcher at the Massachusetts Institute of Technology's computer science lab, the Internet is an ideal target for terrorists or Information Warriors. "I think we are in deep trouble. . . . What do terrorists like? They like events that cause publicity. Will this be the decade of the cyberterrorist?"[5]

Hackers have been using the Internet as a gateway into thousands of computers for years. One example occurred in mid-1992 when the National Oceanic and Atmospheric Administration found that a hacker had come through its modem pool (a large group of modems connected to the same network) and breached their network in search of a free door to the Internet.[6] Hacker archives, police reports, and the media are full of similar reports, few of which were ever followed up to the point of prosecution. It's just too labor- and time-consuming.

Eugene Shultz, a former security manager at the government-sponsored Lawrence Livermore National Laboratories, agrees that the Internet breeds hackers and their brethren, cyberpunks. "It's very possible to see a hundred or more attacks in a single day."[7]

And Shultz ought to know. In a confidential Livermore internal memo, Shultz speaks about a string of recent break-ins. ". . . one hacker from the Netherlands was bragging that he had been using AUTOVON, the unclassified U.S. military telephone network, to break into systems; subsequently, other sources within the U.S. Army have informed us that they have recently found that AUTOVON has been illegally used for data transfer between computers."[8] The memo further speculates that, according to Livermore sources, the attacks against their networks might be financed by either the German news magazines *Der Spiegel* or *One Magazine* or "countries hostile to the U.S. are supplying the money and funneling it through one of these magazines."[9]

Network break-ins of this type came to a head during the Gulf War. Congress got into the act when it was discovered that Dutch hackers had penetrated at least thirty-four military computer systems by bobbing and weaving through the Internet from April 1990 through May 1991. The Senate Governmental Affairs Subcommittee on Government Information and Regulation held hearings chaired by Senator Herb Kohl (D-Wisc.) who said, "The hackers had access to crucial information regarding military personnel, the type and quantity of equipment being moved, and the development of important weapons systems."[10]

No major U.S. company has gone unaffected by the remote touch of a hacker at his keyboard as was so duly demonstrated in early February of 1994. The Internet experienced security breaches of unprecedented scope when perpetrators unknown cracked into hundreds of computer sites nationwide to steal tens or hundreds of thousands of passwords. Using sophisticated monitoring software, sniffers, and malicious software such as Trojan Horses, the large-scale digital robbery sits in a class by itself for scope, audacity, and potential damage. Their huge collection of purloined access codes would permit illicit entry into government, commercial, financial, and educational computers across the entire Internet.[11] For the first time, countless thousands of Internet users are being forced to change their passwords, which augers future security awareness in Cyberspace. Unfortunately, the sophistication of these Information Warriors will likely precipitate further incidents that will cause extensive damage financially and socially. This time we were lucky.

"The switch" is perhaps the biggest network of them all. The switch generically refers to the networks that carry voice, and now digital, signals to almost every home in America.

The switch is owned and operated by AT&T, Sprint, MCI, and the seven Baby Bells or Regional Bell Operating Companies (RBOCs). It is run by the dozens of small local telephone companies and the cellular phone companies who connect their pieces of the switch to the other pieces of the switch. The data components of the switch are run by such major players as British Telecom, Tymnet, and others who are competing for control of Cyberspace. All of these disparate companies work in a competitive harmony (government regulations and common sense dictate their behavior) to make the switch the largest computer and network in the world, and also the easiest to use. Today the switch and its owners are facing the onslaught of first generation Information Warriors, and their networks face exactly the same challenges as do corporate America.

It is the goal of the Information Warrior to get control of the switch, since he who controls the switch wields immense power. He can listen to and tape conversations, turn a home phone into a pay phone or, as happened to thin-haired security expert Donn Parker of SRI, have all calls to his home number forwarded to the Hair Club for Men. I have called hackers at home only to be forwarded to the White House switchboard. The switch contains billing records, payment histories, addresses, and other pertinent personal data for everyone with a phone. Every call you make, every call you receive, is on record in the telephone companies' computers. They have immense power.

The maintenance circuits for the switch are supposed to be accessible only to telephone company repair people, who can turn phones on or off, reroute them, or give them free billing. But hackers and phone phreaks have taken advantage of the maintenance ports to such an extent that many have had to be shut down in defense. Even unlisted numbers are stored within the switch, and unlisted numbers are still connected with a name and an address—if you know where to look.

Instructions on how to use (and abuse) telephone equipment are allegedly proprietary company information, but many of the secrets have been published in underground journals such as *Hactic, 2600,* and *Phrack.* I have received a number of documents, from various underground sources, that give step-by-step-instructions on exactly how to break into and use Tymnet switches. Once a hacker has access to the switch, he can eavesdrop on any conversation in the U.S.

Companies use their networks to make information and services available to their internal employees; they also want to provide certain information to their regional offices, traveling salespeople, and to some clients and suppliers. The modem is what permits computers to pass information and provide services over conventional telephone lines.

Until quite recently, companies did little if anything to protect the modems that give outsiders access to their networks and information. So, the Information Warrior knows that if he can find the right telephone number of the right modem within the right company, he stands a pretty good chance of breaking through into the network and getting access to the information itself. It happens every day, and major companies admit that they have been the victim of such penetrations, with varying amounts of damage.

The Demon Dialer is a common piece of underground software that scans thousands of phone numbers to determine which ones connect to a telephone and which ones connect to a computer. The software automatically makes a list of the number that have computers at the other end, while other software attempts to break into each computer network by cracking passwords. This information, and the software to obtain it, is then shared by the various types of cyberpunks who populate the computer underground. The hackers and phone phreaks then go after their ultimate target: the computers and networks themselves.

Using Demon Dialers, two young hackers scanned Seattle phone lines, "found a Federal Court computer and gained easy access to it. Once inside they found a list of passwords that were encoded in an unspecified manner. They then allegedly went into Boeing Aircraft's systems and used a super-powerful computer to decode the passwords so they could be used to get into sensitive Federal files, apparently with success. The two gained unrestricted access to Federal Court computers including files from the Grand Jury."[12]

Demon Dialers are typically home-brew devices made from common electronic components for a few dollars, as are a wide array of Colored Boxes that hackers and phone phreaks use to combat the phone system. In the U.S. these "toys" are illegal, but one enterprising Dutch firm, Hack Tic Technologies, makes what hackers call the Ultimate Phreaking Box. One hacker said, "Anything you can imagine doing to a phone or a switch, you can do with this box." According to one hacker, Devil's Advocate, "If you're searching for the phone phreaker's equivalent of an all-terrain vehicle, then you may just want to test drive this rocket."[13] The cost of this magic box designed to defeat billions of dollars worth of communications networks? A mere 350 Dutch Guilders or about $180 U.S. Getting them into the U.S. is easy, since all customs will see is a set of seemingly harmless electronics parts. But place one call to the Netherlands, enter the correct numerical sequence, and unlimited possibilities are opened up. Given the proliferation of such programs and tools within the underground, it is not difficult at all to appreciate the predicament of organizations with large numbers of networks and modems.

Breaking into networks and computers is quite common in the commercial sector, but industry does its best to keep it quiet. Occasionally, they can't. The Masters of Deception, a group of five New York hackers, were indicted on up to eleven charges for invading networks over a period of months in 1991 and 1992.[14] According to the Federal indictment, victims of this series of attacks included Southwestern Bell, British Telecom North America, New York Telephone, Pacific Bell, US West, ITT, Martin Marietta, TRW Information Services, Trans Union Credit, Information America, New York University, and Bank of America, among others.

In May of 1990, the Secret Service culminated a two-year investigation called Operation Sundevil. Arrests were made while forty-two computers and 23,000 disks were confiscated across New York, Chicago, Los Angeles, and ten other cities. The operation was supported by twenty-eight search warrants and 150 agents. The alleged crime ring "may account for losses of over $50 million in fourteen cities," said U.S. Senator Dennis DeConcini (D-Ariz.). Stephen McNamee, a U.S. Attorney in Arizona, said that the illicit use of computers might well become the white collar crime of the 1990s.[15]

For white collar crime, fax machines offer the Information Warrior an almost unlimited supply of information. A conventional phone tap listens in on voice conversations that can be taped, broadcast, and then used as needed. The same is true for fax transmissions. An entire industry is built around devices especially developed to intercept faxes. STG, a company that offers fax interception devices for "sale, lease, or rent," also claims in their brochure. "This fax interception device is so reliable . . . you can take it to court."

It is fairly simple for someone with a modicum of electronics training to build his own fax interception device, but for the Information Warrior who prefers to use off-the-shelf equipment manufacturers such as Burlex International, Mentor Links Inc., Sherwood Communications, El-Tec International, Knox Security Engineering, and others make the task that much easier. Given this widespread capability, one must wonder about how the federal government views the potential for abuse of these products on the part of the bad guys, whoever they might be.

In 1990, President Bush signed National Security Decision Directive 42, which addressed Federal concerns about telecommunications systems within the U.S. This document essentially replaced an earlier version, NSDD-145, signed by President Reagan. Portions of NSDD-42 were declassified on April 1, 1992, due in large part to the efforts of Marc Rotenberg at the D.C.-based Computer Professionals for Social Responsibility.

The opening paragraphs of NSDD-42 are standard boilerplate commentary on the importance of computers; however, the authors admit that the emerging technologies ". . . pose significant security challenges." Further explaining these challenges, NSDD-42 notes, "Telecommunications and information processing systems are highly susceptible to interception, unauthorized access, and related forms of technical exploitation as well as other dimensions of the foreign intelligence threat. The technology to exploit these electronic systems is widespread and is used extensively by foreign nations and can be employed, as well, by terrorist groups and criminal elements."[16]

This fear was realized in several major telephone service outages. In January, 1990, millions of customers were cut off from long distance service for over nine hours when software in an AT&T SS7 switching computer malfunctioned and the contagious failure spread throughout the massive telephone network. A year later in New Jersey, one of AT&T's high capacity fiber cables was accidentally cut. Then on September 17, 1991, telephone service was disrupted in New York when, according to AT&T, "power failures" caused two major switches to fail. Beyond customer inconvenience, the danger of losing telecommunications services became all too clear: The major airports in the New York area rely upon ground-based telephone lines for air traffic control. So, planes couldn't land, planes couldn't take off, and the resulting "stack-em and rack-em," as such a jam is called in air traffic lingo, created aeronautical chaos that spread around the globe for days.

A *Network World* editorial on September 30, 1991 summed up the incident quite succinctly. "The network is the life blood of the U.S. economic system." And so, again, such an obvious commentary was put to the test and proven. (A U.S. Army Intelligence officer told me in August 1990 that there was reason to believe the January 1990 outage may have been the deliberate work of software saboteurs. He claimed, without proof, that some of the hacker bulletin boards his intelligence agency monitored had actually predicted the outage and the sequence of cities to be affected. This allegation has never been proved, but it clearly demonstrates that the U.S. military has some awareness of the vulnerabilities to this country's communications networks.)

On September 29, 1992, as a result of these displays of vulnerability, the Defense Information Systems Agency issued a Statement of Work and followed it up on October 5, 1992 with a solicitation for a contract, Request for Proposal entitled "Public Switched Network Software Vulnerability Collection, Analysis and Modeling." In short, they wanted to find out what can go wrong with the phones. The strategic importance of the phone systems and its apparent vulnerability to the capabilities of the Information Warrior must have been of major interest to the government since DISA, an intelligence agency heavy-weight, was involved, and the winning contractors had to hold a U.S. secret clearance.

From the DISA Statement of Work in the Government's request:

> "The hacker threat may continue to evolve as technology evolves. There is a growing indication that the hacker community is becoming more organized and sophisticated. They have demonstrated the ability to penetrate software systems controlling the switches of the PSN (Public Switched Network, telephone companies). It is critical that the vulnerabilities be identified so that the software systems of the PSN can be modified to effectively lessens the threat to NS/EP (National Security) telecommunications systems."

The proposed contract called for the contractor to find system bugs, errors, and penetrations, and to search BBSs for information about who was likely to attack and by what means. Once the data was collected, the contractor would ". . . perform in-depth analysis to determine potential vulnerabilities within the PSN. The study shall also concentrate on determining trends and patterns that may develop from hacker activities."

The Information Warrior may be able to exploit an even

more subtle weakness within the nation's communications networks. On a recent cross-country trip, I sat next to a senior executive with a major telecommunications company and learned something I didn't know. Of all of the threats to phone switches, the phone company and the switch designers most fear the cutting of a major cable where hundreds and thousands of copper lines connect homes and businesses. Each phone switch is a computer with tens of thousands of phones connected to it, and each telephone unit represents an electrical load to the switch, just as a lightbulb or a refrigerator presents a load to the power company. If tens of thousands were suddenly disconnected from that switch, the load factor would immediately change, to the detriment of the switch and the phone company's other customers.

According to this executive (who wants to remain nameless for obvious reasons), this is what partially caused the domino-like failure of AT&T's network in 1990. One switch went crazy and effectively disconnected itself from other switches, which then had their own electrical temper tantrums. AT&T couldn't publicly admit that they knew they had built-in problems for fear of unleashing a rash of similar attacks. The phone companies fear that someone wanting to strike out at them would discover the location of the huge cables feeding the switch and go snip them. The plane-riding telco executive claims that the switch would essentially implode and be unable to provide service to its customers, whether they were connected to the cut cable or not. The switch itself would simply cease to function.

Why does this condition exist? Because the designers just can't consider every possible worst-case scenario. It is impossible to test for every possible contingency and in some cases the extra cost to protect against the unlikely just doesn't make prudent business sense. Besides, when the current breed of switches were designed, no one gave serious consideration to the idea that the phone company might be a target of an Information Warrior. Here once more, we find the same philosophical and mathematical bottleneck that affects software reliability: Goedel's Theorem strikes again.

Not all of the switch connections are made through and across wires of copper and fiber optics. Communications increasingly use the airwaves, as we see in the proliferation of cellular phones, Motorola's multi-billion dollar Iridium Project, and microwave and satellite transmissions. The electromagnetic ether represents a new battlefield for the Information Warrior.

Cellular phone conversations, for example, are wide open to interception by $179 scanner devices that can be bought from Radio Shack, *Monitoring Times* magazine, or dozens of other sources. Courts have upheld that there is no reasonable expectation of privacy when one is talking on a cellular phone.[17] In fact, the problems are so prevalent that back in 1987, Radio Shack sent out internal memos instructing salespeople not to assist in modification of their scanners, and informing them that future models would not be modifiable for this questionable activity.[18] Cellular phone conversations remain absurdly easy to intercept from a car, a backyard, or an office. Densely populated urban areas with high concentrations of cellular phones are a breeding ground for the Information Warrior.

The political implications of interception of cellular phone calls was brought into the national limelight when two political foes took to Cyberspace to fight their battles. On June 7, 1991, Governor Doug Wilder of Virginia charged that someone had tape recorded his private cellular phone calls and passed them on to his political adversary, Senator Charles Robb.[19] According to *The New York Times*, June 23, 1992, over one thousand cellular phones were used at the Democratic National Convention. Perhaps for reasons best left unsaid, the Republicans banned all cellular phones at their convention later that summer.[20] (What do the Republicans know that the Democrats don't?) And the British tabloids had a field day when transcripts of cellular conversations between Princess Di and her alleged lover were made public.

Cellular fraud is a related weapon of the Information Warrior. The goal is to make "free" phone calls although either you (the victim) get billed or the cellular company does, in which case the rates go up anyway. So you pay or you pay. Here's how it works: when you make a call, each cellular phone also broadcasts its internal electronic serial number or ESN. The ESN is used to legitimize the call by verifying the phone number and billing. The ESN is periodically rebroadcast along with other critical information, making its theft ridiculously simple. The Information Warrior then sucks the subscriber's phone number, the ESN, the station class data, and the manufacturer and dialed number out of the air.

Curtis Electro Devices of Mountain View, California, is one company that makes an ESN reader in a battery-driven, hand-held box, complete with antenna and digital readout. This is a perfectly legal device, ostensibly made for the repair and programming of cellular phones, but in the hands of the Information Warrior it can cost us all a great deal of money. The bad guys only have to reprogram some counterfeit chips, plug them into other cellular phones, and off they go: billing you for their calls to the drug czars in Colombia or Pakistan.

In the major U.S. metropolitan areas, rings work out of limousines focusing on poor immigrant areas, attracting people who cannot afford a phone or who might be here illegally yet still want to phone home. For as little as $5 per quarter hour, phone service is offered to anywhere in the world. Since the limousine is driving around the city, police cannot zero in on it. Income of $10,000 to $50,000 per day in cash, per operation is not unrealistic. The illicit chip may only be good for a few days until the miscreant behavior is discovered, but by then, a new stream of ESNs have been pulled from the air and the Information Warriors are ready to steal from a new set of victims, including the Government. In California, the highways have been outfitted with cellular phone boxes for use by stranded motorists. One phone bill they received was quite a surprise. It included an extra 11,733 calls for 25,875 minutes that cannot be matched with legitimate usage.

If Saddam Hussein had been listening to the microwaves in mid-1993, he might have been able to find out about the impending raid on Baghdad. Secretary of State Warren Christopher was receiving updates and advice from his staff in Washington, D.C., prior to the raid, and the cellular conversations were intercepted by a hacker who was scanning phones.

Maybe listening in isn't what all Information Warriors want to do. Maybe, as we discussed, their aim is more destructive. Truckers use CB radios to steer clear of cops and radar guns, but during the heyday of the 1970s CB rage, a popular game was to increase the power output of the CB to such a level that it would literally cause a passing motorist's CB to smoke. Truckers, of course, had the proper circuitry to handle the massive signal strength their fellow CBers were transmitting.

As satellite communications become the rule, the Information Warrior finds opportunity there, as well. On April 27, 1986, HBO viewers were rudely interrupted during the broadcast of *The Falcon and the Snowman*, when their screens suddenly displayed the message:

Good evening HBO From Captain Midnight $12.95/Month No Way! (Showtime/Movie Channel Beware).

HBO's satellite signal had been overridden by a satellite hacker who was displeased with the scrambling of pay-for-view satellite transmissions.[21] The industry instantly convened to discuss the situation. It turned out that a threatening phone call was made prior to the jamming episode by a caller who only identified himself as "Carl." The caller warned, "This is electronic warfare."

Carl alleged that he was associated with the American Technocratic Association, based in Wilmington, Delaware. The group claimed that for a mere $25 million, they could "completely knock every satellite off the globe."[22] Showtime experienced similar interference with their satellite transponders in December of 1985, but not to the same degree.[23]

In an article entitled, "Declaration of Electronic War," author Bill Sullivan cited the concerns of the satellite industry about such threats. After the Captain Midnight interruption, the attendees at the meeting "wanted to keep a low profile and did not want that vulnerability disseminated to the general public . . . because [they] are so vulnerable to jamming." The ATA claimed that they were going to proceed with destructive jamming, by overloading the satellite transponders, and the consensus was that this was possible. John Roberts of United Video said, "I think a knowledgeable person could put together a satellite transmitter inexpensively . . ." and *Radio Electronics* magazine said, "One report stated that the [Captain Midnight] feat required a great deal of technical expertise and about $60,000 worth of equipment."[24] A Federal Communications Commission spokesman, Ron Lepkowski, admitted that, "We've always recognized the possibility."[25]

So, when we add it all up, just how bad is the situation? The SRI, under the leadership of Don Parker, published a report based upon interviews with hackers in the United States and Europe. In an abbreviated version of the paper, "The State of Security in Cyberspace," they concluded that the PSTNs (Public Switched Telephone Networks) are the least vulnerable to interception, PDNs (Public Data Networks) are somewhat more vulnerable, the Internet is "somewhat insecure," and the cellular phone system is the most vulnerable. Highlights of the report state:

- Malicious attacks on most networks . . . cannot be completely prevented now or in the future. . . .
- It is possible individuals or groups could bring down individual systems or related groups of systems on purpose or by accident. . . .
- We found no evidence that the current generation of U.S. hackers is attempting to sabotage entire networks. . . .

- There is some evidence that the newest generation of hackers may be more motivated by personal gain than the traditional ethic of sheer curiosity. . . .
- The four major areas of vulnerability uncovered in our research have little or nothing to do with specific software vulnerabilities per se.[26]

The most comprehensive public study on the actual costs of communications compromises was written under the expert guidance of lawyer John Haugh. In 1992 a two volume reference, *Toll Fraud and Telabuse: A Multibillion Dollar Problem* was published by Telecommunications Advisors. This study, which did not even include the Internet, documented how pervasive a problem telecommunication technology crimes really are. The opening line of the preface quotes an MCI statement from 1991: "There are two kinds of customers; those who have been the victims of toll fraud, and those who will be."

Haugh and his group's research supports that claim, with the statement that "the total cost of toll fraud and teleabuse is more than twice the estimated annual cost of the AIDS epidemic." They can support this statement, too, with detailed analyses. For example:

Stolen Long Distance	$1,800,000,000
800 Toll Fraud	350,000,000
Victim Costs	51,000,000
Carrier and Vendor Fees	32,000,000
Cellular Fraud	700,000,000
Credit Card Toll Fraud	400,000,000
COCOT Fraud	60,000,000
Subscription Fraud	300,000,000
Telabuse	5,200,000,000
Total	$8,893,000,000

That's almost $40 per person per year in the United States alone and, according to Telecommunications Advisors, these are highly conservative figures.

Haugh's group examines why toll fraud has remained a secret. The reasoning is similar to computer crime cover-ups: embarrassment, a tendency to blame the other guy, technological ignorance, and from the vendor standpoint, fear of hindering sales by telling potential customers that they could become victims.

Toll Fraud points out that lawsuits are pending and hundreds more are expected as fraud costs mount. Unless solutions are found, the courts are going to be jammed with fraud cases where ultimately, the perpetrator will not be caught, yet someone will have to pay: either the carrier or the victim. The problem is improving somewhat with Sprint, AT&T, and others offering insurance policies against telabuse. *Toll Fraud* warns companies and individuals who use long distance services that the problem is real and it's getting worse. "We see that the severity of the problem is decreasing; each event causes less financial damage," says Haugh, "but the frequency is dramatically increasing. Ultimately that means greater losses for everyone."

Private phone companies, the PBXs used by American businesses, are also ripped-off by amateur and professional Information Warriors. Just like the switch, a PBX is a small switch serving one company, and it has maintenance ports and a feature called DISA that allows employees to dial in and use the company's data and voice networks. The Information Warrior has found it profitable to break into these private phone companies and steal millions of dollars in services. The victims have to pay the bill or fight the fraudulent charges in court because the perpetrator is long gone.

Voice mail, a popular feature, has also fallen victim to hackers. Some companies have been blackmailed by hackers who have taken over their voice-mail systems. The hackers insist that unless they are permitted to use a portion of the PBX for their own purposes, the entire PBX will be destroyed. One well-known case involved two teenagers who, when they did not receive a promised promotional poster from a company, broke into the offending company's PBX and voice mail, held the company hostage, and eventually caused extensive damage.

But let's take Information Weaponry one step further, and ask ourselves what would happen if the theft of information were effected so discreetly, so invisibly, so insidiously, that there was no way at all to determine the losses? The losses to your organization might be deep, potentially fatal, but you'd never, ever know you'd been a victim of Information Warfare. You might just think that your firm was the victim of bad luck. The Information Warrior relies upon such uncertainty. He really doesn't want us to know what he's up to, and that further complicates our efforts at understanding his real goals and motivations.

7

The World
of Mr. van Eck

"Who would have thought that a sprinkler system would contain useful information?"

—MORGAN DEATH

OK, so the Information Warrior can tap a phone or a fax machine, royally screw up a computer system by fidgeting with its software, change your home phone into a pay phone, and generally wreak all sorts of havoc. Let's step back for a moment, and review the ideal characteristics of the weapons used by the Information Warrior:

- Invisible
- Passive
- Untraceable
- Readily Available and Inexpensive
- Disposable
- Remote controlled
- Insidious

To varying degrees we have already found that malicious software, network sniffing, and playing with the switch meet many of these ideals. But let's look at another weapon; one that is still considered classified by the government just because it does meet these goals so well.

137

Electromagnetic Eavesdropping

Any electrical current produces a magnetic field. A television station broadcasts a very small magnetic field from its antenna atop the World Trade Center or in a corn field in Iowa, and a portable TV set in your home can pick up and display *Mr. Ed* reruns or *Murphy Brown* in startling clarity. Let's take this thought one step further. Computers, printers, fax machines, and video monitors are also electrical devices that conduct current and they too emit magnetic fields. Guess what? These magnetic fields can be picked up by a special receiver, too, and can be read in startling clarity, invisibly, passively, and with little fear of detection. Sounds like an ideal tool for the Information Warrior.

A computer is actually a miniature transmitter broadcasting all of its information into the air, where it is ripe for the picking. From an electrical standpoint, the CRT or monitor of a computer is the "loudest" component, meaning that the magnetic field it produces is the strongest. Back in the early days of computers, in the days of Radio Shack TRS-80 ("Trash 80s"), Commodore Pets, and VIC-20s, users often experienced severe interference from their computers on their TV sets.

Many of us set up our computers in the living room so we could spend quality time with our families, watch *M*A*S*H* and play with our latest adult toys. But we also noticed that unless the computers were a safe distance from the TV, the picture was virtually unwatchable. Wavy lines scrolled across and up and down the screen and "noise" filled the picture. If we rotated the computer and sat at a different chair at the dining room table, the interference was less objectionable. If we moved the computer into the bedroom, the interference often went away. To satisfy our desire to watch TV and still peck away at BASIC, we would twiddle for nights on end trying to optimize the picture on the boob tube by minimizing the interference. That might mean finding the only place in the room that would allow us to enjoy both diversions at once, or it might mean using three rolls of properly placed and shaped rolls of Reynolds Wrap around the computer and on the TV aerial. We were trying to shield the television set from the electromagnetic radiation emitted by the computer and its monitor. Little did most of know then that we were experiencing a phenomenon that the National Security Agency had buried deep within their classified Tempest program. The government had known about the national security problems associated with computer-based electromagnetic radiation for years.

Electromagnetic eavesdropping is a formidable weapon to the Information Warrior. Twenty years later the government still shrouds much of the issue in secrecy, and it is only due to the efforts of independent researchers not controlled by the secrecy laws concomitant with government employment that we understand just how much of a risk electromagnetic eavesdropping really is.

Since every computer unintentionally broadcasts information into the air (except those few especially built to tightly-guarded NSA Tempest specifications), the Information Warrior has the means to detect, save, and read every bit of information that passes through a computer and onto a video monitor. And he can do it passively, from some distance, without your ever being the wiser.

Detecting and recovering this data is not possible only for the intelligence community or super-high-tech whiz bangers. The ability to read computer screens from a remote location is available to anyone with a modicum of knowledge of basic electronics. Your television repairman is an ideal candidate for assisting your local Information Warrior. Morgan Death, a former Vice President at Hughes STX, wrote, "Many individuals and corporations have no idea how easy it is to obtain information from electronic radiations. They thought of Tempest protection as a black art that only the intelligence community had to worry about."[1]

In its simplest form, an electromagnetic eavesdropping device consists of no more than a black and white television set and a handful of parts costing less than $5. The interception we experienced with the Trash 80s was the actual video signal (the characters that cross the computer screen) being picked up by the TV antenna. The computer monitor leaks this information at about the same frequencies used by channels two through seven on the TV. All we need to do is tune them in and voila!, we have an echo of what appears on our computer screen. The reason we couldn't read the Trash 80 characters on our TV set was that the detected signals had lost their "sync," or synchronization. The information was there, but it fell apart. The Information Warrior simply puts it back together again.

A television set modified to pick up computer screen emissions needs to have two signals added to those unintentionally leaked by the monitor under surveillance. The first is the vertical sync which, on a TV set, is called vertical hold. The second signal needed is the horizontal sync. If either of these signals is maladjusted, the TV will endlessly "roll" up and down or left to right, as the case may be. (Readers who owned early generation television sets can easily relate to the frustration.) The radiated signals from a computer combined with these two sync signals will produce a perfectly readable copy of whatever appears on the computer with no wires connecting the two. To add more fuel to the fire, the data displayed on the video screen can be detected even when the video monitor itself is turned off.

Many audiences to whom I speak find this simple item alarming and discomforting, thereby leading to a degree of incredulity—until they see the demonstrations. In September of 1991, on Geraldo Rivera's ill-fated TV show, "Now! It Can Be Told," I demonstrated what I believe was the first national broadcast of electromagnetic eavesdropping.[2] Despite the fact that atomic bombs were going off in the background, the demonstration was real.

The publicity surrounding electromagnetic eavesdropping first reached a furor in 1985 when a Dutch scientist, Professor Wim van Eck, published an unclassified paper on the subject.[3] He stated that, based upon his studies, "it seems justified to estimate the maximum reception distance using only a normal TV receiver at around 1km. . . ."[4] As a result of the publication of this document, electromagnetic eavesdropping was popularly dubbed "van Eck radiation." According to Tempest engineers certified by the National Security Agency, the NSA department responsible for the security of the Tempest program went ballistic. They classified the Van Eck report, which included very exacting details and mathematical analysis that they had considered to be exclusively under their domain. Tempest engineers were forbidden, as part of their security agreement with the Government, from speaking about or acknowledging any details of van Eck's work.

But the cat was already out of the bag. The prestigious and scholarly journal *Computers and Security* discussed van Eck in its December 1985 issue, to the continued chagrin of the intelligence community, and in 1988, the British Broadcasting Corporation aired a segment on the phenomenon which is similarly classified in England.[5]

This impressive demonstration was conducted in London, with the detection equipment set up in a van that roamed the streets. The technicians in the unassuming van would lock into "interesting" computer signals, emanating from law offices and brokerage firms located in London high rises, from a distance of several hundred feet. They then recorded the impressively clear computer-screen images on a video tape. When company executives were brought into the van, they viewed a playback of the video tape that demonstrated the capability for remote passive eavesdropping of highly sensitive information. The impact of such capability was evident on their shocked faces and in their commentary. According to Tempest technicians, the NSA classified this tape along with van Eck's publicly available papers.

Swedish television broadcast a similar demonstration on a show called "Aktuellt." These demonstrations provided conclusive evidence that the risk to privacy and the sanctity of information was real. Despite our government's efforts at hiding the potential risk to American businesses, van Eck radiation was becoming widely known everywhere and to everyone else but us.

In 1990, Professor Erhard Möller of Aachen University in Germany published a detailed update to van Eck's work with such eavesdropping. To this date, the NSA still classifies these protective measures in their Tempest program. They allegedly went so far as to classify portions of a university text book written by the legendary expert in electromagnetic control, Don White.[6]

On the home front, Hughes STX (a division of Hughes Aircraft) demonstrated van Eck emissions using a circa-1955 Dumont tube television console set and a small portable black and white unit as receptors. Not only are van Eck radiations broadcast into the air, but water pipes, sprinkler systems, and power lines are excellent conduits, offering ideal tap points for interception. Attaching a wire to a hot water pipe and watching computer screen images appear on a television set is a most disquieting experience, but one that cannot be ignored.

Jim Carter, president of Bank Security in Houston, Texas, has also been publicizing the phenomenon at such events as HoHoCon, the annual hacker's conference, and Jim Ross's Surveillance Expo in Washington, D.C. His experiences with Van Eck were highlighted in 1991 when, in cooperation with Benjamin Franklin Savings and Loan, he demonstrated how to successfully attack a Diebold ATM machine. He says that, using Van Eck radiation, "we got all of the information we needed to reconstruct an ATM card." Carter says that he notified Diebold of the vulnerability to their machines and to their customers. They flew a couple of engineers down "but after two years, we're still waiting for them to get back to us. They really don't give a damn if they fix the problem or not."

Today, if you don't have the expertise to build your own, you can actually buy a van Eck unit, priced from $500 to $2,000, from any number of catalogs. The results range from godawful to darn good. One company, Spy Supply in New Hampshire, no longer sells their unit. According to one of the company's principals, Bob Carp, they were approached by the

NSA and strongly urged to discontinue sales immediately or risk the wrath of the government.[7]

Another company, Consumertronics in Alamogordo, New Mexico, claims to sell a van Eck detection unit for educational purposes only. However, reading their literature and catalog of product offerings suggests other motives.[8] On the high end, sophisticated and expensive test equipment such as that built by Watkins-Johnson of Gaithersberg, Maryland, and an assortment of other U.S. and foreign companies, provide an excellent means to detect a wide range of signals and reconstruct video signals of good quality.

The NSA has gone to extraordinary lengths to maintain the secrecy surrounding van Eck radiation, such as asking Spy Supply to cease and desist and classifying portions of engineering text books that might give too much away. By attempting to bury the issue as completely as possible and allowing discussions of value to occur only under the veil of national security, they have done this country and its industries a great disservice. To the best of my knowledge, they have never openly discussed the realities of van Eck radiation, thus reducing its credibility as a threat in the eyes of corporate America and the protectors of its information. The unfortunate rationale of many security professionals is "if it's not officially acknowledged, then it can't be real."

A few years back, after the initial flare-up of concern about electromagnetic eavesdropping, Chase Manhattan Bank ran some internal test to determine their vulnerability. Based upon their home-brew tests, they determined, "Quite frankly, at the bank, we're not overly concerned about screens being read."[9]

However, in the fall of 1992, Chemical Bank found themselves the apparent target of exactly this type of eavesdropping by unknown Information Warriors. According to Don Delaney of the New York State Police, bank officials were alerted that an antenna was pointed at their midtown New York bank offices, where a large number of ATM machines and credit card processing facilities are located. For reasons that the bank will not discuss, they elected not to pursue the matter al-

though the police offered assistance.[10] From external appearances, it seems that Chemical Bank was the target of what has
generically become known as a Tempest attack.

Because van Eck detection is so simple, so insidious, and
so passive, the number of reported incidents is bound to be
low. In addition, most people aren't even aware of the capability so they wouldn't recognize it if they saw it. A major U.S.
chemical company, however, did know that it was the target of
industrial espionage using van Eck techniques. The security
director of the firm was an ex-CIA employee, well-trained in
surveillance techniques. He said that he was alerted by the
sight of a Toyota van sitting in the parking lot near one of the
company's research and development buildings. What caught
his attention was an antenna on the roof of the van, which
appeared to be scanning the area and fixing itself on the R&D
facility. Although he can't prove his countermeasures solved
anything, the van quickly disappeared after he shielded the
targeted labs from emitting van Eck radiations.[11]

There are plenty of methods to protect against Information
Warriors who want to eavesdrop on screens, keyboards and
printers, but a question of legality arises. According to one
author, "In the United States, it is illegal for an individual to
take effective countermeasures against Tempest surveillance."[12]
This statement is ominous if taken at face value. It implies that
electromagnetic eavesdropping is commonly practiced in domestic surveillance activities. Could this be one reason why
the NSA has been so rigorous in its efforts at downplaying the
matter?

Perhaps. The NSA and other government agencies do use
these techniques and do have their own surveillance vans,
complete with van Eck detection equipment. A specially-
constructed chassis is made by Ford Mother Company, so that
the eavesdropping van cannot be eavesdropped upon. The
vans are then outfitted with the very best surveillance technology that the Pentagon's billions can buy. Who are they
listening to? No one I know will say, but their capabilities are
most impressive. The NSA recently developed a custom

integrated circuit employing specialized Fast Fourier Transforms (FFTs), that will enhance the clarity and range of the van Eck detection equipment substantially, as well as significantly reduce the size of the surveillance equipment.[13]

I assume that by now the problem becomes explicitly clear. The computer screens that we once thought were private are, in fact, veritable radio stations. The keyboard strokes that we enter on our computer are also transmitted into the air and onto conduit pipes and power lines. An *A* at the keyboard sends out an electromagnetic *A* into the air or down the sprinkler pipes and any digital oscilloscope, in the hands of a professional, can detect the leaking signals with ease. A keyboard *B* emits an electromagnetic *B*, a *C* at the keyboard sends out its unique signature, and so it goes for the rest of the keyboard. PIN numbers or other potentially sensitive information can be detected, stored, and decoded with the right equipment in the right hands.

Printers, too, betray the privacy of their users; generally unbeknownst to them, but all too well known by the Information Warrior in search of information. The NSA uses a classified technique called digram analysis to assist in eavesdropping on van Eck emantions from printers. Each printer type has its own unique sets of electromagnetic patterns, depending upon how it was designed and built. The NSA will buy one of each, analyze its patterns, and then be more easily able to decode the intercepted information patterns.

As the story goes, during a very intensive security sweep of the American Embassy in Moscow in the early 1980s, a small transmitter was found inside of a classified telex machine. Allegedly, it listened to the electromagnetic patterns generated by the telex machine and retransmitted the raw signals to a secondary listening post where the Soviets performed their own digram analysis to read sensitive U.S. Government messages.

Since there is virtually no way to know that a computer or printer is being "van Ecked", there is no reliable method to determine what losses might actually have been incurred due

to electromagnetic eavesdropping. The possibilities for speculation are endless. Exploitation of van Eck radiation appears to
be responsible, at least in part, for the arrest of senior CIA
intelligence officer Aldrich Hazen Ames on charges of being a
Soviet/Russian mole. According to the affadavit in support of
Arrest Warrant, the FBI used "electronic surveillance of Ames'
personal computer and software within his residence," in
their search for evidence against him. On October 9, 1993, the
FBI "placed an electronic monitor in his (Ames') computer,"[14]
suggesting that a van Eck receiver and transmitter was used to
gather information on a real-time basis. Obviously, then, this is
an ideal tool for criminal investigation—one that apparently
works quiet well.

In 1991, I designed a few scenarios for a defense think tank
in order to define the needs of an urban Information Warrior
who wants to use this approach. The simplest approach
involved a portable van Eck detector with its own transmitter
and receiver, so that it could be remotely tuned into the
computer, printer, or video monitor of choice. Smaller detectors are more expensive but offer advantages to the Information Warrior, who could easily plant a small receiver in the
basement of a building, leave it there unattended, and sit a
comfortable distance away, scanning and listening for the information he wanted.

Consider the following. An Information Warrior who has
profit as his motive uses van Eck detection equipment to listen
in on the computer of a brokerage firm. They are planning to
issue either astoundingly good or astoundingly bad news on
one of their clients, which will soon have a major impact on its
stock price. Now that he knows this "insider information," he
makes the appropriate financial decisions and buys or sells or
shorts a big block of stock with the intent of making a financial
killing. Can the Information Warrior be prosecuted for this?
There is no clear answer at this time.

Perhaps the CEO of a major company is worried about the
outcome of future litigation, and would give anything to know
what the opposing counsel was planning. Electromagnetic

eavesdropping could easily provide him with that information— and there is hardly any chance that he would ever be caught. Invisible, passive, and insidious.

Van Eck detection also lends itself nicely to the exploitation of Binary Schizophrenia or other social malaises we discussed earlier. Imagine that the goal of the Information Warrior is to exacerbate friction among upper management of a company. If certain sensitive and supposedly private information were acquired by our insidiously invisible detection equipment and "accidentally" leaked into the wrong hands, all members of the management team would suspect one another of being likely culprits.

Or if a customer's personal financial data were acquired from a bank's computers and properly leaked to the right people, the bank would be suspected of and possibly legally responsible for fiduciary irresponsibility. That it would lose a customer in the process goes without saying. While the press might not use such techniques itself, sometimes they don't know and don't care where and how information is obtained. Companies are embarrassed enough when stories appear on activities that aren't meant for public disclosure. Electromagnetic eavesdropping only provides one additional means to effect breaches of privacy and confidentiality.

According to Mark Baven, an editor at *Government Data Systems*, "In today's volatile financial market, where inside information can lead to millions of dollars of profits, a raid on a corporation's vital data . . . could be extremely worthwhile. The cost of implementing Tempest technology would be far offset by the potential savings that such security would provide."

The one thing we can be sure of is that the technology to listen in on computer leakage will only become better and better and cheaper and cheaper, just as all technology does. At one point or another, business is going to have to decide that its only protection against passive information interception is an active defense.

Cryptography

"The best way to keep a secret between two people is if one of them is dead."

—COMMON SENSE MY MOM TAUGHT ME.

IF YOU TINKER in your garage and come up with a nifty new way to build a nuclear bomb, all of your efforts are automatically classified. Classified at birth, if you will. You can't talk about it and you can't write about it. While this appears to be in violation of our First Amendment rights to freedom of speech and prior restraint, the courts have upheld the government's positions arguing that "thermonuclear annihilation of us all justifies an exception."[1]

And so it almost goes with cryptography. Cryptography is the art and science of scrambling information to keep a message secret. The better the cryptography, the better the secret is kept.

As far as the Department of Defense is concerned, cryptography and nuclear technology are two of the most sensitive areas in science and research since they both represent military strength. The bomb and its power are obvious, but is the cryptoquote puzzle in the daily paper really a threat to national security? No, because that is weak cryptography— call it "crypto" if you want to sound knowledgeable—meant to be solved by Grannie at the kitchen table. The government only cares about the "strong" crypto. The National Security Agency, the country's listening post charged with keeping our secrets and breaking "theirs," is concerned about strong crypto, and expends great effort on its job.

If it weren't for cryptanalysis (the art of breaking codes), World War II could have cost the Allies many more lives and years of war. In order to protect themselves against Allied interception of vital strategic messages, the Axis used secret codes to 'encrypt' their military communications. Only those with the right key could unlock the message to decipher it. The Germans developed a coding or encryption scheme that was so good, the British had to organize a huge analytical apparatus consisting of thousands of men and women just to crack their messages. Ultimately, through serendipity, the British recovered a piece of German naval equipment responsible for building the indecipherable coded messages. That machine was called the Enigma, an invention light years ahead of other cryptosystems of the day. Alan Turing is the intellectual giant often credited with shortening the war by deciphering German messages.

Instead of using advanced technology, the United States employed Native American Navaho to communicate military transmissions in the Pacific Theater, and the Japanese never caught on. The Japanese coding system, on the other hand, proved fairly easy to crack and during much of the war in the Pacific, the U.S. was regularly intercepting and reading Imperial communications. This information remained secret for years.

The use of cryptography to disguise messages is as familiar as the Sunday paper cryptoquote that uses a single level of letter-substitution: For example, an *A* stands for *K* and *L* stands for *C* and so on for all twenty-six letters. Letter substitution was used by Julius Caesar to send secret written messages to his field generals. The key to reading the message was knowing which letter stood for which other letter. Today, the crypto may be such a complex stream of mathematical symbols that an enciphered message would takes the world's most powerful supercomputer years to crack.

Cryptography is all about secrets—keeping them or trying to find out about the other guy's. Cryptography was originally considered a military weapon and, to a great extent, it is still a deeply guarded secret today. The government and the NSA take cryptography so seriously that they tried unsuccessfully to have cryptography placed under the same umbrella as atomic research. That would have put all cryptographic work under the control of the Department of Defense, removed it from the public domain, and established a stranglehold that might still be in place today.

But the Government made some fatal mistakes along the way. Along came computers and the need to protect the information that they contained. In the early days of computers, circa 1970, the biggest private commercial use for computers and thus the demand for cryptography came from the financial community. They recognized that in order to insure an accurate and reliable means of moving money through Cyberspace, their Electronic Funds Transfer (EFT) systems needed protection.

In 1976, the National Bureau of Standards, today known as NIST or the National Institute of Standards and Technology, contracted with IBM to modify their Lucifer encryption algorithms to become the national standard for data protection. (An algorithm is the rule by which the encryption scheme works.) And so was born the Data Encryption Standard, or DES (Pronounced dezz or d-e-s). DES, a strong encryption scheme in its day, was endorsed by the Department of Treasury and has subsequently proven to be an adequate protector of the hundreds of trillions of dollars electronically transferred in the U.S. every year.

The NSA, though, had its concerns, and succeeded in having DES categorized as a weapon system. Therefore, NSA approval is required in order to export DES outside of the United States, in addition to that of the Departments of State and Commerce. DES is controlled by ITAR, the International

Traffic in Arms Regulations, and violators receive harsh penalties. Essentially, the thinking went, the U.S. doesn't want DES to get into unfriendly hands so they can encrypt and disguise their data from our professional eavesdroppers.

But here's where they really screwed up.

Since DES was a national standard, it was entered into the public domain and the DES algorithms were openly published for anyone to see. For the price of a stamp, any American or even a foreign national could, and can, write to NIST and receive a copy of the DES standard. Despite the fact that DES was controlled as a weapon, we published—and gave away free—the instruction manual and parts lists, enabling anyone or any country to build their own. That's like sending a Patriot Missile kit to Libya or Iran with a note saying, "Please don't build this."

The export controls for DES and for products that used it made it nearly impossible for manufacturers of encryption products to sell their wares outside of the United States and Canada. After years of frustration on the part of our friendly allies, they took the obvious route. Since the majority of the commercial sector was unable to legally import DES from the United States, they decided to build it themselves. After all, it is a public domain algorithm.

So what do we find today?

We see American-designed, public-domain DES being manufactured all over the world. The best DES comes from Germany, the cheapest from Taiwan and Hong Kong. Computer stores in Moscow sell Kryptos, a Russian version of the American national encryption standard. According to the Software Publishers Association, of 210 foreign encryption product from at least 33 countries, 129 use DES.[2] So what's the point in restricting the sales of DES? The political gerrymandering surrounding DES is a classic example of inane policy making.

In the mid-1980s, the NSA attempted to have DES decertified as a viable means of protecting financial transactions. That would have meant that vast investments in encryption equipment on the part of the Department of Treasury, the

Federal Reserve Board, and thousands of banks were for naught. They would have to start from scratch developing acceptable means of protecting our money. The NSA argued that DES was no longer considered secure, and that in its estimation computer technology had sufficiently evolved to render DES's effectiveness impotent. The Treasury Department dug in its heels and, after protracted fights, NSA acquiesced and DES was recertified. The battle will be over in 1997, by which time a replacement for DES will be in place. In fact the battle may be over now, because DES is breakable.

At the March 1993 RSA Data Security Conference, Dr. Martin Hellman presented a theoretical approach to cracking DES by using parallel processing. On August 20, 1993, Michael Wiener of Bell-Northern Research in Canada published a paper "showing how to build an exhaustive DES key search machine for $1 million that can find a key in 3.5 hours on average."[3]

With increasingly powerful Computers Everywhere it was just a matter of time before the key to cracking DES encryption was out of the bag, and the NSA knew it. They had warned the Treasury Department almost a decade earlier, but never came up with enough rationale to force action. The NSA has had its own DES cracking machines for years, costing between $50,000 and $100,000 each and using the same techniques that Hellman and Weiner describe. The Harris Corporation built a system for the government that can crack DES in less than fifteen minutes using a very fast, very smart Cray Y/MP supercomputer.

To the Information Warrior, all of this is good news. To the Federal Reserve Board and every other financial institution who relies upon DES to protect their transactions, these revelations spell a potential disaster. For about $1 million, the Information Warrior now has the ability to eavesdrop upon and make modifications to critical financial transactions. If only the NSA had been more open in sharing their knowledge, we could have been well on our way to the next generation of encryption. But in the interest of their limited interpretation of

National Security, they kept their secrets to themselves. The Government (read the NSA and law enforcement) had its own agenda and plans and wouldn't share them—until April 16, 1993, that is.

On that day, President Clinton's press secretary released a statement announcing "a new initiative that will bring the Federal Government together with industry in a voluntary program to improve the security and privacy of telephone communications while meeting the legitimate needs of law enforcement." The needs of the Justice Department spurred the development of a new encryption technique for wide-spread use. That initiative is called "Clipper." Clipper was announced just after Janet Reno was appointed Attorney General, and might have been announced earlier if Clinton hadn't had trouble with prior designees.

Clipper is a hardware chip based upon the classified "Skip-jack" encryption algorithm, common in such government arenas as the Defense Messaging Agency and in unclassified networks such as ARPANET. In theory, it is stronger than DES but because skipjack is classified, it will not be available for the public scrutiny enjoyed by all widely accepted encryption schemes such as DES or the de facto standard RSA public key methods. Without open academic analysis, the encryption strength is subject to question and the success of Clinton's Clipper program is in jeopardy. Clipper was born back when the NSA tried to decertify DES and law enforcement agencies such as the FBI were fearful that criminals would use encryption themselves. Wiretapping is a favorite tool of law enforcement but eavesdropping becomes more difficult if criminals' conversations are encrypted. If drug dealers keep their records on a computer that employs encryption, deciphering the information is an enormous undertaking. Law enforcement understandably wanted action taken so their jobs would not become even more difficult.

In 1991, as a result of in-government lobbying, the Senate Judiciary Committee attempted to add a rider to Senate bill 266, a piece of anticrime legislation: "It is the sense of

Congress that providers of electronic communications services and manufacturers of electronic communications service
equipment shall ensure that communications systems permit
the government to obtain the plain-text contents of voice, data,
and other communications when appropriately authorized by
law." The Government wants to be able to decrypt conversations and digital traffic so they can continue their eavesdropping activities. This wording, added two years in advance of
the Clipper announcement, was in anticipation of the technology becoming available.

The offensive wording was removed from the bill as a
result of vocal objection by the ACLU, CPSR, (Computer
Professionals for Social Responsibility), and other privacy
advocate groups, but government efforts have not abated. They
have pushed ahead with what they call "voluntary compliance" with Clipper for communications and its brethren
Capstone, used for computers.

There are several huge problems with the Government's
position.

First, unless everyone uses Clipper, the entire effort is
futile. In order for everyone to use it, it would have to become
a mandate or law, therefore making other forms of encryption
illegal. That will never happen in an open society. Second, for
Clipper to be accepted, the Government has to be trusted not
to abuse their capabilities to decrypt private transmissions
without proper court authorization, as is required today.

The proposed method for protecting the average American's privacy is through a complex process of "key escrowing"
the means of decypting a Clipper conversation. The Government's plan is to designate "two trusted third parties" who
will each hold a piece of the key that could decrypt specific
Clipper transmission only. The problem here is that whoever
becomes the trusted parties becomes a target for the Information Warrior, because all of the keys to the digital Clipper
kingdom would be sitting with two specific groups. The press
office of the Attorney General said in April 1993 that they

were having trouble finding groups willing to take on that responsibility and risk. Mother Teresa is unavailable.

The third major problem with Clipper is that since no one outside of a select few will be able to examine the internal workings of the Clipper system, we have to take on faith that the Government doesn't have a so-called back-door to bypass the entire escrow system.

Immediately after the announcement, the business community was unexpectedly united in opposition to Clipper. Over thirty-one companies, including IBM, DEC, Apple, Hewlett- Packard, Microsoft, and Lotus have written, in cooperation with the Electronic Frontier Foundation, a letter to the White House and Congress, outlining their concerns about the Clipper plan.

Clipper finds few adherents, and even some NSA, NIST, and other Government officials admit privately that Clipper worries them. One Clipper adherent is Dorothy Denning, an elegant computer scientist from Georgetown University who has taken the unpopular position that Clipper is a reasonable trade-off between personal privacy and the legitimate needs of law enforcement. At one security conference she said, "If Radio Shack sells a cryptophone that the government can't crack, I think we'll have a real crisis on our hands."[4] For her unpopular stand she has suffered undue amounts of "flaming," public ridicule and accusations that she secretly works for the NSA.

Padgett Peterson, Information Security Specialist with Martin Marietta, is a less vocal adherent, but apparently more acquiescent to the Government position. He envisions the day when everyone will be using Clipper, like it or not. "Doctors, lawyers, CPAs, and everyone else will use Clipper," he maintains.

Even the international community is outraged. The French Government isn't about to permit the use of Clipper in France if the U.S. holds the only keys to the kingdom. Other countries voice similar sentiments.

The big question asked by civil libertarians, the ACLU, and

others aware of technology's immense intrusions on our lives and privacy is, "Will the White House drop the other shoe?" The other shoe, of course, is the mandate that Clipper is in and all other encryption is out—by law.

AT&T supported clipper when it was announced, probably due to the fact that the Department of Justice had placed a multimillion dollar order for special encrypted Clipper telephones with them. AT&T even discontinued the DES version of their original secure phone, the Model 3600. But when the Clipper chips were delayed by almost nine months (manufacturing problems yielded a ninety-six percent failure rate), they supported an intermediary encryption technology instead of the original DES version that was already a saleable product. Washington insiders speculate that AT&T was pressured into their actions by the intelligence community with threats of unfavorable Federal contract review.

Perhaps the Government is engaged in a campaign to desensitize the American public, a sophisticated form of Information Warfare. First they attempt to pass a law, then they back off when attacked by privacy advocates and adverse publicity. Next, they make the very technology available that would have been used to implement the proposed law, if it had been passed. Then Clipper is announced and the flak hits the fan, so they back off again. They try to convince the public that Clipper really is OK. Then maybe they'll try to sneak in another law, perhaps in a few months or a year. See what happens. Sooner or later, the reasoning goes, the public will cease to care and Clipper will become the law of the land. It is a scenario that does not take great imagination to conjure. It depends upon who is behind Clipper, the depth of their pockets, their political wherewithal, and their motivation and resolve.

Ultimately I think that the Clipper situation is another misguided effort on the part of the government. Before Clinton's April 16 announcement, not too many Americans were aware of encryption and what it could do. Today front page articles are hitting the general media and awareness of privacy and eavesdropping is at an all-time high. Everyone knows about Clipper. Now the White House says, "While encryption technology can help Americans protect business secrets and the unauthorized release of personal information, it also can be used by terrorists, drug dealers, and other criminals."

That's right. And with Clinton's and Bush's and the NSA's well thought-out plans for Clipper, we can all sleep easier at night knowing that organized crime, the drug cartels, Islamic fundamentalists, and other friendly Information Warriors will sign up for Clipper before plotting their strategies.

To the Information Warrior, cryptography represents the same two-edged sword that our military has had to deal with for decades. The Information Warrior must increase the power of his analytical arsenal to penetrate the secrets we so dearly want to protect with encryption. Is $1 million too much to invest to disrupt the financial transaction between banks?

Crypto works for the Information Warrior. He can, as any of us might decide to do, encrypt all of the voice conversations between the members of his army. He can encrypt cellular calls, telephone calls, computer conversations, and everything on his own computer systems. If he is arrested, or if his equipment is legitimately confiscated in the investigation of a crime, the information will be unreadable and therefore unavailable as evidence, presenting an admittedly deep dilemma for law enforcement. Right behind Clipper is the computer-data version called Capstone. It will add more government-approved encryption tools to the suspect Skipjack algorithm and escrow system. Although Clipper is allegedly strong enough to resist attack through the next thirty or forty years of computer advances, the Clinton administration has a long way to go before it is adopted in the private sector.

On Friday, February 4, 1994, the Clinton Administration, after months of study, returned a favorable verdict to adapt Clipper for Government use, and to strongly encourage the private sector to follow suit. The Department of Commerce named the Department of Treasury and NIST (National Institute of Standards and Technology) as the two trusted key-escrow holders despite originally preferring at least one non-Government-trusted third party. The debate certainly isn't over, and Senator Patrick Leahy, Democrat, Vermont said, "The only good aspect of the Clipper Chip program is that it is not mandatory, yet that is exactly why the program is doomed to fail."[5] Wide spread public use is still the law-enforcement officer's idea of the perfect dream: so attractive yet so unreachable.

The government appears to be suffering from its own brand of Binary Schizophrenia regarding cryptography, thus unmasking the internal confusions between agencies. Software engineer Phil Zimmerman designed a scheme he called PGP, or Pretty Good Privacy, that the government thinks is *too* good. PGP has worldwide support and its adherents use it religiously to protect their information transmissions. The government, however, wanted to know whether Zimmerman violated the law by placing PGP on the Internet, thus making it globaly available.

A voice of sanity comes from Congresswoman Maria Cantwell (D-WA) who, on November 22, 1993, proposed a bill that would largely remove export restrictions on DES and other commonly available software encryption schemes. Propelled in part by industry concern over America's competitive disadvantage, the bill attempts to deregulate controls over technology that has already been let out of the bag, so to speak. Although Cantwell's efforts are to be applauded, the bill in its inchoate form still allows arbitrary export restrictions to be imposed by the NSA through the Departments of State and Commerce. Sooner or later, the government will have to realize that they cannot control Cyberspace in the same ways they have controlled aspects of our physical Cold War world.

The Information Warrior knows that cryptography is a powerful tool and he will use it to his best advantage, regardless of what Washington does. Because crypto can be made "strong" with software, and software is not illegal, anyone with the skills can generate strong cryptographic privacy with little trouble. Government and industry must come together and focus on their common interests, not their differences. The ramifications for us as a people and a country are far-reaching.

Is the day coming when, if any of us encrypts our voice or data communications, we will be immediately suspected for a crime? Will the mere fact that we desire privacy suggest we have something to hide?

When the legitimate concerns of national security, corporate protection, and personal privacy suddenly merge, no one answer will keep everyone happy.

Except the Information Warrior. He frankly doesn't care.

9

Chipping: Silicon-Based Malicious Software

"I'm a dues-paying member of local thirteen, Villains, Theives, and Scoundrels Union."

—BORIS BADENOV, SPY
"ROCKY AND BULLWINKLE"

OVER THE LAST COUPLE OF YEARS, I have had the opportunity to speak before a number of government groups and present some of the concepts behind what I call "Chipping." In many ways I overestimated the knowledge of my audiences, especially those experts in the intelligence community who claim to know something about computers, software, and technology in general. To my chagrin I found that a fairly small percentage of my Federal audiences had the insight to recognize the yin and yang of that technology. Those dedicated civil servants who do understand the dangers inherent in chipping have become so frustrated with the system (translate: do nothing) that they find it infinitely easier to lay back, get promoted to a G-14 pay grade, and wait until their pension is primed for a profitable retirement buyout.

Unfortunately, the Information Warrior is less laid back. He is on the offensive and has an excellent grasp of the technology. Chipping is just another Information Weapon that can be used against the econotechnical information infrastructure of our society.

At the heart of just about everything electronic sit tiny,

sometimes minuscule, components known as integrated circuits. An integrated circuit is the building block upon which toys, cameras, televisions, and computers are made. If you refer to integrated circuits as either ICs or chips, you'll sound like an expert. Chips come in thousands of flavors, but a mere handful dominate the innards of information systems.

We've all heard the term memory chip. A memory chip is an integrated circuit that is designed to act as a storage device for information. A memory chip that can hold 64K of information is called a 64K RAM chip. (RAM stands for Random Access Memory.) We speak of a 256K chip or a one meg or four meg chip, and so on. Designers are now working on RAM chips that can store tens of megabytes (thousands of pages) on a single piece of silicon the size of a thumbnail. Dozens of different kinds of memory chips are used in computers that require high speed storage measured in the megabytes and gigabytes. A gigabyte is a thousand megabytes, and a terrabyte is a million megabytes.

The nomenclature for chips is sometimes incomprehensible to anyone but an engineer—SRAM, NovRAM, 256KDRAM, EEPROM, UVEPROM, FlashRam and so on—but don't let that bother you. RAM is just RAM. Just like a lamp, whose primary purpose is to illuminate a room regardless of its styling and design, a RAM chip is an electronic memory device regardless of the technical intricacies involved. RAM is RAM is RAM.

The most familiar chip in the world might be the CPU, or Central Processing Unit. The CPU is the brains inside the computer or, as Intel says in their ads, "The Computer inside the Computer." CPU chips carrying the Intel trademarks of 286, 386, 486, and Pentium drive the majority of desktop computers today. Apple is a major user of Motorola's 68000 series of CPUs and IBM, Sun, and DEC all have their own CPU chips meant to compete with Intel's virtual monopoly.

Etched onto a small wafer of silicon, with a thickness measured in molecules, is a dizzyingly complex pattern of paths, connections, gates, and millions of switches. The process of CPU design and manufacture is so complex that other computer systems calculate and lay out the digital road maps.

If the CPU is removed, the computer is deader than a door-nail, and arguably no longer even a computer. If the CPU is disabled, the computer system becomes unreliable and fails. The parallel to the human brain is unavoidable; no head, no brain, no life. No CPU, no computer.

Other chips provide the glue to make computers compute, ovens cook, cellular phones call, or airplanes fly. These small logic chips switch signals from on to off to on again, when told to do so by the CPU. Even with the immense power of today's CPUs, unless the so-called glue chips are working properly, the electronic device in question will idly sit on the closet shelf or find its way back to the store for replacement.

Input/output chips let you print on your printer, talk to another computer via modem, or make your television cable-ready. An input chip will listen to the rinse cycle time you enter onto the numeric keypad on the washing machine. An output chip signals that dinner is ready or sends information from a fax machine through Cyberspace across the Global Network. Video chips provide dazzling color and animation on computer monitors. An entire modem is available on a single piece of silicon, or in one chip. Hundreds of manufacturers worldwide offer an unlimited number of chips that perform almost any conceivable function.

Some chips are smarter than others. The RAM chip doesn't have what we might call native intelligence; it doesn't think for itself. The command to write to a RAM chip or read the information stored in it must be made by the CPU. CPU chips are very smart. Built into their microscopic circuits is a set of instructions called microcode. These are a comprehensive set of rules by which the CPU chips live and breathe.

The microcode is a kind of language. Just as a New Yorker might not be able to answer a Russian tourist's request for directions, a CPU chip might sit and do nothing if it is asked to perform a task for which its microcode is not prepared.

Other chips give the impression of being smart, such as

ROM chips. The term ROM Bios describes a set of instructions or rules that tell a particular computer how to function when asked to perform certain clearly defined and prespecified tasks. A ROM chip is really not all that smart, though—no smarter than a library. The information is there but for it to be of any value, you have to know how to access and use it. That is the job of a CPU. The CPU will address the ROM chip and look up the particular information of interest.

More and more chips appear daily. Portable camcorders are possible because of the development of extremely compact and specialized integrated circuits. Color correction circuits keep blue, blue. Gyrostabilizing circuits let you strap a camera to the back of your pet for a dog's view of the world without too much jitter.

Chip specialization is so inexpensive today that it is within the reach of the average electronic hobbyist, not to mention the Information Warrior. For a few dozen dollars, an electronics tinkerer can buy an integrated circuit that he can program himself.

EPROMs (Erasable Programmable Read Only Memory), PALs (Programmable Array Logic) can cost as little as a few dollars, or as much as $100 or more for sophisticated chips with thousands of gates. For more sophisticated engineers, ASIC, or Application Specific Integrated Circuits, can be designed, prototyped, and turned out in large quantity in less than three months for between $10 and $25,000. ASICs are found in almost every electronic device because it reduces manufacturing costs and other waste in the long run if conventional off-the-shelf chips are used.

For big manufacturers who produce millions of copies of the same chip, the use of VLSI, or Very Large Scale Integration, is popular. VLSI techniques permit thousands upon thousands of circuits to be condensed into smaller spaces. The tool-up costs for a custom VLSI chip start at $100,000 and go up from there. However, volume production techniques reduce the per unit cost of each chip, sometimes down to pennies. It's a matter of economy of scale.

Why all of the hubbub about chips? Because, chips are not always what they appear to be. They can neatly provide the insidiousness required by the able and resource intensive Information Warrior. What sort of damage can be caused by Information Warriors using chips or integrated circuits as a weapon? The answer, as you would expect by now, is plenty.

Recall that the essential difference between malicious software and a programming error is intent. The same concept holds true for chips. Occasionally, a chip will fail. A physical imperfection in the manufacturing process will cause the chip to internally break, malfunction, or cease to function altogether. The result? If the chip is a critical component, the device will fail—the television sound just stops, or the readout on the copy machine is blank. A failed chip in a car's electronic ignition will not allow you to start the car and pull out of the driveway. Similarly, if the central processor of a large computer fails, the entire system comes to a grinding halt. A glitch in a single chip is enough to shut down the most extensive electronic system.

Unfortunately, unlike the amateur television repairman of the fifties and sixties, you can't run down to the corner drug store, test the tubes, and replace the one that doesn't glow. Today's circuits are so intricate and intertwined that they need complex test equipment and highly trained technicians to isolate and repair the offending equipment. In the meantime, to the rest of us, it's just broke. Often it doesn't pay to fix the offending chip; the cost of repair is sometimes higher than the cost of replacement. How many of us would consider sending a $19.95 calculator back to the factory for repair? Most of us give the broken one to the baby and buy another at K-Mart.

But what if the chip was meant to fail, or to act differently than it was supposed to? What if the intent of the chip was to fail or malfunction on cue, as if it were following rules that only it knew about? The modification, alteration, design, or use of integrated circuits for purposes other than those originally intended by the designers is called "chipping." And chipping provides the Information Warrior with a bevy of opportunities to wage his war.

A simple example will suffice. In New York and other major metropolitan areas, phone fraud is rampant and costs industry hundreds of millions of dollars yearly. Cellular phones have been particularly hard hit and chipping is at the core of the rip-off. Once the electronic identification number of a cellular phone is in hand, that number must be programmed into chips using a PAL or EEPROM programmer, a tool used by hobbyists and engineers. The newly programmed chip then replaces the original chip that contained the phone's original EIN, in the new modified cellular phone. A phone has been chipped to bill an unsuspecting victim. In this case, the chipping was definitely malicious in both intent and effect, and the act itself runs afoul of quite a few laws.

But let's get imaginative for a moment, and think up other devious chipping activities that might lend themselves to an Information Warrior's agenda. Let's say that our Information Warrior has ample resources and is not looking for immediate gratification. That is, he is content to wait a couple of years before the results of his chipping become apparent. Counterfeit chips would work quite well.

Small chip makers, often from the Pacific Rim, build copies or clones of popular, pricey chips that are widely used and rarely examined. Often the ersatz manufacturer will not have obtained the rights or licenses to legally build the chips, but build them they do. Some are so brazen as to even label the counterfeit chips with the markings and insignias of the legitimate manufacturer. The counterfeiters make a few gazillion chips and sell them illegally, at a discount, as the real McCoy. Deep discounting can be a red flag, but overproduction is often used as an excuse, and raises few eyebrows when there are big profits to be made. The counterfeiters make and sell the chips to manufacturers for use inside VCRs, automobiles, computers, telephone answering machines, even military hardware. To all outside appearances, the chips are legitimate.

Counterfeit chips are generally sold to make quick profits, but they have a more insidious use for the well-armed Information Warrior. What if, in addition to making a counterfeit version of a chip that is in particularly high demand, a few additional functions are added to the chip, functions that would give the original designers a bad case of cardiac arrest?

Let's say that Kumbaya Electronics designs a fancy new chip that combines all of the functions of a clock radio into one component: the tuner, the amplifier, the clock, and its alarm circuits. Works great. Let's say that another company buys one of Kumbaya's chips and reverse-engineers it; takes it apart so thoroughly that they know everything about its inner workings. At a fraction of what it cost Kumbaya to develop the chip, the counterfeiters clone the fancy new chip but, since they are Information Warriors or they are being paid by them, they add extra circuits and instructions not in the original design.

Those instructions might be that at midnight on December 20, 1999, the chip would stop working—period. If the clock radios that used the Kumbaya chip sold well, the clock-radio manufacturer is going to have a lot of returns on his hands. Thousands of dissatisfied customers won't know about each other, but the manufacturer will find out soon enough that he has a problem. In addition to an immediate negative financial impact, whether from extensive returns at Sears and Circuit City or from a bad rash of publicity, the manufacturer faces a potential public relations problem. If the clock-radio manufacturer traces the problem back to the chip, and they undoubtedly will, Kumbaya Electronics will also have a problem. Despite their best efforts, word will get around that their chips are unreliable and shouldn't be used.

Who would want to do such a thing? A competitor is a pretty good place to start the list of suspects if the motivation is an economic battle between companies. Such sabotage is very effective and hard to detect and prove. The clock radio example is a pretty simple one, without earthshaking effects, but the same chipping technique can be used with devastating results.

Imagine that the battle between Japan and the U.S. for the automobile market becomes more heated than ever. U.S. trade restrictions have hurt Toyota, Nissan, Honda, and the rest. Detroit has gotten its act together, and sales of Rising Sun cars to aging baby boomers and the younger generation are way down. Since the Japanese economic system, *keiretsu*, is based upon interlocked relationships between thousands of smaller companies and their seven huge parent companies, the economic impact is felt throughout the small island nation. As a matter of international pride, Japan does not wish to lose face in the economic battle for motor vehicle superiority. Something must be done about the resurgence of the American automobile industry. This is a matter of Japanese Economic National Security.

Several Japanese companies now supply chips to American car companies; they provide the brains for electronic ignitions and braking systems as well as other chips for less mission-critical functions. Whether unofficially sanctioned with a wink on a national level, or as a knee-jerk reaction at the industrial level, a simple plan is hatched. Sell the Americans the chips they want, except there will be a little "surprise" waiting for drivers of certain American cars. The chips will look and function the same as ever and pass the necessary tests to be qualified for use, just as they always have. But, at some time in the future, according to a set of rules inserted into the chip by its designers, the chip will fail.

Maybe the windshield wipers will go haywire every day at 6:30, but only when the car is traveling at fifty-five MPH. Or the left blinker and the right blinker will intermittently cross their wires, further maddening the victim when he can't reproduce the symptom to his mechanic. Depending upon the desired results, the victim cars could become a joke as a result of their peculiarities, or gain an impossible-to-shake reputation for being deadly, such as happened to the Audi 5000. The results could be fatal—not only to passengers but to the car company.

Tens of billions of dollars could be lost if the Ford Taurus were subject to a rash of sudden uncontrollable failures when operating at a high-speed, or certain maneuvers resulted in accidents and deaths. The resultant publicity could be devastating—all because a chip was told to fail.

Chipping is the Trojan horse of microelectronics. Like the Greek gift to their Homeric enemy, the chip allows the electronic terrorist to slip his devastation in undetected. The more common the chip, the easier it is to counterfeit and distribute. What if, however, the Information Warrior did not want to destroy his target? What if his Trojan Horse had a different purpose, perhaps one of tracking or surveillance? The chipper might add, for example, a circuit that electromagnetically broadcasts a distinctive signal or pattern as a tracking device, like those often used in Hollywood's great car chase scenes.

Electromagnetic eavesdropping, or van Eck detection, is a useful tool for gathering information in a clandestine manner, but the state of the art has a way to go and chipping is one way to get there. While the chip performs its expected tasks, our silicon Trojan Horse will perform two unexpected functions. One, it will be tuned to listen for a specific type of Van Eck radiation. Two, it will transmit that information, to make distant reception easier. Conceptually, this is the equivalent of a phone bug, except that it is a computer being tapped.

There is immense value in knowing the channel on which every computer in foreign consulates broadcasts; it makes interception all the easier. The signal is cleaner, less data reconstruction is required, and the cost of surveillance is reduced. The only hitch? Getting the bug into the computer. In Gordon Liddy parlance, that requires a "bag job," or physical entry into the target. Replacing or adding a chip to a computer or printer is not too difficult for a repairman or computer dealer. Or, as the CIA supposedly did, you can sell the printer with the chip to the guy who's gonna sell it to the guy who's gonna ship it to the guy who's gonna buy it. Or you can fill the sales pipeline and listen in on everybody.

Some military planners recognize the power of chipping in

the furtherance of their goals. These are not the types of projects that one will routinely hear about in the *Washington Post* or in a Congressional hearing. Chipping is a carefully guarded technique that the NSA, the CIA, and their brethren whisper about in shielded windowless rooms. The funding is "black," meaning that R&D efforts into chipping are not line items in a general ledger. Accountability for chipping lies within the intelligence agencies, not within the Congress that funds it. Compared with the high cost of B-2 bombers, submarines, and satellites, chipping is chump change. Perhaps that is why it is so carefully protected. The powers that be don't want the other side's Information Warriors to do unto them what they are doing unto others.

The arms industry is an ideal market for government-sponsored chipping. The international dealers either sell indiscriminately to the highest bidder, or they are sponsored by governments in the pursuit of their political agenda. The U.S. is no exception in its sale of weapons systems to political allies and foes alike. Modern armaments are highly sophisticated electronic devices, the Patriot missile perhaps claiming first place in name recognition.

Let's assume for a moment that CIA and Pentagon Information Warriors want to play a trick on the customers who buy American weapons. A few of the electronic goodies inside the weapon system have been chipped; they have been modified perhaps to fail in three months time, or to shoot off course by three degrees, or to blow themselves up after two shots. Or maybe they have a radio beacon installed in them that identifies their exact location to overhead satellites. If the U.S. had built Iraq's Scuds and chipped them, it would have been a far sight easier to take them all out on day one. Imagine if North Korea's IBM 360 mainframe computers which control their missiles contained a "back door" to which only the U.S. military had access. Some close to the Department of Defense maintain this is exactly the case.

Chips have no sense of right or wrong, no morals or conscience. The chip only does what it is designed to do, and the intent and purpose of the chip is imbued in silicon by its designers. It is no more difficult to design a malevolent chip than to design one that works flawlessly for years. The cost to make the chips is the same, and only a little extra effort is required to maintain invisibility and insidiousness. Other than that, the distinction between a good chip and a bad chip is in the eyes of the beholder—or of its victims.

From the Information Warrior's viewpoint, chipping takes advantage of unexploited vulnerabilities that exist in virtually every electronic system. Chipping offers a wide range of capabilities and is usually a reasonably priced tool. When gigadollars are involved, chipping is an insignificant cost in the equation. Due to the insidiousness of the technique, it ranks as a highly effective weapon for the Information Warrior.

10

HERF Guns and EMP/T Bombs

"Lock phasers."

—CAPTAIN JAMES T. KIRK, *STAR TREK*

THE AZURE SEA GLISTENED 10,000 feet beneath the U.S. Navy P-3 patrol plane. Rays of light streamed from the sunset crimson skies in the west, creating mosaics of color that shimmered across the surface of the warm Caribbean waters. But the pilot and the two drug enforcement agents in the cockpit had little time to appreciate the beckoning views.

They were too busy concentrating on the video screens, digital readouts, and communications equipment that filled the forward section of the highly-customized airplane. The interior of the specially outfitted craft was darkened to facilitate use of the racks of sophisticated electronic equipment.

A conflict was brewing.

"Bogey heading twenty degrees-seventeen miles due north. No ID," the voice crackled over the cryptographically secure communications line. Everyone in the plane listened to all comm.

"Roger that, Blazer. Casa One in pursuit," the P-3's pilot answered immediately, as he sharply banked the plane to the right.

"Make it clean, Casa One," the invisible voice retorted.

"Always have been, Blazer. We're batting a thousand."
Knowing glances were passed around the cockpit.

The P-3 began a rapid descent; the motors roared as the
plane flew through the thicker air.

The DEA agent in charge spoke into his mouthpiece. "Are
we ready?"

The other agent scanned the wall of displays and pressed a
couple of switches. "114%, nominal. Charge rate 1.7 seconds.
What's the target?"

"Let you know when we know."

The plane descended to 2,000 feet on the same heading as
the Bogey. "Eight clicks upwind," the P-3 captain said, pointing at the full color radar screen sitting between his and the
copilot's seat.

The radar screen was filled with a number of small
symbols, geometric figures with numbers attached to each one.
The numbers indicated the call, the sign, and other identifying
information on each aircraft in the area. Except one. A single
symbol, flashing bright red, reading: UNIDENTIFIED.

"Got a broken transponder, y'think?" the DEA agent in the
rear of the cockpit asked.

"I sincerely hope so, for his sake," said the bearded senior
DEA agent. There wasn't any trace of humor in his words.

"Four clicks. Got a visual," the pilot said casually. Both
DEA agents looked out the front of the plane and the pilot
instinctively pointed.

"He see us?"

"Not yet. I got in silent."

"What is it?"

The pilot leaned forward, as though a few extra inches
would improve his view of a plane over two miles away.
"DC-3. Couldn't outrun my grandmother's Vespa."

"Yes!" shouted the second, younger DEA man. "They leak
like a sieve. I need less than a mile." He proceeded to make a
few adjustments to an oscilloscope, mumbling to himself.
"Point nine six five gig . . . four millisecond. . . ."

"OK, Ace, bring us in. I'd like to ask a few questions."

The P-3 lurched forward and the old DC-3 rapidly got closer and closer. "Wave him?"

"Go for it." The wings of the P-3 appeared to flap, trying to attract the attention of the target DC-3. No response. The DC-3 flew straight. "Again." No response. "The book says three, do it again." Nothing.

"OK, let's see if he's got his ears on." The head DEA man was in charge, absolutely professional. He adjusted his radio. "Ah . . . the DC-3 without markings . . . yeah, you. Please identify yourself." He looked over at the plane, now only a few hundred yards to his right. "I repeat, please identify yourself." Nothing.

He spoke to the pilot. "Get me in visual, Ace." The plane inched toward the DC-3 until the outline of the other pilot's face was visible. "Flare him." The other DEA man adjusted a dial and pushed a button secured by a hinged plastic Molly-cover.

"Flare deployed," he said casually as a large flare traced its way on a near-interception course with the cockpit of the DC-3.

"That'll get his attention." By now the DEA chase plane was so close that the DC-3 pilot's reaction, one of near terror, caused the head DEA man and his pilot to guffaw. When the flare shot past the front of the DC-3, the pilot's fear turned to anger, eliciting an unfriendly hand gesture in response.

"Well, I do believe that he's not on his way to Disney World with the family. Wouldn't you agree?" Nods all around, and the tension was somewhat abated. In these cases, you have to make sure that Ozzie and Harriet aren't out for a spin or you are in real trouble.

"He knows damn well we can't shoot him down."

"Maybe he'll listen to reason now."

"Think so?"

"No, but it's worth a try."

"Ah . . . you in the DC-3 . . . this is the Drug Enforcement Administration. We are operating under the authority of a multinational enforcement group and within the laws and powers granted us. We'd like to have a word with you if you don't mind. There's a little island about forty miles ahead where you can land. Please indicate your willingness to comply by responding immediately."

The senior DEA man gazed over at the DC-3 pilot. Nothing. Par for the course.

"Hey dirtball. Drop the load, now." Nothing.

"OK, here's the deal," he said calmly. "I will give you fifteen seconds to respond. If you do not respond in a positive way, expect the following to occur. First, your radio systems will fail. You will notice that because the static will disappear and no reception will be possible. Not even from us. Got it?"

They looked for some response and got none.

"I will give you one minute after your communications fail to give us the sign that you will comply. At the end of one minute, you will then find that your avionics will fail, all electrical systems will fail, your engines will stop, and your plane will sink into the water beneath you at a high rate of speed. If my memory serves me right, the laws of physics say you will not survive the crash. Do I make myself clear?" No response.

"Hey, Señor Stupid in the DC-3. Your fifteen seconds begins . . . Now!" He clicked off the radio and said to the pilot, "Take us out about a half mile. Is that good for you?" he asked the other DEA man at the equipment.

"Who could ask for anything more," he responded in the singsong voice of an old Toyota commercial.

The plane slowly glided away from the DC-3.

"Five seconds." Silence in the cockpit.

"Got it fixed on target."

"Two . . . one . . . fire."

The technical DEA man again raised a hinged panel and pushed a large red button. "Full power . . . front antenna struck . . . 4.5 megawatts. A poodle in a microwave would have fared better." There was no sound, no bullets, no missiles. Just an invisible beam of energy shot at the misbehaving DC-3. "Charge complete. Again?"

"For good luck." Again the red button was depressed and the DEA man repeated his report of an invisible bullseye.

"Let's see if he comes around to seeing things our way," the head DEA man said, relaxing back in his chair. The DC-3 turned suddenly to the right and accelerated. "I guess he wasn't convinced. Stay with him, Ace."

"No problem," the pilot said, following the DC-3 in a steep turn.

"Thirty seconds. Get in front of him." The Navy P-3 airplane accelerated and it soon seemed that they were the ones being chased; they were in front of the DC-3. "Avionics next."

The other DEA man said, "Power up to 180%, directionality .083, 1.21 gig. Ready when you are."

"Ten seconds."

The more maneuverable P-3 matched every move of the old lumbering DC-3, and maintained a forward position. "Five . . . four . . . three . . . oh, screw it . . . fire." Again, the red button was pressed.

"Shouldn't be long now," said the head DEA man.

They watched for several seconds, until the starboard propeller began to sputter and decelerate. The plane dipped to the left and they then saw the port propeller turn more slowly and the poor DC-3 twisted in the opposite direction. In many ways, this was the sad part of every operation for all three in the chase plane. Their target had no chance, none at all, but he just wouldn't listen. It would be over in a few seconds.

The DC-3 propellers were coming to a stop and the plane was plummeting rapidly. A plane of that size falling into the water makes a substantial splash.

"Call it in, Ace."

The pilot flipped a switch on the secure communications panel. "Blazer, this is Casa One."

"Copy you, Casa One," the static voice answered.

"Bogey fell into the drink, Blazer. Apparently a total systems failure."

"Copy that, Casa One. Survivors?"

"Not likely."

"Well, that's a darn shame. C'mon home Casa One. Good work."

Fiction? A true story? Maybe. Maybe not.

Even though the antidrug effort has cost tens of billions of dollars and the Pentagon spends some $1.2 billion annually to support such endeavors, America's War on Drugs has been less than successful.[1] One of the rules of the war is that we don't use bombs, bullets, or missiles to shoot down airplanes in international airspace. Unless of course they shoot first.

But where does it say that it's illegal for a drug courier's plane to go haywire and crash?

The beauty of the scenario above is that there is no obvious trace of foul play. There are no bullet holes or missing fuselage. The plane is largely intact, and when and if it is found, a close physical inspection will show the plane to be in pristine physical condition.

If the electronics packages are removed and subjected to intensive testing, all that will be found are components that failed without an obvious cause. Drug barons will not likely perform rescue and surveillance operations, at least not initially. The cost of such a flight is comparatively modest: $500,000 for the drugs, $1.5 million for the plane, $400,000 for the pilot, all for an ultimate $12.5 million-per-plane load payoff.[2] Losing planes, pilots, and drugs are part of the cost of doing business.

In our scenario, though, the DEA, the DoD, and antidrug forces have access to a weapon that is ideally suited to waging Narco Warfare. It is powerful, it is remote, and it is invisible. And ultimately, it is deniable—a government favorite. And there's not a whole lot the drug guys can do about it.

HERF Guns

Equipment such as that described in this tale is in use today and has become part of the arsenal of the U.S. military and other law enforcement agencies.

When I first presented the concept of High Energy Radio Frequency (or HERF) Guns as an Information Weapon to a Congressional Committee, their initial reaction provided pure comic relief to an otherwise dull Government hearing. On June 27, 1991, the day following a widespread telephone outage in the Northeast, Congressman Dan Glickman's and Tim Valentine's Technology and Competitiveness Subcommittee held hearings on the effectiveness of the Computer Security Act of 1987. This Act is designed to force all government agencies to develop information security policies for their respective operations, submit them for approval, and then implement them. The CSA-1987 has no impact on or authority over commercial and private computer systems. Serendipitously, the timing of the telephone outage heightened anticipation of the hearings.

Congressman Glickman, a Democrat from Kansas, opened the session with a statement that showed his true concern for the security, integrity, and sanctity of computer systems in both the public and private sectors. The events of the day before, and the prior system crashes, framed his remarks. He established the tone of the session, and then it was my turn.

Taking his words to heart, I pointed out and described how a magnetic gun could be harmful, if not deadly, to computer systems. I called them HERF Guns. I have dubbed the really big HERF guns with greater range and greater power EMP/T (pronounced 'empty') Bombs.

One of the first questions asked was, as you might expect, about HERF Guns. Congressman Glickman asked, "Do you think we ought to consider banning these kinds of devices?" I replied, "If you did you would be banning the microwave and communications industries from existence." Laughter rippled for some time and certainly lightened the load for the rest of the hearing.

If I may put on my Congress-bashing hat to offer an aside, I would like to see a greater number of engineering types elected to office instead of the infinite stream of pork barrel lawyers we get today. Very few people are aware of the fact that guns and bombs can be built that target only computers, communications, and other electronic systems. The situation sort of reminds me of Jimmy Carter's neutron bomb—kill all the people but leave the buildings standing.

A lesson in HERF: HERF stands for High Energy Radio Frequency. It's an easy acronym that's even fun to say. A HERF Gun is a very powerful weapon in the Information Warrior's arsenal, and it can come in all sorts of different configurations to meet one's needs. At a very basic level, a HERF Gun shoots a high power radio signal at an electronic target and puts it out of commission.

Electronic circuits are sensitive to interference from external magnetic fields. We have all experienced interference in radios, televisions, or portable phones. When the radio crackles, that's electromagnetic interference. When the television aerial gets twisted every which way, or a lightening bolt strikes nearby, or a cellular phone call is cut off when the car crosses a bridge or enters a tunnel, that's interference. Or, as mentioned earlier, the earliest models of computers could cause substantial interference to our television reception.

But electronic circuits can also be overloaded and forced to malfunction. If you take the 110 volts from the wall and plug it into a VCR's video input, your VCR will cease to be a working VCR. It might even exhibit the telltale sign of the ultimate electronic failure: smoke. When jump-starting a car, we all make sure that plus is connected to plus and minus to minus, because of the dire warnings on the battery. Similarly, lightening and cable television systems do not get along well at all. Power strips have surge protection circuits to keep sensitive electronic equipment from being blasted into silicon heaven when the power company glitches or lightening strikes the pole transformer on the corner.

Electronic circuits are more vulnerable to overload than most people realize, and that weakness is exploited by a HERF Gun. A HERF Gun is nothing more than a radio transmitter, conceptually similar to the real tall ones with blinking red lights on top to keep planes from hitting them. Your portable CB or your cellular phone are also radio transmitters, with different purposes, working at different power levels. The HERF Gun shoots enough energy at its target to disable it, at least temporarily. A HERF Gun can shut down a computer, cause an entire computer network to crash, or send a telephone switch into electronic orbit. The circuitry within modern computer and communications equipment is designed for low-level signals; nice and quiet 1s and 0s which operate within normal limits. The HERF Gun is designed to overload this electronic circuitry so that the information system under attack will become, at least temporarily, a meaningless string of babbling bytes.

For the Information Warrior, a HERF Gun need only meet a couple of criteria to be effective. First, the HERF Gun should put out as much energy as possible—the more energy it puts out, the more damage it can cause. Secondly, a HERF Gun should have some directionality or control over where its magnetic bullets are going. Some HERF Guns are like shotguns, spreading out their radiation in all directions; others are highly focussed like a precision rifle. A HERF Gun can be a remarkably simple device or a complex one that takes up truckloads full of equipment, but they all have the same basic pieces: a source of energy, a method of storing the energy until the gun is discharged, and an output device or an antenna. Everything else is up for grabs.

In 1991, I put on a briefing for a defense contractor which covered various approaches and uses for HERF Guns. In conventional military-think, the following objectives can be met with electromagnetic weaponry:

- Personnel and Transportation Interdiction
- Harassment of Opposition
- Communications Disruption
- Destruction of ADP Capability
- Interruption of Transportation Services
- Sabotage
- Terrorism/Anti-Terrorism
- Air/Land Defense
- Military Offensive
- Enemy Ordinance Activation
- Communications Interference
- Electronic Component Destruction

If a HERF Gun is too small to bring about the damage the Information Warrior wants to inflict, he might find himself interested in the ElectroMagnetic Pulse Transformer, or EMP/T Bomb. The EMP/T Bomb is essentially the same as a HERF Gun, but a thousand or more times more powerful.

The electromagnetic pulse or signal, catapulted at the speed of light from an EMP/T Bomb, is so incredibly strong that any computer in its path will likely be rendered useless forever. Its internal organs, the chips, will be electrically melted beyond repair. But there is more. With an electromagnetic signal of that strength, all floppy diskettes, hard disks, tapes, and tape backups will be thoroughly erased. *All* the data will be gone—forever. An EMP/T Bomb is a powerfully insidious weapon in the hands of a dedicated Information Warrior, and, as in so many cases, these advanced technical weapons are created by the denizens of the Pentagon.

The military has for nearly two decades been interested in what is euphemistically called Nonlethal Weapons; that is, weapons whose primary function is not to kill a human adversary, but to disable their ability to wage war. In a January 4, 1993, *Wall Street Journal* article, Colonel Jamie Gough explained that "without killing people, such weaponry would disrupt telephones, radars, computers, and other communications and targeting equipment." Other defense officials say the damage would be inflicted by "a new electromagnetic pulse generator that disables equipment without hurting people."[3]

It turns out that during the Gulf War, the United States did indeed use such Information Weapons. The April 15, 1992, issue of *Defense Week* stated that "The U.S. Navy used a new class of highly secret, nonnuclear electromagnetic warheads during the opening hours of the Persian Gulf War to disrupt and destroy Iraqi electronics systems, including air-defense weapons and command and control centers, military and industry sources say."[4] The experimental weapons were supposedly mounted on a few of the Navy's Tomahawk cruise missiles.

For the record, officials from the program deny any such warheads exist. However, in a private conversation, a Defense Department official told me that such weapons had indeed been used. In order to get our cruise missiles and planes into Baghdad without warning Hussein, we needed to shut down the Iraqi air defense systems that ringed the country. So, as a test of the technology under actual battlefield conditions as well as a real weapons systems deployment, the Navy targeted two main air defense stations on the southern border of Iraq. The magnetic-tipped EMP/T bomb cruise missiles exploded near the defense stations and immediately the lights went out, radar screens went blank, electrical lines went down, communications to Baghdad were cut, and Iraqi soldiers went searching for the circuit breakers. By the time they realized what had happened, it was too late. The real cruise missiles were making right turns at the El Rashid Hotel and our F-117s were strafing armaments factories.

As a result of these successes,

"The U.S. Central Command, the unified command for the Middle East that formerly was headed by General Norman Schwarzkopf, has told the Joint Chiefs of Staff that it wants a wide-area-pulse capability—that is, the ability to fry enemy electronics by detonating a warhead outside the atmosphere. The Central Command's statement didn't expressly say so, but only a nuclear explosion would be powerful enough to do the job. 'You're probably talking about a few tens of kilotons,' says Earl Rubright, science adviser to the General Command."[5]

The Navy seems to be ahead of the pack in the development of such weapons. They realize that the warfare of the future may be much less dependent on traditional bombs and bullets than on nonlethal electronic- and information-based weapons. After all, transportation, communications, and finances are largely reliant upon the correct operation of computer and communications systems. Thus, if those systems are knocked out, the opposition will feel the immense effects of the systemic collapse of its infrastructure.

In response to the fact that antagonists of the United States already have the capability to wage limited forms of such warfare, the Office of Chief of Naval Operations published in April of 1992, an internal draft of a document entitled "Space and Electronic Warfare: A Navy Policy Paper on a New Warfare Area."

The internal Navy document is less than thirty pages long, but the table of contents alone is enlightening. Sections are entitled "Navy SEW Policy" (SEW stands for Space and Electronic Warfare), "SEW Disciplines," "SEW Technology," "The Surveillance Grid Concept," "The Communications Grid," "SEW Battle Space Modeling," "EW Techniques," "Electronic Combat Subsystems," and more.[6] Obviously, the Navy had begun some serious efforts under Admiral Tuttle's command to restructure Navy conflict goals and techniques. The Navy, in fact, has been the victim of HERF, as has been the Air Force, albeit accidentally.

In the early fall of 1992, a U.S. naval ship entering the Panama Canal Zone forgot to turn off its radar systems, which operate on the same principle as HERF, but in the form of HPM, or high power microwaves. In this case the Canal Zone computer systems got zapped! The radar hits were so strong that nearby computers were fried and had to be replaced.[7]

Earlier we discussed the software-intensive fly-by-wire aircraft that the military, and even civilians, are increasingly using. The maze of wiring that runs the planes is susceptible to HERF damage. In the 1980s, the Army's UH-60 Blackhawk helicopter was the victim of a series of crashes and mishaps. "Critics charge electromagnetic interference with software-driven controls may have been responsible for five Blackhawk crashes that killed twenty-two servicemen. In fact, tests found that radio waves could trigger a complete hydraulic failure which could lead to loss of control of the aircraft. . . . In all, forty out of the Blackhawk's forty-two systems were susceptible to electromagnetic interference from radio and radar transmissions."[8]

Air Force planes are routinely fitted with EEDs (electro-explosive devices) that are used to trigger ejection seats, release bombs, and the like. A sophisticated Air Force radar system, known as PAVE PAWS, can detect a baseball from a thousands miles away and also has the capability to blow one of our own planes from the sky. PAVE PAWS is so powerful that it can accidentally detonate an EED with potentially disastrous results.[9] The B1 Bomber's radar system was so clumsy that it even interfered with itself![10]

So guess what HERF and EMP/T, designed for the express purpose of doing damage, can do to a computer or a computer network, not to mention a telephone system, a cash register, a bank's ATM network, or a communications system? If the military, who is supposed to be prepared for such contingencies, is having trouble with interference, how well would the myriad computers on Wall Street fare under a HERF attack?

Don White, one of the premier experts on electromagnetic shielding, is an extraordinary man. Short and in his mid-fifties, with willowy white hair, Don exudes the enthusiasm of a man half his age. White has written several widely-used text books on the subject, which are openly available in engineering libraries. But some chapters of his books, used for government training are actually given classified status by the National Security Agency.

White feels that HERF represents a real challenge for the commercial sector, especially if used by terrorists. He agrees that HERF, since it is both invisible and insidious, is a much-overlooked threat. In one editorial he wrote,

So, if there is an adversary whose operation is located inside a building you want to disrupt, merely drive your radar van and park it within a quarter mile (even the lay are accustomed to seeing dish antennas). Erect the stored parabolic dish on top of the van and point it at the target building. And presto! You did them in. Better yet, to make it less conspicuous, place the dish inside the van and use plastic sides in the van rather than metal.

Of course, you could be much more subtle about it and cause your adversary to have EMI intermittents. That way, he would economically suffer without being shot down, which might otherwise precipitate greater investigation.

With a radar van temporarily parked on an overpass, a field strength in excess of 1000 V/m could be laid down on Brand X automobiles passing thereunder. Think of the resulting adverse publicity about Brand X cars, which have problems with antiskid braking microprocessors.

The opportunities become mind-boggling, especially if done in "good taste." However, in the hands of terrorists, (industrial as well as political), the whole subject becomes outright scary.[11]

Maxwell Laboratories, a defense contractor specializing in high energy weapons, published an arcane paper in 1992 entitled, "Utilization of High Power Microwaves Sources in Electronic Sabotage and Terrorism." The authors describe the history of HERF-style weapons, beginning in the early 1970s.

High power microwaves sources have been under investigation for several years as potential weapons for a variety of sabotage, terrorism, counter-security and combat applications. However, in recent years, there has been an increasing awareness of HPM (a form of HERF) as a tool for commercial sabotage and civil terrorism.

Several similar papers have been written which describe the techniques that make such Information Weapons possible. The language used by Defense Department contractors is highly technical, describing detonation methods such as slug-tuning, magnetrons, klysterons, gyrotrons, vircators, and magnetically insulated oscillator tubes. The scary part is the detachment with which these papers are written.

It is expected that for all civil attacks, with the possible exception of sophisticated terrorists, electronic sources (of power) . . . will be used. For short ranges and directional attacks, submegawatt levels can be used. For longer ranges or omnidirectional radiation, higher, but still achievable, powers will be achieved.[12]

Even though "due to classifications restrictions, details of this work are relatively unknown outside of the military community and its contractors,"[13] advanced technology is extremely hard to contain, especially since many other countries are paralleling the U.S.'s classified work on HERF. "In many instances, if the military has it, it will rapidly find its way into terrorist hands."[14] In a draft document, high-energy expert E.R. Van Keuren further fans the flames by stating that "when discussing terrorism and sabotage . . . our adversaries are much less reluctant to make their weapons available to terrorist nations than the United States."[15]

HERF Guns and EMP/T Bombs meet the Information Warrior's criteria as the ultimate weapon. What are his potential targets? James Rawles writes for *Defense Electronics,*

Likely terrorist targets are key financial centers such as Wall Street in New York, the City district in London, or the Paradeplatz in Zurich. This would cause incalculable damage to computer hardware and software associated with stock and commodities markets, banking, international currency exchanges, and pension funds. Rebuilding computer systems and restoring software databases from paper records would doubtless take many months.[16]

HERF Guns are portable and can sit inside a van, making them virtually invisible to passersby. Who pays any attention to a small truck with an antenna, and television or film crew markings on the side? But what about at the end of a runway? Or even on a commercial airliner itself? With terrorists beginning to arrive on our shores thanks to their state-sponsored travel agents, we have to consider all of the possibilities. When HERF Guns can be carried in a suitcase or a backpack, our cause for alarm rises to critical levels.

Companies near airports have known for a long time that radar systems can cause computer systems to crash for no apparent reason. Poof! They're just down. The FAA has known as well, but hasn't been very public with its knowledge. According to sources, the FAA is replacing the glass in its control towers and offices in and around airports, investing millions of dollars to protect itself from the nasty side effects of radar signals so that their computers and navigation and guidance systems stay "up" at all times.[17] The only problem is they're not telling much to anyone else, and therein lies the danger to John Q. Frequent Flyer, who careens coast-to-coast unaware of any possible danger.

On a recent series of commercial airline flights, I heard a new spiel from a flight attendant. "We're descending below 10,000 feet for our approach into (safe major metropolitan airport). Please turn off all laptop computers, CD, and cassette players. Thank you for flying US Air."

In the July 26, 1993 issue of *Newsweek*, the following appeared.

On an uneventful flight over the southern Pacific last February, the 747−400 pilot stared wide-eyed as his navigational displays suddenly flared and crackled. The data made no sense. But a flight attendant was already whisking a passenger's laptop computer up to the flight deck. When the crew turned it on, the navigation displays went crazy. They returned to normal when the crew switched off the laptop. The plane reached its destination safely. Investigating the incident, Boeing engineers bought the same model laptop and tried to replicate the glitch in another 747. They couldn't.

. . . In a holding pattern 13,000 feet somewhere above the southeastern United States, the pilot saw the guidance computers and controls that maintain the craft's lateral stability shut down. A passenger in row one—directly above the flight computers and near the navigation antennas— was using a radio transmitter and receiver, a flight attendant said. The first officer hurried back and the told the man to shut it off; the systems blinked back on. Five years later, no one can explain how, or even if, the radio zapped the computers.[18]

So what's happening here, HERF? A CD player is certainly not a HERF Gun, but to a poorly shielded avionics package in a fly-by-wire airplane, with the 145 miles of wires and cables that are in the latest Boeing 747–400s, it could all be the same.

While the FAA and most airlines deny any safety concerns, malfunctions of avionics systems do bring up serious public-safety issues. Since 1990 the FAA has compiled almost one hundred reports of such occurrences with a six-fold increase this year alone.[19] Why? Very possibly because fly-by-wire airplanes are indeed affected by computers and digital music systems. It's no wonder that the engineers at Boeing, NASA, and Apple are having such a time trying to figure out what's happening: we live in an electromagnetic sewer. God knows we shouldn't be saying "let's not worry about it" with computers flying planes at 37,000 feet.

The FAA knows better, and I would hazard to guess, wants to do everything within its power to avoid a panic, or loss of public faith in the airline industry. Imagine some nut who brings a specially modified laptop onto an airplane. Airport security in the United States is so dismal that anyone can get just about any electronic device through it with no trouble. But this laptop is modified to emit very high levels of radiation, either automatically or upon command. A real fanatic who is totally committed to his cause might be willing to go down with the plane; more than a few people meet that criteria. Or, if his survival is important, he might check his luggage through with a HERF device, timed to go off at some point during the flight—without him on board, of course. Luggage scanning can't tell the difference between a good electronic device and a malicious one. If the FAA has cause to worry, this certainly qualifies.

In a scenario described by the FBI during a CPSR meeting in Washington, D.C. on June 7, 1993, agents revealed a case in which a rocket launcher was nearly placed at the end of the O'Hare runway in Chicago, ready to shoot down commercial airliners. Let's replace that weapon with an even more powerful HERF Gun. Situated in a van, powered by a V-8 and an alternator, the HERF energy could have a devastating effect on planes taking off and landing.

Acquiring HERF Guns is pretty simple. You can go out and build one: I have seen home-brewed versions capable of firing twelve megawatt blasts. Electronic hobbyist magazines occasionally provide construction details of high voltage-high current power generators. It's an exercise in Electronics 101. Or you can buy one. Where? Kits are available from catalogs, or you can construct one courtesy of the U.S. government: a military surplus high-power radar system can be modified by someone familiar with electronics. Don White offers a four-day course called "HERF and Electromagnetic Terrorism," which teaches how to protect against electromagnetic weaponry.[20]

Cyberspace has indeed come of age, and modern airplanes are as much a part of it as computer networks.

So there you have it—the basic Information Weapons for the well-armed Information Warrior. From malicious software to EMP/T Bombs, with dozens of tricks in the middle, even the least technically astute reader gets a pretty fair idea of what the Global Network and Computers Everywhere will be facing in the coming years. It doesn't take a rocket scientist to make or use Information Weapons, just a little knowledge and resourcefulness, the kind that is taught in high school and college science classes all across this country. There is no magic required, just a fundamental working knowledge of electronics and software, and a target. Anyone with the motivation has access to these technologies.

Thus far, we have concentrated on capabilities instead of intention. So now, let's take the next step in our exploration of Information Warfare and take a look at what kind of enemies and adversaries we will be coming up against in the Battle for Cyberspace.

What we want to know now is—who are the Information Warriors?

11

Hackers: The First Information Warriors in Cyberspace

"Convicted Hacker and Computer Consultant. Available July 10, 1992."

—LEN ROSE

AD OFFERING SERVICES AFTER HIS INCARCERATION.

THE BEST EXAMPLE of how computer crime can be waged through social engineering was provided by an ex-hacker whom I will call Jesse James. One afternoon in Newport Beach, California, he put on a demonstration to show how easy it was to rob a bank.

Jesse took his audience to a trash bin behind Pacific Bell, the Southern California Baby Bell service provider. Dumpster diving proved to be an effective means of social engineering because within minutes, an internal telephone company employee list was dredged out of the garbage. On it, predictably, were hand-written notes with computer passwords.

In the neighborhood was a bank, which shall go nameless. After some more dumpster diving, financial and personal profiles of wealthy bank customers surfaced. That was all Jesse said he needed to commit the crime.

At a nearby phone booth, Jesse used a portable computer with an acoustic modem to dial into the telephone company's computer. Jesse knew a lot about the telephone company's computers, so he made a few changes. He gave the pay phone a new number; that of one of the wealthy clients about whom

190

he now knew almost everything. He also turned off the victim's phone with that same number. Jesse then called the bank and identified himself as Mr. Rich, an alias.

"How can we help you, Mr. Rich?"

"I would like to transfer $100,000 to this bank account number."

"I will need certain information."

"Of course."

"What is your balance?"

"About ____," he supplied the number accurately.

"What is your address?"

Jesse gave the address.

"Are you at home, Mr. Rich?"

"Yes."

"We'll need to call you back for positive identification."

"I understand. Thank you for providing such good security."

In less than a minute the phone rang.

"Hello. Rich here."

The money was transferred, then transferred back to Mr. Rich's account again, to the surprise and embarrassment of the bank. The money was returned and the point was made.

Other than the governments of the world, hackers can arguably be given the unenviable title of the first Information Warriors. Hackers seem to get blamed for just about everything these days. The phones go down—it's a hacker. There's a new computer virus—it's a hacker. Dan Quayle's credit report shows up on TV—it's a hacker.

According to most hackers, the media gets it all wrong. Lay people are still too grounded in snail-mail and big business; the Feds are still embroiled in paper-based bureaucracies. Even hackers themselves can't agree on the proper terminology to describe themselves.

Today, the nom-de-guerre "hacker" takes on a somewhat sinister connotation. Most people, when asked, say something like, "Isn't a hacker someone who breaks into computers?" Right or wrong, that's the image. Locked into the modern lexicon by popular usage, the term "hacker" may well be forever doomed to suffer such pejorative overtones. Hackers are often blamed for credit-card fraud and other more conventional crimes, in which the use of computers were merely incidental. As one would imagine, hackers are not happy about such misperceptions, blaming what they term "clueless Feds and the idiot police" for destroying the original ethos of hacking.

To begin with, the term hacker is derived from the word "hackney," which means drudgery, "hackneyed" means "worn out from overuse; trite." A writer who knocks out lackluster words for pay is a hack. An old, worn out horse is a hack. A taxi driver is a hack who drives a hack. How about the golf hack who can't score below 100 even with two Mulligans a side and an occasional foot wedge?

Anyone can be a hack and the connotations aren't always negative. Most of us are hackers in one way or another. The car enthusiast who tinkers and tunes his car every weekend is a hack. He constantly wants to improve his knowledge and techniques, sharing them with others at car meets or races. He relentlessly pursues the perfect engine, or transmission, or whatever else makes a car tick. A hacker, regardless of area of interest, is curious by nature. Rop Gonggrijp, a well-known ex-hacker and editor of *Hacktic*, a Dutch computer hacker magazine, said it this way.

Pretend you're walking down the street, the same street you have always walked down. One day, you see a big wooden or metal box with wires coming out of it sitting on the sidewalk where there had been none.

Many people won't even notice. Others might say, "Oh, a box on the street." A few might wonder what it is and what it does and then move on. The hacker, the true hacker, will see the box, stop, examine it, wonder about it, and spend mental time trying to figure it out. Given the proper circumstances, he might come back later to look closely at the wiring or even be so bold as to open the box. Not maliciously, just out of curiosity.

The hacker wants to know how things work[1].

And that is exactly what pure hackers say. They only want to know more about computers: the ins and the outs, the undocumented features, how can they push the system to its outer envelope and make it do things the original designers never envisioned. Hackers try to cram ten megabytes onto a 1.4 megabyte disk.

The original generation of computer hackers could be said to include John Von Neumann (the acknowledged father of the digital computer), Alan Turing, and Grace Hopper, among other computable notables. These pioneers pushed the limits of computer science. However, most hackers envolved out of academia in the 1960s and 1970s, when terminals were connected to distant huge computers that filled rooms with vacuum tubes, core memories, and immense power supplies.

The undisputed catalyst for mass-market hacking was the introduction of the microprocessor by Intel, and the subsequent development of the personal desktop computer. Millions of PCs and Apples were bought by businesses, students, and former and future hackers during the incubation phases of the Global Network and Computers Everywhere. The nascent personal computer field was a petri dish full of ripe agar solution encouraging unbounded creativity, learning . . . and hacking. But then the money motive kicked in, which according to Rop meant the loss of true hacking creativity. Some hackers soon became budding millionaires, motivated only by the search for the Almighty Buck.

Over the years, new technology and the Global Network allowed a new breed of hackers to emerge. For the hacking phenomenon to increase logarithmically, one last piece of the equation was needed and was already well on its way to market: Infinite Connectivity. How do we get all of these computers to talk to each other? Novell took care of that with the proliferation of inexpensive Local Area Networks, or LANs, for PCs in the office. Modems allowed simple computer-to-computer conversations, as well as the creation of thousands of database and bulletin boards accessible by anyone with inexpensive equipment. Wide area networks (WANs) began to connect through the phone companies and the switch, entwining the globe in a spider's web of communications based upon systems with such uninviting names as X.25, ISDN, TCP/IP, OSI, T1, and 10 Base T. Such interconnectedness now gives anyone who wants it access to the Global Network via an incomprehensively complex matrix of digital highways. The hacker-purist, however, would likely prefer the word *free*way.

Hackers, long confined to their lone desktop PC and its limited communications capabilities, knew there was a world to explore out there—and explore they did. They traveled throughout Cyberspace and the growing Global Network, and found that the computers at the other end of the line were indeed fascinating targets of investigation. Every imaginable type of computer system was no more than a phone call away and there were thousands of others willing to help you on your way to conquering the next system. You could talk to a VAX over at the hospital, a 3090 over at the IRS, or the Tandems running the credit card division over at American Express. That euphoria, that sense of power, had been given to anyone with a couple of hundred dollars.

Billsf, a thirty-six-year-old post-Woodstock American expatriate and self-described phone phreak who now calls Amsterdam home, speaks for many from the first generation of hackers. He says the thrill is in getting into the system and doing what "they" say can't be done. For him voyeurism is not part of the equation. Of breaking into a computer he says, "The first time it's a hack. The second time it's a crime." In his mind that legitimizes and proves the innocence of the hunt. He continues to defend hackers who enter computers without permission. "If there is unused computing power out there, it should be free. If I have the smarts to get it, I should be able to use it." He uses the same argument to justify phone phreaking, where the aim is to figure out how the phone systems work and then make calls for free. "If there's an open phone line, I should be able to use it for free. Otherwise it's going to waste."

Victims and potential victims of computer hackers are not so generous. The most common accusation is that hackers are nothing more than glorified criminals. The debate often goes like this:

"It's like my house. If I don't invite you in, don't come in or it's called breaking and entering and I'll call the police."

"It's not the same thing. What if I went into your house, ate an apple, and watched some TV. Then I make two phone calls and went to the bathroom. Before I left, I put $2.14 on the counter to cover the cost of the apple and the phone calls and water. I was just looking around. That should not be illegal."

"Yes it should! And is. The same laws should apply for you coming into my computers uninvited."

"What if my presence kept your house from being robbed? Would that make a difference?"

"You still invaded my privacy. I would feel violated. My house belongs to me and so does my computer. Please stay out."

"My entering or not entering your computers is a matter of ethics—not the law. It is up to my sense of responsibility to keep a clean house when I'm in your computer."

Breaking into a computer system, cracking its password scheme, or learning how to beat down the front door, is often referred to as "cracking" in distinction to "hacking." This is far from a universal definition, as there are many dissident hacker factions, but I'm going to use it anyway. Hackers, like any other group, come in many flavors but despite their claims to the contrary, they can be accurately described by category. Let's examine a few of them.

Amateur Hacking

I know that term will offend some, but amateur hacking is a part-time effort and does not provide income. The term amateur hacker, or perhaps semi-professional hacker, is not a derogatory one nor does it belittle their skills. It merely distinguishes them from professional hackers who utilize the same techniques and tools to make a living, either legally or illegally.

Consider the following profile of a typical hacker as offered by some of their own. Hackers are

- mostly males between twelve and twenty-eight
- smart but did lousy in school
- misfits and misunderstood
- from dysfunctional families
- and of course, they can't get a date

I know a lot of hackers, and in many cases, they tend to work and play on the edges of society. Some hackers—apparently too many—"consume their own body weight in controlled pharmaceutical substances," according to one underground member who himself imbibes in same.

According to Dr. Mich Kabay, Director of Education for the National Computer Security Association, some hackers could be suffering from a clinical narcissist personality disorder. He suggests that the classic hacker personality is anathemetic to society, characterized by such traits as:

- a grandiose sense of self-importance
- preoccupation with fantasies of unlimited success
- need for constant attention and admiration
- strong negative responses to threats to self-esteem
- feelings of entitlement
- interpersonal exploitiveness
- alternating feelings of overidealization and devaluation
- a lack of empathy

No, not all hackers are nuts nor do they universally suffer from clinical personality disorders. They are a varied group but they do tend to think and live "on the edge." According to Dr. Percy Black, Professor of Psychology at Pace University in New York, "they're just kids," no matter what their age. He explains that malicious hacking may come from "inadequate endogenous stimulation." Simply put, either their home life, diet, or social life is such that their brains don't secrete enough "get-excited-feel-good" chemicals to create an internal feeling of satisfaction in any other way.

Some say that Ian Murphy, a 36-year-old former hacker with the nom-de-hack Captain Zap, is the perfect example of such a chemo-social imbalance. His claims to fame include federal prosecution for, among other things, electronically "stealing" computers and breaking into White House computers. His stories stretch the imagination. Murphy was featured in a 1992 *People* magazine profile and is, to say the very least, a loud, personable character. He has graced the cover of *Information Week*, a popular trade magazine, and claims to make over $500,000 a year as a hacker-advisor to corporate America.

As one probes the history and behavior of hackers, we see that a gang mentality quickly envolved. A subculture of people with common interests gathered in their favorite electronic watering hole to "hang out." BBSs and the Global Network provided the tools to allow anyone to organize a database, add a modem, and start a digital party. The term "virtual community" has come into vogue, referring to a common electronic location in Cyberspace where kindred spirits can meet. As Cyberspace developed, cliques evolved and cybernetic hierarchies formed. The teenage 414 Gang earned their rep—and national attention—for their penetrations of the Sloan-Kettering Cancer Center and Los Alamos military computers in 1982.

Competition among teenagers being what it is, whether on skateboards or with the opposite sex, it is only enhanced in Cyberspace. On hacker group might feel challenged by another's claim, so they would then have to go out and better it.

Membership in a particular group quickly becomes a status symbol, one that has to be earned. Ostracism from a group is considered a major embarrassment in the Global Network. So competing hacking groups popped up all over the country, and indeed the world. Sherwood Forest, Anarchy Inc., Bad Ass MF, Chaos Computer Club, Damage Inc., Circle of Death, The Punk Mafia, Lords of Chaos, Phreaks Against Geeks, Phreaks against Phreaks Against Geeks, Elite Hackers Guild, and Feds R Us were but a few of the estimated thirty thousand private BBSs operating in 1990.[2]

As competition in Cyberspace grew, the country's networks and computers became the playground for all genres of hackers and cybernauts. Occasionally the competition got out of hand, as it did in the case of the Legion of Doom versus the Masters of Destruction. From 1989 through the end of 1991, a so-called Hacker War was waged on the battle field of corporate America's information infrastructure.

On July 8, 1992, five New York hackers who belonged to the MoD, an organized hacking group, were indicted in Federal Court on eleven separate serious charges. (Depending upon who you listen to, MoD stands for Masters of Destruction, Deceit, or Deception.) What adds intrigue to this story is the claim that other hackers were responsible for turning the MoD in to the authorities. The Federal indictment said that the five defendants, who pleaded not guilty at their July 16, 1992 arraignment, conspired to commit a range of computer crimes, including

- Eavesdropping on phone conversations from public switch networks
- Eavesdropping on data transmissions
- Intercepting data transmissions
- Owning computer cracking hardware and software equipment
- Reprogramming phone company computer switches
- Stealing passwords
- Selling passwords

- Stealing credit profiles
- Selling credit profiles
- Destroying computer systems
- Causing losses of $370,000[3]

One of the defendants was quoted as saying the group could "destroy people's lives or make them look like saints." All told there were eleven counts with up to fifty-five years in prison and $2.75 million in fines if the defendants were found guilty. All five have since pled guilty or lost their court cases. Their jail sentences are intended to be an example to other would-be hackers.

The Defendants named were

- Phiber Optik (aka Mark Abene)
- Outlaw (aka Julio Fernandez)
- Corrupt (aka John Lee)
- Acid Phreak (aka Elias Ladopoulos) and
- Scorpion (aka Paul Stira)

Aged eighteen to twenty-two, they all come from lower to lower-middle class neighborhoods in Brooklyn, the Bronx, and Queens in New York City.

"That's absurd," a defensive Mark Abene (aka Phiber Optik) told me. "There is no group in New York and there is no computer underground. I have never been a member of any organized group." Phiber vehemently denied his involvement. However, Abene, after pleading guilty to reduced charges, was sentenced on November 3, 1993 to a year and a day for his escapades. Emmanual Goldstein, editor of *2600*, called it a "dark day for hackers."

Chris Goggans (aka Eric Bloodaxe) and Scott Chasin (aka Doc Holiday) disagree. They are ex-members of a rival hacker group, the Legion of Doom. Although other members of the LoD have periodically vacationed at government expense, neither of these two have ever been prosecuted. In mid-1991, they disavowed their hacking days and started a security consulting company, Comsec Data, which survived less than a year. Business was bad. Corporate America could not bring itself to hire ex-hackers to work on their security problems, and the security community loudly ostracized them. The founders were young and inexperienced in business, and the press was generally negative.

But during the demise of their company, the Comsec Data boys were busy. Very busy. They were collecting evidence against their underground adversaries, the Masters of Destruction and especially Phiber Optic. Evidence, they claim, that they turned in to the authorities.

According to Chris Goggans, twenty-three, his first contact with Phiber was back in early 1989, when he heard that Phiber Optik was claiming to be a member of the Legion of Doom. After recommendations from another member of LoD, Phiber was able to prove his technical knowledge and worth and was permitted into the group. Soon thereafter, Phiber and Goggans agreed to share some information: Goggans knew how to access the Nynex switches, bypassing all security and authentication. Phiber knew the syntax and knew his way around the host mainframe computers themselves. A deal was struck to trade information.

Goggans says Phiber never lived up to his end of the bargain—a big no-no in underground cyberspace. "He told us to go to hell." As a result, the LoD threw Phiber Optik out in mid-1989. Phiber denies much of this account, saying he wasn't a member of LoD, just an occasional acquaintance. But according to Goggans, Phiber Optik began an electronic smear campaign against him, Chasin, and others connected with the LoD as a result of the public embarrassment. The sophomoric pranksterism included such antics as placing menacing messages and commentary on BBSs.

Enter Corrupt.

A new BBS called the 5th Amendment, or 5A, was created by Micron (an anonymous hacker) and Chasin in December

1989, with access limited to the "cream of the crop of hackers." Phiber was not invited. In February 1990, Corrupt was admitted to 5A because of his knowledge of holes in VMS systems and security. In April 1990, a number of 5A and ex-LoD hackers were illegally using a telephone voice conference bridge owned by a local Texas oil company. Anyone with the right phone number can dial in and participate in a conferenced conversation—a very common way to rip off big companies.

Alfredo de la Fe, eighteen, who was convicted on June 19, 1992, for trafficking in stolen PBX codes, agrees with other hackers who were in on that conversation that someone broke into the conference and said, "Yo! This is Dope Fiend. MoD," with a thick ethnic accent. Apparently someone responded with, "Hang up, you stupid nigger." The caller was Corrupt, who happens to be black, and who took great offense. He had been "dissed" in public and revenge was necessary. However, it may be that Corrupt misunderstood, because another member of the group, who actually is white, had been dubbed SuperNigger.

The wording distinction is important, because Phiber Optik insists that his future problems with Goggans, Chasin, and their Texas Legion of Doom friends were racially motivated. "They're just a bunch of racist rednecks," Phiber told me in a four-hour telephone interview that his lawyer advised against.

Goggans bristles at the suggestion. "We never even knew that Corrupt was black." Other hackers present on the call maintain that the racial epithet was only a "friendly" insult. Nothing racial, just kidding, if you will. Others say that the New York-based Masters of Destruction took the comment as fighting words.

Corrupt apparently sought revenge.

Shortly after the conference call, the LoD, their cohorts, and their neighbors began receiving harassing calls. Goggans says, "They (the MoD) were pulling our phone records, finding our friends, and then their friends." LoD's underground reputation grew, apparently in part because the growing MoD population (fourteen on August 1, 1990, according to the written History of the MoD) were attacking computers and leaving messages that laid blame on the Legion of doom. Phiber swears that the name MoD was an insult aimed at the LoD, intended to make fun of them. "Goggans is a strangely deluded kid from Texas. Besides, he's an asshole."

The animosity, Phiber says, came from the LoD's racial slurs against MoD members, only one of whom does not belong to a minority. Plus, "they weren't very good and bragged and took credit for anything and everything. Just rednecks who should keep out of our way." Goggans says the attacks increased in early 1991 because of the escalating tensions between the two groups. Insults were hurled at each other over BBSs, E-mail, and voice-mail circuits.

Goggans further charges that the MoD changed his long distance carrier from Sprint to AT&T, to make access to his billing records easier. Goggans says MoD bragged about the hack and claimed, "We rule MicroLink!" (Microlink is a subnet of Southwestern Bell's network.) The 1992 Federal indictment specifically charges MoD with tampering with Houston-based phone switches, and Southwestern Bell alleges $370,000 in damages. The indictment says the MoD "altered calling features, installed back door programs, and made other modifications." (This should sound familiar: malicious software being put into a switch.)

Credit reports were the next weapon allegedly used by the MoD against the Texans. Chasin, his mother, her friends, and neighbors were all victimized by MoD's access to credit databases. TRW admits that its computers were penetrated and that credit reports were improperly taken. The Federal indictment includes details surrounding 176 separate credit reports that the MoD had in their possession, not to mention database access codes. Goggans says that during this phase of the conflict, "they would call us and admit what they had done. . . . It had gotten totally out of hand. The MoD were hurting innocent people and we had to do something about it. No one else could have."

According to Chasin, "They are electronic terrorists."

Corrupt's own words seem to explain the hacker paranoia that inflamed this incident. "It's not just winning the game that counts, but making sure that everyone else loses," he wrote into the MoDNet computers.

De la Fe, an acquaintance of Corrupt, claims, "MoD was listening to the Feds and their computers. They were planning to wreck government computers." Morton Rosenburg, eighteen, was sentenced to eight months in prison for purchasing passwords to TRW computers from MoD's Corrupt and Outlaw and using them to illegally access credit reports. He says that the MoD was highly organized in its efforts. "The MoD had printed up price lists for passwords." Conflict, another hacker, adds, "Knowledgewise they were incredible—but with a bad attitude. They harassed hackers everywhere." Chasin says, "They were into 'outing' hackers."

Phiber says about Goggans, "He's a pain in the ass. This is none of his damn business. He should stay out of other people's lives."

As a result of the harassment they felt they were receiving from the MoD, Goggans and Chasin documented the Mod's electronic activities—in effect, snooping on the snoopers in Cyberspace. They turned this information over to security officers at the regional Bell Operating Companies (RBOCs), and the Secret Service and FBI were brought in to investigate. Tymnet (a notoriously weak communications network, according to hackers) was also notified by Goggans, as were a number of other companies who were allegedly the victims of Phiber and crew.

"We gave the Feds everything," Goggans claims. "We had all of the files, the dates, the times, the logs. We could have responded electronically but we decided to play by the rules. We called the authorities." The FBI will only admit they began their case in May 1991, the same time that Southwestern Bell and Goggans called them.

Goggans claims that in order to find out more about the MoD, he penetrated the weak security of a supposedly impenetrable MoD computer. He gave the FBI, Tymnet, and the Computer Emergency Response Team (CERT) MoD's lists of Tymnet passwords and IDs for Goddard Space Center, Trans Union Credit, CBI-Equifax (another major credit database), MIT, and a host of other targets.

According to the Federal indictment handed down in New York, many of the passwords found in the possession of the defendants were collected by "sniffing the switch" or monitoring data communications circuits on Tymnet. Since the defendants allegedly had access to the Tymnet computers, they were able to eavesdrop on the Tymnet network and record packets of information, including the passwords and access codes of thousands of users.

After cooperating with federal investigators, Goggans was on the receiving end of what he considers bodily threats. On Sept. 7, 1991, Phiber sent E-mail to Goggans saying, "You need to get the shit beat out of you. Count on it," and "Never know when someone will plant a bat in your skull." Other threats allegedly included a promise to give Goggans a trip home from a computer conference in a body bag. Phiber admits making the threats, but says in his defense, "he sent me an ad for an LoD T-shirt and I went totally crazy. It was just a joke." Some joke.

The so-called LoD-MoD hacker war was over. Rosenberg was put away even though he once claimed, "I stay out of jail because I do too much LSD. They're afraid to lock me up." Phiber Optik claimed innocence even though his codefendant Corrupt pled guilty to many of the eleven indictments. I received a copy of Corrupt's handwritten confession, which further showed how much control some hackers have had over the phone networks and computers. He admits:

I agreed to possess in excess of fifteen passwords, which permitted me to gain access to various computer systems, including all systems mentioned in the indictment and others. I did not have authorization to access these systems. I knew at the time that what I did was wrong.

I intentionally gained access to what I acknowledge are Federal-interest computers and I acknowledge that work had to be done, to improve the security of these systems, which was necessitated by my unauthorized access.

I was able to monitor data exchange between computer systems and by doing so intentionally obtained more passwords, identifications, and other data transmitted over Tymnet and other networks.

I was part of a group called MoD.

The members of the group exchanged information, including passwords, so that we could gain access to computer systems which we were not authorized to access.

I got passwords by monitoring Tymnet, calling phone company employees and pretending to be a computer technician, and using computer programs to steal passwords.

I participated in installing programs in computer systems that would give the highest level of access to members of MoD who possessed the secret password.

I participated in altering telephone computer systems to obtain free calling services, such as conference calling and free billing, among others.

Finally, I obtained credit reports, telephone numbers, and addresses, as well as other information about individual people, by gaining access to information and credit reporting services. I acknowledge that on November 5, 1991, I obtained passwords by monitoring Tymnet.[4]

One of the saddest comments to come from this entire affair was made by MoD member Outlaw, who said, "It was only a game. Not a war."

Inner-City Hacking

Inner cities are truly a study in disaster. This disaster, though, is no longer the exclusive province of any particular racial or ethnic group. Our inner cities have become melting pots, where the populace—regardless of race, color, or creed—behaves as if all hope is gone. When a ten-year-old boy carries a gun to defend his drug-dealing turf and sees little chance of survival past his teens, he has lost the ability to function in society. He sees himself as the victim of a government and a culture that have abandoned him. Why should he care about anything?

Now imagine the same angry inner-city kid, armed with a computer instead of a gun. The inner-city hacker, unlike his middle-class brethren, is angry over his social condition, intensely dislikes "the system," and has generally been powerless over his station in life—until now. For the first time he has the power and ability to affect people and events by remote control. The power of Cyberspace is in his hands.

The inner-city hacker has the same knowledge and power as his technoprecedents, regardless of the poor state of education in his neighborhood. He has little or no social conscience and the specter of jail is hardly a deterrent. It might even be an improvement over his current situation. I have had conversations with these hackers and their sense of arrogance, disdain, and alienation echoes that of the social dissidents of the 1960s. However, many radicals in the sixties were middle-class kids rebelling against the comfortable lifestyle of their parents. If things got tough, they could always go back to their well-manicured ranch-style house. Inner-city hackers have nowhere else to go. So, Cyberspace is an ideal destination. It gives them a new place to live and a turf of their own. It is the only place where they have power and can make the rules.

Eurohacking

Eurohackers offer a unique perspective. From my interactions with them, I find them to be more worldly, and enlightened than their American counterparts. This observation is consistent with most Americans' image of the sophisticated European. Eurohackers are generally motivated much more by philosophical or political concerns than by the American hacker's desire for profit or simple revenge. Cliff Stoll's Hanover Hacker in *Cuckoo's Egg* was linked to the East German Stasi and the KGB. The world's best computer hackers are supposed to be in Amsterdam, Holland. I went to find out if that was true.

I was introduced to a hacker group portrayed on a late-1991 Geraldo Rivera show.[5] Rop lived, with a couple of other hackers, in a reasonably-sized apartment overlooking Balmar, a suburb of Amsterdam. Computers, phones, wires, and shelves full of three-ring binders dominated one wall of the large living room. Attached to the phones were various electronic contraptions which, I would learn, allowed me to phone home for free—on whose dime I do not know.

The wallful of books, as it turned out, were chronicles of their activities: logs, schematics, accumulated information on computer and phone systems worldwide, just about anything you'd need to break into any computer anywhere. I certainly did not expect this level of organization. As it turns out, though, Rop and his small group of friends are not part of any large, coordinated hacking effort. They speak to and share information with hackers around the world, but they basically work alone.

Rop—an ex-hacker—is the philosopher of the group, spry-small in stature but big in the ideas and ethos departments. His sandy-blond shoulder-length hair was the only sign of antiestablishmentarianism. "I don't drink, I don't smoke anything, and I don't do drugs," he boasted.

Rop and I ended up with strongly diverging viewpoints throughout our discussions. For instance, he strenuously argued that hacking is a way of life and not a crime. In his view, society has got it all wrong. Despite our differing views, I found Rop to be a most likable person, with a tremendous body of knowledge. He was the promoter behind the "Hacking at the End of the Universe" convention in August 1993, which was attended by several hundred hackers from around the world. They camped in a field at eighteen feet below sea level to discuss the latest and greatest, the law, the philosophy of Cyberspace, and anything else that popped up.

One of the other hackers present was a tall, thin, pale American expatriate from Berkeley. Billsf is and has been a phone phreak since the 1960s, when he was twelve. He looked and acted the part of an extra from a Love-In, with long black hair and an attitude that reflected the naive altruism of a free Haight-Ashbury concert. He told me that his middle-class father was politically to the right of Attila the Hun and that he prefers the freer lifestyle in Holland to that of his homeland.

If I had to peg Billsf with a political label, it would be that of the anarchist. But basically, he is what I would call lost: the Great American Dream was never right for him. There had to be bigger, better, and greener pastures out there and he went in search of them. From all appearances, he found what he was looking for in Europe and Cyberspace.

Billsf, Rop, and the other hackers present were as congenial as could be. On many occasions we simply agreed to disagree and then moved on. The Euroview of hacking is much richer and more complex than that of their American counterparts. Indeed, in many cases, they view American hacking with varying degrees of disdain.

My questions about "good" (nondestructive)-hacking versus "bad" (malicious)-hacking struck a dissonant chord to Rop, for whom there is no substantial difference. "First of all," Rop said, "you must know that hacking is value-free. When you speak of good and bad, it really doesn't mean anything within the context of true hacking. Hacking is beating technology. The Germans have a phrase for it: 'Treating technology without respect.' . . . It's a system of laws as flaws," Rop said cryptically. "Breaking into a computer should not be a crime! No one gets hurt and we all learn something. But hurting people with the data or hurting the computer should be illegal. Having a negative impact should be illegal."

"You have a lot of benign people going to jail," Rop said, obviously displeased. "They're not real criminals. They are explorers who are being persecuted for thinking." These political overtones became increasingly clear as we talked further. Rop and Billsf and their comrades live by a code of ethics that is self-restrained, occasionally inconsistent, and generally difficult to pinpoint. They continuously refer to individual responsibility and the need for each person to determine what is right and what is wrong, and to act upon those beliefs. To these Eurohackers, the system is self-balancing. Anarchy can well be tolerated in Cyberspace because most people act responsibly.

According to Rop, the U.S. establishment has an antihacker attitude that borders on paranoia, which makes hacking on U.S. systems all the more attractive. Just like the school bully who always picks on the whiniest kid in class, Eurohackers "pick" on U.S. computers because, instead of just doing something about the problem, in their eyes we constantly whine about it.

The phone companies are a good example, they maintain. The U.S. phone system is the biggest and best, and therefore the most fun to hack-phreak. Although AT&T, Tymnet, and the other public carriers get real annoyed when their piece of Cyberspace is invaded, the hackers say they are just using empty wires not filled with either voice or data. It's not like the phone companies are losing money.

Sometimes, hackers go into systems for kicks, just because they know it is annoying. An avid Eurohacker described to me how he likes to go into military computers and use key words that trigger intelligence agents. "Bothering the military is loads of fun. It really seem to get to them. For example, if you get into a classified computer, make it look like you know more than you really do. Use some secret phrases, or talk about the

President or Star Wars or something like that. If you do it right, you'll trip their listening devices and then you can just laugh at them."

In an almost total turnaround the hackers denied any misdeeds on their part. "They treat us like some kind of national security threat."

As the hours passed, I learned that not only were the social mores of the Eurohackers more worldly than those of American hackers but that they were more politically aware, committed to using their talents as a powerful tool in creating change. A modern version of the sixties ethos was dominant, as was the fervent belief that the "system" needs a major overhaul. The biggest surprise of all was that they believed it was okay, in many cases, to interfere with computer and communications systems with which they disagreed politically.

One hacker told me, "I would love to get a group together and crash the entire Justice Department. I see nothing wrong with trashing the U.S. government's computers so the U.S. has to start over again." Another said, "It would be great fun to shave a couple of hundred points off of the Dow and see what happens." He then curled up in a ball in his chair and amused himself with imagining the outcome. So, are Eurohackers a national security threat? Do they work for anyone? Are they benign, or are they causing trouble far beyond what is reported in the general press?

Eurohacker politics could be viewed as libertarian, even anarchistic. "Why should I follow a law that, when broken, doesn't hurt anyone else?" is a foundation of Rop's philosophy. I believe that he believes what he says, but I also see a slight twinkle in his eye that might suggest he carries his point to an extreme for effect. I think he may even see a little bit of the antihacker's side—just a little.

"Everyone hacks TRW. It's a big game." Rop sat back and laughed a mocking laugh; he just can't believe how poor the security is. "We all know that credit records in the U.S. are totally worthless because of hackers." The Dutch hackers maintain that the lax security policies of credit databases make them ideal targets for criminal hackers. "We got into one database and we found a list of credit cards that were assigned to people who were part of the witness protection program. It was all there. Names, addresses, aliases. The government got so freaked they pulled it all and changed databases."

So breaking in shouldn't be illegal? "Who cares if it's legal? The Mafia can do the same thing. And you think they care if it's illegal? The bad guys are going to do it anyway." They have a point. The Eurohackers seem to be warning us about how their skills can be used by truly motivated and dangerous Information Warriors with specific criminal goals.

But couldn't hackers do the same thing, just for "fun"? "Sure we could and maybe we should. It would wake a lot of people up," Rop said, adding that this was his opinion alone. "There are many instances where breaking into a computer is almost a necessity. And then once you're in, there are many good reasons to do a lot of illegal things. . . . There are a lot of bad companies. Companies that make things bad for people and for the planet." Rop focused on what might be called the military-industrial complex for his examples of bad companies. "Chemical companies that make poison gases for warfare; I see no reason not to take down their computers."

Nowhere did Rop suggest that he has, is now, or is planning to implement his concepts. There wasn't even an indication of a threat to carry any of them out. To him it is pure intellectual speculation, and Rop does not appear to be the kind of person bent on vengeance, malice, or misguided high jinx. According to him, he is merely an ex-hacker with a system of beliefs that are contrary to many laws.

The motives of Eurohackers seem to be purer than those of their American counterparts who sell and buy credit card numbers. "I don't get my jollies by harassing people," said one of Rop's group. "That's not the kick. Breaking in and looking around; that's the object." Rop cynically added, "There are some machines much more interesting than people to talk to."

On the other hand, Rop warns that "there are a lot of

mercenaries out there, people who live by the credo "hacking for dollars." (The Masters of Destruction appear to fit into that category.) He added, "I am sure I could find a team of people to do specific things to computers. They could target the military computers, the draft computers, anybody's. . . . Putting a team together can be done." Rop would not say how such a group would be organized or who might be a candidate for membership. However, he and his friends did say that if they were approached by the right person with the right goals and with the right sense of right and wrong, then maybe it might be a group worth joining.

Another hacker with strong sociopolitical beliefs smiled broadly. "I could see a real nice virus whose only purpose in life is to waste military computers." He smiled even further. "Yeah . . . that would be great."

The Eurohackers to whom I spoke did not have anyone else's agenda in mind. They did not have mastery over an enemy as a goal, nor were they power hungry. Instead, they feel that if they or others were to so choose, they could dramatically disrupt the social fabric of Western society. The hackers said it would be great fun to sit back and watch the resulting chaos, how people and society coped. Then, they say, society would be better off for the experience.

"You see," said on of the more radical ones, "computers are to be used as a tool for revolution. It is up to us to stir up the social system. It's not working. We have to make the waves."

We discussed a few hypothetical situations. In one, the computerized food distribution system is forced down, as is transportation. Food is not getting into major urban areas and Los Angeles, for example, is teeming.

"It's a great social experiment. After a few days the farmers will bring in their trucks and set up on the streets, real farmer's markets. In a few weeks everyone will get used to the new way of shopping for food." But can we reasonably expect such a rational social response to such inconvience, if not deprivation? I think not. Our altruistic hackers are being naive.

In another instance, it was suggested that the heavily-computerized broadcast industry might be a viable target for social revolutionaries. They agreed, partially. "Take out the television. The radio can stay. It's not as harmful." NBC-TV in New York, for example, uses a massive Novell network for scheduling. No schedule means no ads, which would hit GE's pocketbook. Throwing the system out of whack might just be considered great fun. Get to the antennas . . . or the satellites. . . .

It's hard for me to imagine getting many of the drug-crazed American hackers I know to organize cogent arguments, much less put forth a minority political platform, but Rop did successfully apply some Boolean logic to define himself.

"I am a computer revolutionary. If a revolutionary is a terrorist, then a computer revolutionary is a computer terrorist and therefore I am a computer terrorist."

Professional Hacking

Why have I spent so much time on hackers? Because as bad as some hackers have been, and as bad as hackers can be, I believe hackers are merely endemic of the real problems that our economic and technical infrastructure face today. Hackers have shown the chinks in the electronic armor. Their pioneering activities have defined Cyberspace as much as have the billions of dollars worth of fiber networks which comprise the Global Network. They have penetrated the establishment's technocastle and crossed the moat with little resistance. They have shown that the walls that protect our resources are not as solid as the managers of the information would have us believe. As we will see, threats to the fabric of Western society come from places that we might not have known about without the hackers. This is not a defense of hacking activities, but one could certainly make a case that hackers have made us aware of issues about which we otherwise might still be blithely ignorant.

No, the issue is not hackers, but hacking.

Hacking is one of the tools which the Information Warrior will use against his targets. We should be concerned with their capabilities, the skills and techniques used by hackers in the pursuance of their particular interests, whatever they may be—criminal or political, educational or for-profit, malicious or benign. Bruce Sterling ended *The Hacker Crackdown* with seven words that cannot be more explicit: "It is the end of the amateurs."[6]

Simply put: if a bunch of kids have the ability to cause the kinds of damage they have, how much damage can dedicated, well-financed—perhaps mercenary—professionals cause at their master's bequest? You will soon discover the disquieting answer to that question.

12

Who Are The Information Warriors?

"There's a war out there, and it's about who controls the information. It's all about the information."

—COSMO IN *SNEAKERS*[1]

"We're in the information business. Then we put it on the table and analyze it."

—JIM KALLSTROM, SPECIAL AGENT, FBI[2]

Yes, hackers can be called the original Information Warriors, and many of us consider this relatively benign group the end-all and be-all of potential dangers to our information infrastructure.

Unfortunately, this is simply not the case.

As we examine who the Information Warriors are—or could be—several surprises will crop up. We will find that many of them are blue-suited, starched-shirt executives who, since they are working within the framework of the law, see nothing dangerous or insidious about what they are doing.

The military has spent millions of dollars playing war games against real, potential, or imagined enemies and fighting them on real, electronic, and virtual battlefields in order to fine-tune its capacity to win a war. The Pentagon deals with capabilities, possibilities, probabilities, plausibilities, and of course deniability. Cold War scenarios largely concentrated on the threat of Soviet expansionism. It was only a question of where we were going to fight the Russkies (In Eastern Europe? On the Autobahn? In Paris? Under the polar ice cap?) and who we could count on as an ally.

A few short years ago, only a handful of even the most insightful intelligence analysts considered the possibility that the world would peacefully evolve into a unipolar military structure, in which our principal adversary would all but disappear. In decades hence, we may well look back on the Cold War as the good old days of "us" against "them." The concept of mutual assured destruction provided a nervous, but reasonably solid, reason for the two world powers to keep their fingers off of the Button. It also kept 140 other countries in line. If they supported Iran, we supported Iraq. If we supported Israel, they supported an Israeli foe. If nothing else, such common-sense-defying logic kept the peace.

But look what we got in exchange for an end to the threat of thermonuclear conflagration! There is a rash of ethnic, cultural, and national regional uprisings on every continent. Our attention is now spread across the globe, as each new conflict competes for our intervention, benevolence, or leadership. Our priorities are no longer as simple as scanning the Arctic Circle for incoming missiles. As we have learned already, our national interests have taken on a decidedly global nature focused on economic influence, with immediate and long-term sociopolitical ramifications. Today we not only have to compete actively with first- and second-world nations for leverage and position; third-world nations are growing at staggering rates and they, too, will be our competitors in the next century.

Today, a major military attack aimed directly against the U.S. is a statistical improbability, conventional terrorism notwithstanding. However, that does not mean an attack against the national security or economic interests of the United States is equally unlikely. In fact, the odds of such assaults have increased.

Information Warfare is still warfare, whether it is waged as a politically acceptable alternative to bombs and bullets, or if it is waged against companies or organizations that represent the power or money of the United States, or if it is waged against individuals. Not every potential Information Warrior will have the same motivations, the same resources, or the same manpower or organizational abilities. But they all have or can develop the capability. As we explore the roster of potential Information Warriors, we will now shift our attention to motivation; capability is a given.

We can identify people, organizations, and ecopolitical groups with the motivation and capability to wage Information Warfare, but we cannot predict who will or who won't become an active adversary. With that in mind, let's examine candidates who might resort to Information Warfare as a means of executing their agenda.

Corporate Employees

Employees hold the keys to a company's success or failure. A company counts on its employees for trust and allegiance in exchange for a paycheck, but that is no longer enough. The recession of the early 1990s found employees cast aside after decades of faithful service, while upper management gave themselves seven-figure bonuses. The prospect of a secure future for the loyal, so common during the 1950s and 1960s in corporate America, was traded for a pink slip—with not even a word of thanks. Some employees felt they had been royally screwed, despite having played by the rules of the game for so long.

Other employees feel underpaid, underappreciated, or want to make a little money on the side. They may have grudges against their bosses, and depending upon their positions within their firms, they can still cause damage if properly motivated. Stressed-out post office employees are getting a reputation for murder and mayhem. Why shouldn't they screw up the computers instead? They are less likely to get caught, there's less jail time if convicted, and it is far more devastating to the reputation of snail mail. A few cases in point:

Thomas Ferguson was convicted of aggravated assault in

1988 and received three years probation. The following year, he was convicted of violating probation and sentenced to three years of prison and another year of probation. Despite this less-than-glorious background, Time Customer Service, a division of Time, Inc., hired Ferguson as a computer analyst in its Tampa data processing office. On June 26, 1992, Ferguson was arrested for attempting to sell computer disks containing credit card information on three thousand Time, Inc. subscribers to undercover detectives. He was selling names, credit card numbers, expiration dates, and other information needed to make purchases. His asking price? One dollar each. The going price on the streets is $20 per credit card number, but according to police, Ferguson wasn't a very sophisticated criminal. Upon further examination of Ferguson's apartment, additional credit card data was found on computer disks, compromising the privacy and security of eighty thousand more people who had entrusted their information to Time. Also found were tape cartridges with a mailing list containing eight million names and addresses.[3]

Technicians in the London offices of AT&T manipulated computers to funnel money into their own pockets by setting up a 900 number to incur charges to the calling party. They then had the main AT&T computers call their 900 number. The British Computer Misuse Law of 1990 is stiff, yet the perpetrators were never prosecuted due to legal technicalities.[4]

In 1979 Mark Rifkin, a Security Pacific Bank consultant, transferred small amounts of money to a New York account until it totaled $10.2 million. If not for his amateurish boasting, he would have gotten away with transferring it all to a Swiss account.[5]

A Pinkerton Security employee was given high level access to company computers and permitted to override her manager's approval codes. She used those codes to transmit money to bogus company accounts. Since she was also the person who reconciled the company's accounts, the scheme went undetected for two years.[6]

At the Charles Schwab brokerage firm, employees used computers to buy and sell cocaine.[7]

Then there's the story about the married couple who worked for competing companies. "While her husband slept, she used her laptop to log onto his mainframe at his company and download confidential sales data and profiles of current and prospective customers." The husband lost his job; she didn't.[8]

Money seems to be a key ingredient in turning a normally trustworthy employee into an enemy of his employer. On December 24, 1987, Frans Noe, a Lloyds bank employee in Amsterdam, attempted transfers of $8.4 million and $6.7 million from the Lloyds bank in New York to an account he had opened in Zurich at the Swiss Bank Corporation using the SWIFT network. Unknown to anyone, though, the software contained an error that halted the transfer of the $6.7 million. That is the only reason Herr Noe was caught and finally sentenced to eighteen months in jail.[9]

Even small companies are vulnerable. At Southeastern Color Lithographers in Athens, Georgia, the company lost hundreds of thousands of dollars in sales. Their accounting records were regularly blitzkrieged by invisible forces, causing a number of employees to quit. They couldn't handle the pressure of computers that just wouldn't work. The employee behind these antics was eventually caught and is now serving five years in prison.[10]

Benjamin Francois, a personnel supervisor at Jeweler's Financial Services in Clearwater, Florida, had access to thousands of East Coast customer records. He altered the customer files, listing credit cards as lost or stolen. His accomplice, John Wise, would then go to expensive stores, armed with the right names and social security numbers, and walk off with thousands of dollars in jewelry.[11]

Kind of gives you a warm and fuzzy feeling about the people you trust with your name, rank, and credit card, doesn't it? If you are doing the hiring, it makes you wonder what's behind the smiling face across the desk.

Sun Microsystems got the chance to review *its* hiring policies when twenty-seven-year-old Kevin Poulson, a computer programmer, was arrested for "conspiring to break into Pacific Bell Telephone Company computers, stealing and trafficking in telephone access codes, obtaining unlisted phone numbers for the Soviet Consulate in San Francisco, and wiretapping conversations of Pacific Bell officials who were investigating them."[12] Despite the fact that he had been prosecuted for a youthful history of hacking, Sun hired Paulson to work on the Air Force Caber Dragon 88 computer system, used to conduct war exercises at Fort Bragg, New Jersey. He penetrated Air Force computers and allegedly retrieved a classified Air Force Tasking Order which specified real-life military targets in case of conflict.

Stories abound about employees getting even. In 1988, a disgruntled employee was found guilty of planting a computer virus that destroyed $168,000 in sales commission records. In another case, a jealous engineer modified another employee's files in the hopes his rival would receive a bad performance review.

At a certain point we must ask, "Are our hiring policies designed to protect our corporate interests?" When companies such as IBM, Apple, Xerox, and dozens of high-tech firms release hundreds of thousands of skilled technical workers into the realm of the unemployed, social blacklash must be considered a very real possibility. What sort of information do they take with them? Did they, and do they still, have access to sensitive company information and computers?

In order to wage more successful attacks, company insiders are a desirable and accessible asset for the Information Warrior. Money talks, blackmail works, and the company suffers. But we also find a huge army of capable ex-employees who, if properly frustrated or antagonized, could easily join the ranks of the Information Warrior. Revenge is sweet, and in this case, a fairly safe means of retribution.

Vendors and Contractors

If you hire an outside organization to perform services, they, too, can wage Information Warfare against you. Revlon, the giant cosmetics firm, was the victim of a software developer who felt mistreated. The supplier, Logisticon, figured it had only one recourse: to shut the Revlon computer systems down. Revlon was effectively out of business for a full day.

The Florida State Department of Health Rehabilitative Services claims that Electronic Data Systems, a division of General Motors, intentionally sabotaged its computer system. EDS's contract with the state was to end on May 31, 1992. In a series of internal audits, it was found that the computers had high failure rates. According to Inspector General Bobby Brochin, HRS employees said that "program bugs by EDS" caused the problems and when the contract period was over, EDS "left it (the computer) with mistakes in it." HRS employees Viann Hardy and others suspected deliberate mischief by EDS, but Jack Pridgen of EDS flatly calls the allegations "preposterous and not true."[13] (EDS subsequently won back the contract.)

A technical vendor can hold a tight grip over computer systems; he has access to most of a company's operation and is often responsible for insuring that all systems are "go." Contractual and payment disputes can become decidedly ugly if the vendor turns to Information Warfare as an alternative means of forcing settlement or compliance. The concept of outsourcing information processing services may no longer be attractive if the vendor can literally shut down an entire organization's operation when and if the business relationship turns sour.

Government Employees

Government employees are supposed to be the backbone of the civil services that keep society on an even keel. A life of civil service was once held in high esteem: the pay was OK, the benefits excellent, and life tenure was expected. When one went into government employ, part of the reward was a sense of gratification in knowing one was working for the common good of society. In the past we tended to trust our civil servants. They have access to an awful lot of sensitive information—our medical records, our tax records, our employment histories, our military service, just about every aspect of our life. But is that trust still warranted?

Without even considering the possibility of international espionage and spying for the "other side" (whichever side that is today), we find that low-level Government employees occasionally act the part of the Information Warrior, ultimately at the expense of our personal privacy.

The Social Security Administration needs to have faith and trust in their employees. Its computers process over fifteen million transactions a day—five hundred per second—including such confidential data as earnings histories, criminal records, addresses, family relationships, and so on. A breach of trust would be devastating, which it was. In December of 1991, eighteen people, including six employees, were indicted for buying and selling confidential data from SSA computers. The SSA employees were based in New York, Maryland, and Phoenix—indicating a broad-based operation—and were allegedly selling confidential information to private investigators.[14] What makes this case even more disturbing is the fact that a Chicago police officer and an employee of the Fulton County, Georgia, sheriff's office were also involved in the operation.

Unfortunately for us, the Social Security Administration feels that it can do little about such security violations. Since some employees legitimately need access to sensitive files and information in the course of doing their job, it becomes a matter of trust. Are the employees acting within the law or outside of it? According to Renato DiPentima, assistant commissioner in charge of the Office of Systems Design and Development, "Admittedly, it would be very difficult to tell, in that situation, when a person got an occasional query, that one of them was not legitimate."[15]

The same argument applies to the IRS or any other federal agency that holds private data on us, the American people. Bill Clinton's White House and the State Department were accused of illegally tapping the phone of former Assistant Secretary of State Elizabeth Tamposi for her alleged investigation into Clinton's passport history.[16]

Even the limited number of reported cases of information abuse makes the hair on one's neck stand on end. According to author Ronald Kessler, members of the IRS Intelligence staff used their position to help friends and associates in law enforcement. They were "willing to provide copies of income tax forms, the same ones the government promised were absolutely privileged and would not be shown to anyone outside the IRS, to help them. Returns led straight to deals, properties, investments, a whole wealth of confidential data." Cops apparently operate by their own set of rules, and their form of Information Warfare belies the trust we place in them and in Washington. "It didn't take much coaxing to get the IRS just to audit the son of a bitch if he was guilty, say, of contempt of cop. IRS cops understood the rules. They were universal."[17]

The Department of Treasury's Financial Crimes Enforcement Network, known as FinCEN, was launched in 1990 and has the privacy community understandably outraged. Although originally conceived as a means of tracking drug barons, terrorists, and money launderers, FinCEN's power grows daily. Users of the network can access very sensitive personal and commercial financial information from several national databases, including the Currency and Banking Database (the CBDB) and the massive federal Financial Database (FDB). They search hundreds of millions of records, looking for banking transactions that smell of illegal activities.

Most disturbing, however, is the proposed Deposit Tracking System (or DTS), which would be able to invade the privacy of 388 million bank account holders in the United States. According to Diane Casey, executive director of the

Independent Bankers Association, "Our open and democratic society would be changed profoundly if any agency of the government maintained the scope of information on private citizens in this proposal. It raises questions about our democracy that would have to be addressed by the highest policy-making levels of government."[18]

Coupled with FinCEN's planned Artificial Intelligence/ Massive Parallel Processing program (AI/MPP), the government could examine any financial transaction on a real time basis. We have to ask, "Can we trust the keepers of the secrets?"

The problem apparently runs deep, within a culture that imbues power without accountability to our civil servants. In many ways, control over our personal privacy is the only sense of power some IRS employees will ever get. "An internal IRS survey . . . found that of every hundred credit reports accessed by IRS workers, five are illegally obtained."[19] Since 1990, despite laws prohibiting it, criminal investigators at the IRS regularly eavesdrop on the cordless and cellular phone conversations of suspected tax dodgers.[20]

The Resolution Trust Company (the RTC), supposed to get the United States out of $500 billion in losses, may have also acted the part of an Information Warrior. According to the Associated Press, Barbara Shangraw, a top RTC legal eagle, received orders from RTC's D.C. office to look into the files of employee Bruce Pederson. Apparently, during Congressional testimony in the summer of 1992, he criticized management policies—and management was none too happy. Barbara E-mailed a request to computer technician John Waechter: "I have been requested by D.C. to get into Bruce Pederson's Word Perfect. Please copy into a directory for me what Bruce has in his Word Perfect." This smells like a direct violation of antiwiretapping law, expanded in 1986 to include computers and electronic mailboxes. She got caught.[21]

To make matters worse, the White House allegedly ordered the IRS to illegally investigate tax records for political purposes.[22] At the height of such executive abuses, former Attorneys General Edwin Meese III and Richard Thornburgh were accused by the Congressional report of covering up allegations that the Department of Justice had stolen millions of dollars in software from Inslaw, Inc. The House Judiciary Committee report came to the conclusion that not only did the Justice Department steal software, but that Meese and Thornburgh lied as to their knowledge of the case.

Civil servants are given power—immense power—and that power will only increase as bigger and faster systems connect more of our digital essences into what has often been referred to as a national database. (Clinton's proposed health care system would put medical records into a single repository, a fine target if ever there was one.) Abuses of this power are symbolic of the social sicknesses that permeate society as a whole. There is no reason to expect government employees to be immune.

Law Enforcement

Even some law enforcement officials, the people who are supposed to protect us, are Information Warriors in their own right. Mike Peros, an expert in electronics countermeasures, runs Privacy Electronics in St. Petersburg, Florida. He performs "sweeps" to find out if someone is bugging you, tapping your lines, or otherwise electronically intruding on your privacy. When hired, he regularly finds taps—some obvious, some better disguised. One day in 1991 he was hired by a Tampa, based firm to search for bugs. Apparently the owners were concerned about their competition. Peros went in and quickly found one crude bug. "It was pretty shoddy work," he said. After he left the firm, he found himself being pursued. The Florida Department of Law Enforcement (FDLE), wanted to know what happened to their bug. When Peros wanted to know if it was a legal intercept, the agents got particularly nervous; apparently, the bug had been placed without proper court approval. When Peros suggested that a court reporter transcribe their conversation, the police said, "We don't want the media involved." The FDLE quickly backed off.

Peros says he's seen plenty of wiretaps and bugs planted illegally by law enforcement, and he expects to see more. According to him, "When the police or the Fed can't get a warrant, sometimes they decide to get creative . . . and bug the place anyway. They collect enough evidence, attribute it to unnamed informants, and then use the illegal evidence to get a judge to sign an order for a legitimate wiretap. It's done all the time."

I hear similar stories from private investigators; moonlighting police; on-duty police; federal, state, and local law enforcement agencies; and professional surveillance and countersurveillance folks. The FBI was issued fewer than three hundred legal, court authorized Federal phone taps in 1991, but according to countersurveillance people, the real count of taps—illegal and legal—is staggeringly high.

Private investigators claim that this type of behavior is par for the course for police trying to build a case, and that it is indeed necessary to prosecute criminal activities. Some police officials I have spoken with deny it, but not convincingly so. After all, they have the power, so why not use it? It's all in the name of serving the public good.

But sometimes the strategy can blow up in their faces. The celebrated Key Bank scandal in Florida resulted in multiple prosecutions, but because the wiretaps used in the case were issued based upon "stale and often uncorroborated information," the evidence obtained through 65,000 intercepted calls was tossed out of court. Hillsborough County, Florida, can brag that due to the overzealousness of State Attorneys Lee Atkinson and Harry Cole (and their habit of "judge shopping" to expedite wiretap orders), they have placed more wiretaps than forty-seven other *states*—not counties—combined. "I've got everyone on tape," said Atkinson in a newspaper interview. To make matters worse, Coe has refused to comply with federal law by suppling Washington with the files on his wiretapping habits.[23]

When law enforcement abuses its power, trust of authority disintegrates. As a result, some people are openly antagonistic toward the government and consider themselves technological survivalists—small, ingenious Davids up against the Big Brother Goliath.

At the heart of the country's criminal investigation labyrinth is the FBI's National Crime Information Center. Think of it as a huge computer database with millions upon millions of records on millions of criminals and their modus operandi. The NCIC databases also contain massive records on people who have never been charged with a crime, but may have been investigated or thought to be of interest to law enforcement. Civil libertarians decry the potential for abuse when mere allegations and hearsay are filed away as evidence, in the event one of us might commit a crime. In addition, the NCIC computers can tie into the vast number of computer systems and databases around the country. Agents can look for missing persons, track large cash transactions, correlate driving records from all fifty states—or find out which hotels you frequent and what your travel itineraries are. Such power in the hands of too many people is an obvious danger, tempting even the most virtuous person to give Information Warfare a try.

In July 1993, the General Accounting Office testified before a congressional subcommittee that the NCIC databases have been the subject of regular abuse by law enforcement workers and their associates nationwide. The NCIC databases are legally accessed by 19,000 law enforcement groups within the United States and Canada, using 97,000 terminals and personal computers. However, security mechanisms at the terminals, other than those directly controlled by the FBI itself, is dismal or nonexistent. The federal government is unable to mandate controls on a local level.

So what happens when just about anybody can ask a computer to find out who's done what to whom?

- A former law enforcement officer in Arizona used NCIC to track down his ex-girlfriend. He later killed her.
- A terminal operator in Pennsylvania used the system to aid her drug dealer boyfriend, by checking to see if his customers were undercover agents.
- A dispatcher in Rhode Island used NCIC for background checks on her fiancé's political opponents.[24]

This is not the behavior we expect, nor wish to pay for with our tax dollars.

On another front, the National Security Agency uses its own collection of toys for domestic surveillance. The data it collects is shared with cooperating agencies such as the CIA and the FBI. The NSA monitors fifty-three thousand communications signals in the U.S. every day. Then, acres and acres of super-supercomputers dedicated to the fine old art of eavesdropping and code breaking automatically look for meaningful information amongst the hurricane of data that enters Fort Meade, Maryland. The NSA can listen for and detect key words in phone conversations. Let's say you're talking to a close personal friend in Libya and he asks you, "Were you able to get that nuclear fuel from the Iraqis for me?" NSA computers will trigger alarms and in seconds a platoon of experts will be dissecting the recorded conversation, perhaps in preparation for a friendly visit to your home or office.

Remember those Toyota vans used to electromagnetically eavesdrop on the chemical company in Northern California? According to NSA employees, the Agency has its own listening vans, which can only be described as highly sophisticated electronic eavesdropping laboratories-on-wheels. From inside one of the NSA vans, you can talk to anyone, anywhere, anytime, or listen in on just about any communication system known to man.

Listening in on a computer using van Eck techniques has been raised to a pure applied science at the NSA. The technology developed by and available to the FBI is startling, and in many cases undetectable by almost any means. FinCEN eavesdrops on legitimate banking transactions without justification. In other words, we are all suspects, and all of our supposedly private business dealings are undergoing government scrutiny without our knowledge or permission.[25]

When we see the police—those dedicated to protect and serve—violate our trust, we have reason for deep concern. The epitome of such abuse of trust may lie with the Los Angeles Police Department. By any and all standards, the LAPD and, most assuredly, ex-LAPD Police Chief Daryl Gates, qualify as Information Warriors. The organization spent over fifty years violating the law and mocking the integrity of every dedicated and honest law enforcement officer in the country.

It started in the 1930s, during the Hoover era, when files began to be kept on those suspected of having gangster ties. By 1957, when the Organized Crime Intelligence Division (OCID) was founded, the files were immense, and growing by leaps and bounds. Dossiers were kept on all the movers and shakers. "Using an elaborate intelligence network of informants, surveillance, and devices to intercept phone calls, OCID operatives monitored all kinds of celebrities—politicians, union leaders, Hollywood stars, professional athletes, team owners, TV and print journalists."[26]

The OCID evolved into a project that was Stalinesque in its nature and scope. "OCID's goal was not to protect the public, it was information."[27] One case with enormous implications was the surveillance of Governor Edmund G. "Pat" Brown. Years later the file on his son, presidential hopeful Jerry brown, involved higher technology such as illegal phone taps and intensive electronic surveillance.

For decades, the LAPD's crime unit ran wild, its surveillance employing state-of-the-art technology. "Bugging became almost a way of life at the OCID."[28] Their offices contained the latest and greatest in miniaturized electronic spy gear, enough to make the KGB proud.

Over 50,000 of the private records were to have been destroyed in 1983, but some people within the LAPD felt they didn't have to follow the rules and the files were subsequently found in a cop's home. (Once an Information Warrior, always an Information Warrior.) The essential characteristics of the LAPD's secret police remained the same, with newer and better technotoys being added to the arsenal at least through 1988, shortly before an explosive book, *The L.A. Secret Police*, was published.

In Los Angeles, one man was labeled and convicted as a sex offender based upon testimony of the LAPD. In a conversation between two officers, the truth came out.

"Do you remember that social worker I popped for lewd conduct?"

"Yes?"

"I lied. The guy didn't actually do anything."[29]

An innocent man's life was totally destroyed by a crooked Los Angeles cop who swore, in a court of law, to the veracity of information he knew was false.

In Los Angeles, the OCID had support from the highest levels. Amazingly, Daryl Gates, ex-LAPD chief and ex-captain of OCID, admitted that bugs and other Information Warrior tricks of the trade were used "for our own edification."[30] Gates and the LAPD were Information Warriors. What is the most disturbing though, is that the attitude that created such abuses has reared its head in countless communities across this country. How many of the nearly 20,000 law enforcement agencies are engaged in Information Warfare? It is a question that must be asked, and more important, answered.

Unchecked power brings tyranny and vigilantism. The police have vast capability to wage Information Warfare against real or imagined enemies, completely innocent citizens, or suspects they have presumed to be guilty. They have the capability to construct an electronic case by manipulation of computerized profiles; such power, if misused, places the police in the position of being the judge and jury as well. One must ask whether a desperate law enforcement agency would contrive a case by compiling an indicting and incriminating digital profile of a suspect. Most of us would say that this is an unacceptable extension of the law, but few of us have any answers on how to curtail it.

Narcoterrorists

The leaders of the world's drug cartels are among the most ruthless people on the planet. They mete out brutal punishments for even the slightest hint of disloyalty, kill scores of innocents every year, and wage a literal war against their own governments with their own well-armed militia. Protecting their multi-billion dollar turf with torture and murder is their normal means of doing business. Is there any reason to think they don't have the motivation or the means to wage Information Warfare against anyone who stands in their way?

The first I heard about narcoterrorists becoming involved in Information Warfare was in 1990, during a conversation with a Drug Enforcement Administration agent based in Miami.

"We finally figured it out," my contact said.

"What's that?"

"Why we haven't been able to catch them. The drug runners."

"I thought you were catching them," I said naively.

"Yeah, right. We get about one percent of what's coming in. They've been way ahead of us."

"How's that?"

"You know that speech you just gave," he said to me. "Where you described how you can listen in on computers by a radio, van Eck?"

"Yeah?"

"Well, they were doing it to us!" he claimed.

"You're putting me on," I said in genuine shock.

"No, they've been listening to our computers. They always know where we are, who's assigned where, and if there's going to be a bust. They always knew, and now we know how."

"But I thought you guys used Tempest computers?"

"On our budget we're lucky to get bullets. But things are

going to be different. We just got budgeted for a ton of Tempest computers, and we think that's going to make a difference."

I'd had no idea that operations as sensitive as those of the DEA could function without a high degree of security, especially with as worthy an adversary as the drug cartels. The bad guys have a ton of money. They can buy the best equipment, pay for the best brains, and launch their own attacks at will. Pick a weapon from our list of Information Weapons, place it in the hands of the drug syndicates, and see what can happen.

Small Time Criminals and Organized Crime

Criminal elements have not lost sight of the opportunities that technology brings them, even without the assistance of government masters. Young foreign nationals have been focusing on credit card and other types of fraud while making their mark as Information Warriors. Arab, Chinese, Japanese, and African groups have gained the attention of the Secret Service while "using confidential data as a weapon," said David Leroy, chief of domestic intelligence for the Drug Enforcement Administration.[31]

According to New York postal inspector Martin Biegelman, organized credit card scam artists "obtain security guard positions that are generally low paying and hard to fill. Then, when they're assigned to a building at night, these individuals are given free reign to patrol the offices and the computers located there. They go through personnel files and even employees' desks to obtain names, job titles, Social Security numbers, home addresses, and whatever other personal information is available."[32] Usually, one group of criminals specializes in acquiring the information, another specializes in distributing the stolen information on their own network, and another sells it on the streets to unsuspecting immigrants in the form of fake but usable credit cards.

ATMs have been favorite targets of these criminals. At any

given time, there sits between $4 and $8 billion in cash in the thousands of cash machines that are scattered across the country, ripe for the picking. In May 1993, a creative Information Warrior made national news by putting a fake ATM machine is a Connecticut mall. The modified machine gave out no cash, but captured and saved account information and PIN numbers from everyone who tried to use it.

While some thieves prefer to rip the ATMs from their moorings with a bulldozer, true Information Warriors take the elegant approach. "Shoulder surfers" look at the numbers punched into the ATM and then, with the help of insiders, walk off with the victim's cash. In 1987, ATM repairman Robert Post walked off with $86,000 using this method.

In 1988 Security Pacific National bank was hit for $237,000 from three hundred accounts using a forged MasterCard. Also in 1988, Mark Koenig and friends forged seven thousand ATM cards as part of a plan to rip off Bank of America for $14 million. An insider tip-off put an end to the scheme.[33] Another criminal, from New Zealand, faked an ATM card out of cardboard and transferred NZ $1 million to his account. He turned himself in out of guilt.

Banks are logical targets for criminals who operate as Information Warriors: Go where the money is. And it's surprisingly safe to rob a bank electronically. If you get away with it, the bank will probably not call in law enforcement because they don't want the publicity. In 1989, six City of London banks and brokerage houses allegedly signed agreements offering amnesty and money to criminals in return for their silence and the secrets of their trade.[34]

Bank officials privately admit that they lose millions of dollars yearly to both internal and external thefts, but they consider it a cost of doing business. I can accept the loss of a few candy bars from a K-Mart to be a cost of doing business, but not the loss of my money. The banks say it's their money—and their profits—but that is a difficult argument to defend. If the bank loses, ultimately so do its customers and stockholders. A bank official in Atlanta told me, "We fudge the books to keep the Feds away. If they ever found out the truth, they could shut us down." A security official from one of the nation's largest banks claimed they experienced losses in excess of $100 million in 1993 alone, but because they are so large they can bury the losses in bad debt accounts. Great way to run a business.

The problem is, of course, that their silence only encourages more daring escapades by other criminals, and invites more professionals and organized groups to join in the profit-sharing. Organized crime likes information because it helps them establish control, through extortion and blackmail, over their victims. Since murder and torture are their historical modus operandi, Information Warfare seems benign by comparison. Acquiring the technical skills is a simple matter of money or motivation. Unfortunately their intentions are just as clear.

There is a balance between the Cyber Police State and anarchy, suggests Bob Lesnick, a private investigator from West Paterson, New Jersey. "People are afraid of a police state emerging from the use of computers by the authorities. But they should be concerned about the flip side; an uncontrollable computer dominated crime wave led by dangerous criminals. That will be much more invasive."[35]

Direct Mailers and Telemarketers

They want to know exactly who you are. They want to know, before they invest a dime in a phone call to you, that you love camping, or you have a penchant for travel, or you just had a baby and your first child is entering first grade. They want to know everything they can know about you before they call to interrupt your dinner and offer a wonderful opportunity to move money from your pocket to theirs. They want to know that you are health oriented and own both a Nordic Track and a set of weights from Sears. They want to know your zip code—which side of the tracks do you live on? Do you lease or own a car? Is your house big enough to handle the newest family member, or does your house need an addition? They want to know whether you are a decent demographic target, and worth their time. But most important, they want to know that your credit cards have enough room on them to purchase whatever they're selling you. In order to get that kind of information, the sales company has to rent a list of names and phone numbers based upon their criteria, which spell out in detail exactly who their ideal customer is: income, family size, buying habits. For a fee, a list is then compiled to meet those specifications.

We all get junk mail. If you buy one kid's toy from one catalog, you will receive a dozen similar catalogs three months prior to Christmas. If you travel more than 20,000 miles per year, upscale travel brochures, resorts, and magazines will solicit your business. If you subscribe to *Time*, bet your bottom dollar that *Newsweek, U.S. News and World Report* and *People* will be on your doorstep with deals for pennies an issue.

Once they have your name, you're on the List forever. Your name and address, buying habits, and credit-worthiness are moved from computer to computer, from store to store, from catalog to catalog, all in the hopes that soliciting you will enrich their pockets.

If you've ever declared bankruptcy Citibank won't offer you a credit card, but other firms who offer overpriced products with their own credit card will be on your doorstep. If you spend $5,000 a month with American Express, they will provide your name to a list broker and you'll receive sales pitches from the crème de la crème. However, if you pay for everything with cash, you get probably no junk mail. They can't trace you and your buying propensities, and therefore you are nearly worthless to them. An entirely new kind of discrimination results when one pays cash because, for all intents and purposes, you don't exist. Bad junk mail. Now that's redundant.

I can't wait for that one to go to court. A class action lawsuit on behalf of the lower economic classes, not even given the opportunity to turn down a sales pitch. Now that's discrimination against what Jeffrey Rothfeder calls the "data-disenfranchised." While many of us receive nasty sneers from mailmen trying to force oversized catalogs into undersized mail boxes, a large percentage of the population sits in an information void, never even aware of the staggering possibilities.

Doctors, Hospitals, and Insurance Companies

Arkansas Republican Tommy Robinson wanted a shot at then-Governor Bill Clinton's job. Tommy had spent six good years in Congress, but his chances for political advancement disappeared when one newspaper article claimed he drank a pint of bourbon a day. His medical file had been leaked to the media, and unfortunately for Robinson, the file was wrong.[36]

This is only one example of the untold grief experienced by honest, law-abiding citizens every day. There are no laws governing how, when, and to whom private medical records are to be handled. With the right sequence of keystrokes, a career or a life can be shattered. A medical record is perhaps the most revealing portion of our digital selves. In addition to the usual identification information at the top of the forms, how much we drink or smoke is included, our family history, with social and medical characteristics, is detailed. Complaints, diagnoses, treatments, drugs prescribed and in what quantities—all this paints a picture that is supposed to be confidential between patient and doctor.

The Medical Information Bureau contains files on millions of Americans, and just as with the credit bureaus, the errors are momentous. If a doctor says you have AIDS, it is entered into the MIB database to remain there forever, even if the data is wrong.

When a low-paid data entry clerk types in a medical code as part of a patient's record, one transposed digit can make the difference between the picture of health and a hemophiliac or drug addict with AIDS. Or, maybe the data clerk had a fight with his or her spouse and decides to make a few errors on purpose. Or, it could be a sort of revenge against society, striking out indiscriminately. As of today, there is no recourse, and Congress really doesn't give a damn.

If you have a dispute with your doctor, he could download an inaccurate medical profile onto a database like the MIB. Instead of suing you, he labels you as a sociomedical misfit and ruins your chances of acquiring insurance or getting a promotion. Quite a bit of power within the hands of the medical community, wouldn't you say?

Hospitals, too, maintain extensive medical records and their computers talk to the government's medical computers and the insurance companies' computers, all in the name of business expediency. But the sinister side of the Information Warrior constantly looms. Imagine a night nurse, so fed up with an irritable patient, that she alters his records enough to make the insurance company refuse to pay the bill. Maybe she turns him into a drug addict instead of a patient with a broken leg; insurance companies love that. Or, as in the medical terror thrillers of fiction author Robin Cook, perhaps the records of a patient's allergies are altered so that a doctor's drug prescription will trigger a fatal response.

Private Investigators

"Get the information. However you have to, and I don't want to know about it." A CEO might utter these words to his aide, who in turn hires an investigator to get the goods. The private investigator is an Information Warrior in every sense of the word. PIs will acquire the information they need to satisfy their clients and pick up their check.

The aggressive PI, not content only to work within the limits of the law, will exploit the same technology and capabilities we have previously described. After all, they meet his needs, insidiousness and invisibility being at the head of the list. The good PI will have a network of databankers on whom he can count to get legally attainable, but presumably private, information on individuals; he will have a contact at the police department who, for a bottle of Black Label or tickets to the Jets game, will delve into the theoretically sacrosanct world of law enforcement databases. Bob Lesnick says that a computer is "the most modern weapon we have. Few people, even criminals, can evade a databank."[37] Or, he will get hired as a security guard and have free reign for an evening in the building of his client's competitor. Illegal bugs and taps? Sure, why not, say many PIs. He will even sink as low as "dumpster diving," the refined art of poring through a target's garbage in the search of either valuable or incriminating information.

Ex-FBI agents, ex-cops, ex-anybodies with the skills and a shingle over the door will, for a price, act as your personal Information Warrior.

Security Professionals

Cops treat cops differently from the way they treat you and me; we're not part of the fraternity. Ex-cops are still cops, always part of the brotherhood, and they can count upon each other for favors. Big companies who hire ex-cops and ex-intelligence agents as heads of security unwittingly aid and abet the Information Warrior.

Law enforcement folks will help each other, even at the expense of our privacy or in violation of the law. One ex-cop working for a bank might willingly give access codes to another security pal—no questions asked. Once into one bank's private network, the Information Warrior can navigate into most other banking systems, including ATM networks.

Joseph Van Winkle, a former FBI agent working for a New York bank, doesn't like what he sees. "Every time we build another computer network, private information is compromised even more; dozens of new lines of data communications are opened up. I don't like it, but I don't know what to do about it."[38]

The Information Warrior with that kind of access can do a lot more than print out bank statements for a friend: loans can be paid off, bank balances increased, credit limits raised. On the other hand, foreclosure proceedings could be instituted against the bank's most creditworthy customer. It's all a matter of motivation. Or, if the bank itself is the target, all banking operations could come to a halt with a handful of keystrokes.

It all depends on capability, motivation, and intention.

Supermarkets

One Midwest grocery chain appears to have joined the ranks of the Information Warrior. Dominick's sent a letter to customers that ominously warned: "We have been confidentially recording the purchases you make when you pay by check and use your Dominick's Check Cashing Card at the register. We are studying this data and will soon make a decision on how to use it."[39]

Soon, you may have no choice but to shop and pay through Cyberspace. In the coming months and years, the debit card and the electronic check cashing card will become the norm in stores from coast to coast. Somewhere in a computer at Grand Union, Vons, Food Lion, or any other chain store in America, you will leave behind a trail that says you buy low-fat everything, wear a size sixty-two shirt, or you're a size eighteen female. Guess what kind of solicitations you'll then be getting? Stuff for fat people.

Each and every one of your individual purchases will be monitored, recorded, stored, compared, and analyzed by a hundred different computers. The results will be sold to direct marketing firms that have a customized catalog, just for you. Pretty soon the supermarket will be capable of delivering your groceries to your door before you even knew you needed them.

Imagine who will get your name and address if you buy condoms from any national drug chain and pay by debit card. Now that's privacy.

Proctor and Gamble, the consumer goods conglomerate based in Cincinnati, Ohio, was publicly humiliated when they were caught engaging in this type of Information Warfare. Their management was convinced that an employee was leaking confidential company information to a newspaper reporter. They recruited a local police department fraud detective to use his tax-payer paid power and law enforcement influence to get the cooperation of the phone company to perform an exhaustive search of over one million telephone numbers and forty million toll calls. (How many Information Warriors are involved here?) Despite this extraordinary effort, and the involvement of those who should have known better, no one ever found the leak, if there was one, and the company eventually had to face the embarrassment of admitting they had randomly invaded the privacy of so many people in an ill-conceived operation.

Politicians

Politics has the reputation of being dirty and unscrupulous; anything is fair game as long as your candidate wins. The Robb-Wilder cellular telephone incident discussed earlier is only a more sophisticated form of Information Warfare as pioneered by the attack on Democratic National Headquarters that spawned the downfall of President Nixon. Watergate was Information Warfare at its best, run by the best operatives around. And today, with the commonly available weapons of the Information Warrior as tools, political adjutants will have little reluctance to use them where they best see fit.

Southern Bell, one of the regional telephone companies, has been actively lobbying the Public Service Commission about a pending rate case. Commissioner Tom Beard, under investigation to determine his relationships with key Southern Bell

employees, resigned under the scrutiny, but not before someone contributed substantial evidence to support the suspicions.
In mid-1993, a floppy disk was provided to investigators that
contained logs of telephone calls to and from the homes and
offices of commission members and lobbyists with an interest
in the case, including the Governor's son, Bud Chiles, a
lobbyist for Southern Bell. Either the records were provided
illegally from an inside source, or phones were tapped. In the
process, Assistant Florida State Attorney General Mike Twomey
also resigned, refusing to disclose the source of the mysterious
disk that apparently contained damning information.[40]

No, the political process will not be immune from Information Warfare; I think that it will assume an even more acute
form of what's been practiced for decades. Only the technology is new and improved. Perhaps with the advent of safe sex,
we can imagine a high-tech Congressional scandal involving
ménage-à-trois E-mail.

Political Action Groups

Radical environmental groups such as Earth First! have
resorted to "spiking" trees in forests they think worth preserv-
ing. Such acts could be called violent, since loggers have been
badly hurt when their chain saws met up with these spikes.
The abortion debate has also sparked violence—even murder.
The antiabortionists have said that since abortion is killing a
fetus, they will resort to nearly any tactic to protect the life of
the unborn. Environmentalists believe that *all* human life
could end because we have so disrupted the ecological balance that Mother Nature provided: Ergo saving whales and the
rain forest are attempts to save mankind.

Any of these groups is a candidate for waging Information
Warfare against their real or perceived adversaries. Given the
power of information and the tools available, it would be folly
to pretend that politically motivated organizations won't avail
themselves of the capabilities of the Information Warrior. The

domestic infighting we experience right here in America, and the international factionalism spurred by the New World Order, will only create more and more splinter groups who want to forge their own agendas. It is these groups, many of them heretofore considered benign, who may use their ability to attack information systems as a modern means of civil disobedience.

Far-right Neo-Nazi and White Supremist groups have become well-known for their brutality, base behavior, and social pathology. As disgusted as we may be by their political agenda, we must not underestimate their ability to wage Information Warfare. It is a tool they apparently are already using. When Peter Lake penetrated the Aryan Nation on behalf of CBS News in Los Angeles, he was asked by convicted killer David Lane to assist in what is certainly a form of Information Warfare. Lane asked the reporter, "What do you know about telephone installations? I want to knock out the telephone system in a major Western city for one hour to silence the bank alarms."[41]

Mercenaries, Freelancers, and Ex-Soviet and Eastern Bloc Experts

If you think *we* have an unemployment problem, just look behind what used to be the Iron Curtain. Hundreds of thousands of people, whose job for years was to listen to and interpret information, are now out of work. The information they gained during the heydays of the Cold War was gathered in any way possible, ranging from pure threat and intimidation to high tech surveillance. No one ever accused the Soviets of being stupid when it came to intelligence gathering—so much of the Eastern Bloc's economic power was placed in the military and intelligence gathering, it's no wonder they were good. And now what are these unemployed Cold Warriors going to do to feed their families?

Terrorists

The rules have changed and Americans are feeling the effects of terrorism on our shores for the first time. Aside from bombings, terrorist groups have the capabilities to acquire and use Information Weapons. The results promise to be as devastating as those seen in New York at the bombing of the World Trade Center.

Walter Friedman of IVI Travel in Chicago thinks that huge databases are invaluable to terrorists. "With this kind of data automatically spread to hundreds of thousands of computers world-wide literally as the bookings are made, the thought of how easy it would be for terrorists to get their hands on it and use to plan kidnappings or worse makes one shudder."[42] Terrorists are not generally known for their subtlety, but with government support and the influx of vast amounts of funds, extremist political and religious groups who use terrorism as a means to their ends can now bring the necessary technical sophistication to bear on their activities.

Alvin Toffler says in his book *War and Anti-War*, "Whatever the terms, it is now possible for a Hindu fanatic in Hyderabad or a Muslim fanatic in Madras or a deranged nerd in Denver to cause immense damage to people, countries, or, even with some difficulty, to armies 10,000 miles away."[43]

We will further examine these unnerving possibilities shortly.

Business Competitors: Domestic

Competitive Information Warfare between firms is difficult to identify, much less prove. Publicly at least, American businesses claim that spying on one another only hurts our national competitiveness in the long run, but skillful use of Information Weapons makes identification of the culprits next to impossible. All too many companies are lax in their security against such attacks, thereby increasing their vulnerability and decreasing the chances of satisfactory recourse.

However, some cases have been publicized. Assistant News Director Michael Shapiro and News Director Terry Cole of ABC affiliate WTSP-TV in Tampa were charged with fourteen felony counts for breaking into a competitor's computer system. According to the *St. Petersburg Times* and *Computerworld*, Shapiro broke into WTVT-TV's computers to steal sensitive competitive news information. Shapiro had once worked for WTVT as the administrator for the station's computers, and police found computer disks and software guides from the rival station's computers at his home.

Domestically, industrial espionage as we think of it is rare; most Americans don't play that way. But it still occurs. Borland International, Inc. and Symantec are rival software companies in California. Both would love to know the other's new design specs, product plans, sales data, and contract bid information. According to a grand jury indictment in March 1993, Borland executive Eugene Wang sent E-mail to Symantec CEO Gordon Banks containing just such valuable competitive information. Why? He was getting ready to jump ship and move to Symantec.[44]

General Motors accused former purchasing executive Jose Lopez of taking crates of proprietary company information with him to rival Volkswagon.[45] Even Macy's found itself in a tussle when one of its key executives who "knew too much" moved to a rival retailer. Thus far in this country, espionage seems to be concentrated on what one knows and how much value it is to a new boss.

In a more celebrated case, Virgin Atlantic Airways accused British Airways of hacking into its reservations systems in an attempt to steal passengers. Airline reservation systems are fairly open; a lot of information is shared between competing airlines so that carriers can better assist their customers, but the names and phone numbers of passengers are supposed to be kept secret. A former British Airways employee, Sadig Khalifia, said that he and other employees were shown how to tap into the BA booking system computer that Virgin rented. Once they had the names and phone numbers of the Virgin customers, British Airways employees called and tried to convince passengers to switch airlines. The case never went to court, but British Airways had to pay Virgin Atlantic almost $4 million in damages and costs.[46]

Finding the real dollar amounts lost by businesses to domestic competitive espionage—or perhaps one might call it creative intelligence—is just not going to happen today. Big business is plainly too paranoid to admit they have a problem, much less the extent of it. According to Charles Cresson Woods, a security consultant in Sausalito, California, we don't hear a lot about these type of industrial espionage cases because "a lot of people don't know they're being wiretapped. These taps can go on for years before—or if—they are ever discovered."[47]

From the examples in this book, the informed reader now can assume capability, add to it motivation and intent, and then estimate probability. Does Chase spy on Chemical Bank for lists of their very best customers? Does 3M have insiders working at Monsanto in the hopes of discovering the next generation of chemicals at a fraction of the time and investment? Ultimately, I believe the answer to these and similar questions is, "Of course. They'd be stupid not to."

Business Competitors: International

Airbus can find out an awful lot about Boeing if it has access to an airline's database and plots out where its executives are traveling. It turns out they have access to even better information than that. Industrial espionage is today the stuff of James Bond. Industrial espionage is much more than company fighting company for the latest whiz-bang electro-static micro-metro pink filistoid distiller, or the recipe to Oreos or Coke.

In the international information marketplace, where industrial espionage is a day-to-day expense, the differentiation between foreign business and foreign government has become distinctly hazy. The success of a particular company may be deemed by that country's government to be of strategic value to national economic security. In such cases where corporate and national interests merge, the United States finds itself at a costly, embarrassing, and distinct competitive disadvantage. I hope this point hits home, because it is critical that we understand our shortcomings in this area. *Any* U.S. company, be it small and innovative or of global reach and impact, may find itself battling for survival against the combined forces of not only another corporation but one supported by the resources of its entire parent government. When it comes to waging Information Warfare, our international competitors vastly outclass even the largest U.S. corporations. Some might complain that we're not playing on a level playing field. But those are the rules in a tripolar, aggressively competitive global economy.

Consider the recent revelations of global spy networks within the oil industry. The vast sums of money involved have invited data brokers to acquire information through any means, and offer it for sale to competing organizations worldwide. These spy networks have penetrated Mobil Oil, USX, British Petroleum, and others through the use of clandestine moles and employees paid off in quick bucks in a Swiss account. The oil industry spy brokers from Boston to Hong Kong, Houston to Singapore, London to Libya trade in illegally obtained information and, in mercenary style, sell it to the highest bidder.[48]

The French have openly admitted to attacks against U.S. business interests. The Japanese have refined Information Warfare into an art. Even our old allies, the Israelies, have been caught as well. Just about every major economic power or wannabe economic power is using Information Warfare in the pursuit of its particular national agendas.

And then, who could forget those Russians? Since the demise of World War II, we've been spying on them and they've been spying on us. In that game, I think they won. How else could their ill-fated supersonic passenger plane be named

Concordski and look exactly like the sleek British Airways original? Why do you think that their space shuttle is remarkably similar to ours? Is that a coincidence or did they hire ex-NASA designers to work in Kazikistan for twenty years? I think not. They stole it, and today they even admit it.

Who Else?

How much money could someone make if they knew what government futures prices were going to be, even if only a few hours ahead of time? Should the person in a firm who consistently makes staggering investment profits be considered a brilliant market analyst, or should he be viewed as a likely Information Warrior? And how do you catch him, anyway? The money to be made with insider knowledge is phenomenal; it's like knowing the winning lottery numbers before they're picked. Some of Wall Street's famous power brokers from the 1980s were sent to prison as a result of their illegal profit-taking enterprises. Doesn't the Information Warfare have a similar motive—windfall profits—with substantially less risk? When billions of dollars and lives are at stake, is any quasilegal act or deniable source of information off limits?

Is our society so sick that an unhappy customer would resort to putting the offending company's computers out of commission? Hackers have already done it; causing millions of dollars in damage because they didn't receive their free poster. Considering that we have seen murder and kidnapping in such cases, perhaps Information Warfare is a welcome alternative.

And what about those serial-killers who indiscriminately kill young girls for the thrill of being chased by police? Will any of the emotionally devastated types who got blasted in the recession turn to Information Warfare as a means of extracting revenge from a cruel society? Or maybe it will just be cyberpunks with attitude, who want to raise hell in Cyberspace.

They're well-trained, experienced, and dangerous. Then there's pure harassment by mean people out to cause trouble, who find that the Global Network gives them the ability and the protection all at once.

These are the Information Warriors.

13

The
Military Perspective

"U.S. Satellites carry twenty sorts of sensors, including electronic eavesdropping equipment that can pick up virtually any individual on-the-ground conversation."

—CIA DIRECTOR R. JAMES WOOLSEY[1]

ON FRIDAY, JANUARY 10, 1992, ABC's "Nightline" reported a story that I thought was a joke. According to *U.S. News and World Report*, the Allies, in preparation for the Gulf War, attacked and disabled Iraqi military computer systems with a computer virus developed by the Pentagon.

That's right. We took out the Iraqis with a computer virus.

According to the tale, the super-secret National Security Agency built a custom integrated circuit or chip that, in addition to performing its normal function, contained a computer virus. Viruses can be placed in hardware by chipping, as we have shown, but the technical and logistical problems of getting the right chip to the right printer to the right Iraqi . . . well, it's not a terribly efficient way to go about it. The chip was allegedly installed in a dot matrix printer in France that was destined for Iraq via Amman, Jordan.

The infected chip was reported to have shut down portions of the Iraqi defensive radar systems. This had to be a put on, a joke. But, no, not Ted Koppel! Something was wrong here. I was deeply troubled that "Nightline" could air a story that was so obviously in error.

249

I spent the early morning hours looking back over my archives and found an old article in which I spoke of airborne viruses and their offensive military applications.[2] In 1990, I had given a speech on mechanisms that the military could use to inject malicious software into enemy computers from thousands of miles away. Still, the back of my brain itched; the story Ted Koppel told just didn't make sense. Although I didn't know what I was looking for I knew I would recognize it if I saw it, so I kept up the frenetic search. About 3 AM, I found what I was looking for.

In the April 1, 1991, issue of *Infoworld*, John Gantz's weekly column was titled "Meta-Virus Set to Unleash Plague on Windows 3.0 Users."[3] Gantz said he had heard that the NSA had written a computer virus dubbed AF/91 that was to "attack the software in printer and display controllers." The column went further, stating "each machine makes the virus a little stronger." I remembered reading this column and thinking, "How absurd!" It continued to allege that the CIA had inserted the virus into an Iraqi-bound printer, and that by January 8, 1991, half of the Iraqi defense network was dead and gone—thanks to the efficiency of the AF/91 virus. "The NSA now believes that any Windowing technology is doomed," Mr. Gantz wrote.

The *Infoworld* article concluded, as many a computer column does, "And now for the final secret. The meaning of the AF/91 designation: 91 is the Julian date for April Fool's Day."[4] Alternately, AF/91 can mean April Fool, 1991; here was the joke!

Ted Koppel and "Nightline" were the victims of mis- or dis-information given to them by *U.S. News and World Report*, who in turn were first duped by their sources. Associated Press subscribers also had the opportunity to read the same "news" as if it were fact. The story went nationwide, and to this day, wherever I lecture, this story is still remembered as fact. Once I demonstrate the absurdity of it all, the audience rolls with laughter.

On Jan. 13, 1992, when faced with the evidence that the story was really just a year-old April Fool's joke rehashed through the military grapevine, or perhaps a plagiaristic attempt at spreading disinformation, *U.S. News* still stood by the accuracy of its story and the credibility of the two senior level intelligence officers who confirmed it. The writer, Brian Duffy, did admit, though, that there were some "disturbing similarities" between the two tales. (No kidding.) I've included a point-by-point comparison of the original *Infoworld* April Fool's story and the one put out by ABC and *U.S. News and World Report.*[5]

InfoWorld	*U.S. News and World Report*
1. By January 8, Allies had confirmation that half the displays and printers . . . were out of commission	1. Several weeks before the air campaign of Desert Storm . . .
2. Virus targeted against Iraq's air defense	2. Virus targeted against Iraq's air defense
3. Designed by the NSA	3. Designed by the NSA
4. Virus built into printer	4. Virus built into a chip in a printer
5. The CIA inserted the virus	5. U.S. intelligence agents insert the virus
6. Printer went through Jordan on its way to Iraq	6. Printer went through Jordan on its way to Iraq
7. Peripherals not protected by electronic fortress	7. Able to circumvent electronic security measures through peripherals
8. Disables real-time computer systems (Mainframes)	8. Virus inserted into (their) large computers. Disables mainframe computers
9. "the NSA wizards"	9. "Cunningly designed . . ."
10. "It eats Windows."	10. " . . . each time (he)
11. Source: Old ADP navy buddy	
12. "So, it worked."	

13. NSA believes that any Windowing technology is doomed: There doesn't seem to be an antidote.
14. It could be four years before users start seeing their Windows blur. Maybe the NSA can discover a cure by then.

April Fool's Joke.

opened a window . . . the contents of the screen simply vanished."
11. Two senior U.S. officials
12. "It worked."

Government Information

Myth, fantasy, hoax, or just plain disinformation? Decide for yourself if Duffy was duped by the Air Force intelligence contacts he used for the story, if his Air Force contacts were also victims, or if the whole story was a prank by someone who read Gantz's article. No matter how you look at it, Information Warfare is a part of the picture.

Desert Storm computer stories abound, perhaps because it was the first high-tech war: You could turn on CNN, watch the action, then flip to "Roseanne" during lulls in the fighting.

Prior to the onset of hostilities, a British officer returned from the Gulf for a briefing at 10 Downing Street. Plans and contingencies for the Allied effort were stored on a laptop computer. Unfortunately, the laptop, along with its military secrets, was stolen from the officer in question. What made it even worse was that the information on the computer was not encrypted.

The British tabloids caught wind of the story and by evening everyone in the U.K. knew what happened. That much has been pretty well established but from here on, the various tales diverge. According to the most entertaining one, a common, third-rate West London petty thief, no tidier than a chimney sweep, appeared at a local police station the next morning with a laptop computer in hand. He politely suggested to the desk constable that this might be what they were looking for. The police were incredulous that the computer, containing the country's most secret intelligence information, had been returned, much less by the crook himself. They wanted to know why.

Mustering the best of British pride, still upper lip and all, the man replied, "I'm a thief, not a bloody traitor."

Rumor has it that the thief was released. In any event, the British officer was demoted and court martialed for his dereliction.

The American military was the target of a less benevolent intrusion during the same period. U.S. and European hackers broke into Pentagon computers by fooling the system into thinking they were Dan Quayle. Unclassified files about domestic antiterrorist efforts were accessed, but what made the event even more disconcerting to the military is that the break-in was broadcast nationally on U.S. television.[6]

The Navy makes an unexpectedly honest self-assessment of how well-protected our computers were in the Gulf War: "While Desert Storm appeared to the public to be a high-technology war in all aspects, many systems were several generations behind available commercial technology, and were in fact, vulnerable."[7] That astute, understated observation reminds us that technology does indeed march on, and that the equipment available to the military may not be of the same quality or caliber as that used by everyone else.

The Navy's SEW, or Space and Electronic Warfare, policy is coincident with that of a class-two corporate Information Warfare effort: "Destroy, deny, degrade, confuse, or deceive the enemy's capabilities to communicate, sense, reconnoiter, classify, target, and direct an attack.[8] And just how is the military going to achieve that aim? With the same tools that other Information Warriors use.

In the fall of 1990, a military contract was awarded to study how airborne computer viruses could be inserted into enemy computers. Not by hand, not by person, not by diskette, not by dial-up, but by air. The $500,000 year-long study may have provided the impetus behind the almost laughable Iraqi Virus Hoax.

In a follow up 1993 contract called Statement of Work (SOW) for the Malicious Code Security Model Development Program, the U.S. Army wanted to study the vulnerability of its Army Tactical Command and Control System (ATCCS) that serves as the technical core of battlefield operations. The army is concerned that Information Warriors on the other side could penetrate their systems with malicious software.

Through computerized simulations,

> These (malicious) codes are representative simulations of potential network intruders (hackers) who could disrupt the ATCCS networks.
>
> The contractor shall research and develop a computer model that simulates potential malicious codes that could disrupt or delay any sort of ATCCS information (e.g. programs, software, etc.) These codes simulate how would-be network intrudes actions could disrupt the ATCCS's command and control.
>
> The contractor shall easily introduce simulated malicious code into the ATCCS type internetwork in order to see the effects on ATCCS.[9]

The military, for all of its security and paranoia, suffers from the very same problems as corporate America. Duane Andrews, a former Assistant Secretary of Defense for C3I, (Command, Control, Communications, and Intelligence), said in late 1992, "Our information security is atrocious, our operational (security) is atrocious, our communications security is atrocious."[10]

A few years ago, a senior level Air Force officer I'll call Bob was in charge of a Tiger Team that was supposed to test the physical and electronic defenses of a facility such as a classified office building or an embassy. In an attack mode, the Tiger Team is to do everything within its power to break in and compromise its defensive posture. In this case, Bob's goal was to determine how well the information within a Texas air force base was protected.

A meeting was scheduled a few hours before the simulated attack just to make sure everything was in place. Bob showed his ID at the facility checkpoint and was admitted. But instead of attending the meeting, he left the facility a few minutes later. When leaving, he was subjected to another search. His briefcase was opened, the Sergeant poked around looking for something, then finally said with a crisp salute, "Thank you sir. Have a nice day."

"Excuse me, sergeant."

"Yessir."

"Could you tell me what you're looking for?"

"Yessir. Calculators, sir. We've been having a lot of them stolen recently."

"Thank you, sergeant. Carry on."

Bob walked to his car and called into the meeting.

"Where the hell are you? You're late."

"There's no need for the meeting. I've already cracked security."

Angry silence on the other end of the phone. "Get in here, now!"

Back inside the facility, Bob went to the meeting and was asked to explain. After gaining access to the facility the first time, he had walked up and down a few corridors and into a few offices, slipping floppy disks into his pockets and his briefcase. The guard who checked his briefcase when he left saw the diskettes, but he was too preoccupied with missing calculators.

"I have here," Bob said, spilling the contents of his briefcase on the conference table, "one hundred and forty classified diskettes full of military information. I respectfully submit, sir, that your facility has no security. This Air Force Base fails."

"But you cheated," a higher-up officer stutteringly complained.

"And the bad guys won't? You expect them to announce their visits the way you wanted mine announced?"

"But the procedures, the rules . . ."
"I lied. You still fail."

In all sincerity I hope it's not that bad throughout the government, but I fear the worst.

The military worries about a lot of things, and one of them is the terrorist threat. Our own list of culprits is long enough, and undoubtedly theirs is longer. We know what terrorist groups are capable of if properly motivated, and we know that the battlefield could likely be the networks and computers of corporate America, our communications infrastructure, transportation support systems, or portions of government Cyberspace.

But questions arise. If such a assault were made, what would our reaction be? Would the military step in? Should they? Is a debilitating attack against General Electric by an overseas Green group considered worthy of a national response? If narcoterrorists from an immense drug cartel successfully shut down U.S. border radar systems, what is the appropriate reaction? How do we politically and militarily deal with a remote controlled foreign incursion into U.S. Cyberspace? How do we deal with a situation where the victims are unquestionably on American soil, but the invaders are physically located thousands of miles away?

International law is even more confused than U.S. computer crime law. Extradition for hackers? Prosecutorial reciprocity? It's hard enough with hijackers and war criminals. Can we reasonably expect a lengthy legal process to be the only recourse in the case of a substantial attack by Information Warriors?

Answers to these questions are either deeply buried in the bowels of the Pentagon, or more likely, we haven't made preparations for such eventualities. We are deft with electronic countermeasures (ECM) in guarding air space and the electromagnetic spectra in a hot war zone, but government-business coordination to protect civilian U.S.-based electronic systems for extreme eventualities is barely on the drawing board. The Government's Software Vulnerability Analysis contract to evaluate the vulnerability of the public-switched networks is a healthy step forward in the right direction.

As the role of the U.S. military evolves into that of good Samaritan and humanitarian as well as soldier, we need a frank and open discussion of the role the military would play in such extreme scenarios. Outside of conventional military countermeasures, electronic warfare, and sophisticated secretive intelligence gathering, military assistance in the protection of the commercial technoeconomic infrastructure will never occur unless and until we implement and enforce a National Information Policy.

14

Class 1: Personal Information Warfare

"The Cold War is over, a lot of people are out of work, but it's hard to break old habits. A former CIA agent was working as a waiter. He took my order and then ate it."

—CONAN O'BRIAN.

THERE ARE THREE FUNDAMENTAL AXIOMS that must be remembered to appreciate the potential effects of Class 1 Information Warfare.

1. There is no such thing as electronic privacy.
2. In Cyberspace, you are guilty until proven innocent.
3. Information is a weapon.

Class 1 Information Warfare is an attack against an individual's electronic privacy: his digital records, files, or other portions of a person's electronic essence. The digital you is composed of far-strewn bits and bytes, each of which, when assembled, contributes to building an electronic picture of each of us. The average American has absolutely no control over his electronic privacy and Congress has chosen to ignore that fact in favor of PAC monies and special interest lobbying groups that today seem to control our elected representatives more effectively than we do. It seems that Congress will not or cannot address an issue that is snowballing, at breakneck speeds, towards a technological future so precarious that we as a society may lose control over our personal freedom.

Most of us Americans believe that we have an inherent right to privacy; however, the nature and extent of that right is only today becoming a front-page debate. According to a *USA Today* poll, 78% of us are concerned or very concerned about the loss of our privacy. That figure was only around 30% in 1970, but rose precipitously after the introduction of personal computers in 1977.[1] At the center of our concern is not only the issue of electronic privacy and the protection of the vast repositories of information across the Global Network, but the accuracy of that information. Credit records, for example, are notoriously inaccurate. I spent the better part of a year proving the electronic claims against me were false.

The premise of assumed guilt in Cyberspace causes many of us to shudder with anxiety, exacerbates Binary Schizophrenia, and is in one hundred percent violation of the foundation of the legal system. Yet Congress won't touch it. Computers contain a seemingly infinite stream of data on us, yet we have no control over its content, its accuracy, its dissemination, or its use. This is a sad, sad state of affairs and our nation's lawmakers should be ashamed of themselves.

Class 1 Information Warfare rains digital fallout upon the innocent electronic bystander whose only sin is to be a name stored in a computer database somewhere. This is the area of Information Warfare that most resembles terrorism. But the genesis of modern Information Warfare is based on simple, time-proven techniques. When we think of electronic snooping, most people I speak with come up with a few of the classic methods.

1. Install a hidden microphone.
2. Install a miniature camera.
3. Tap phone lines.

Not exactly a complete list, but enough to make the point.

With technology's great march forward, the means to bug adversaries is more widely available, less expensive, and more reliable than just a couple of years ago. Miniature cameras are so small that the lens is the size of a head of a pin, and fiber optic wire is almost as thin as a human hair. All this makes detection difficult, to say the least.

Countersurveillance is based upon the recognition that the "bad guys" know how to tap phones, place hidden transmitters, and take pictures discreetly. Countersurveillance teams perform sweeps of a client's residence or office looking for telltale signs that a surveillance is underway. Since today's technology is available to both sides, a gamesmanship mentality prevails, with the surveillance and countersurveillance teams jockeying for technical superiority over the target or suspect. Phone tapping is at the point now where, if a professional is behind it, there is little chance of ever discovering it.

Invading our electronic privacy (if we ever had any) is as simple as reaching for the Yellow Pages to call a data banker, a private investigator, or a hacker, or reading relevant newsletters and magazines. Take a look at the kinds of information available from only one issue of *Full Disclosure*, a proprivacy tabloid. Their banner reads "For Truth, Justice, and the American Way," and their editorial slant is "providing in-depth, inside information on electronic surveillance technology."[2]

- How To Get Anything on Anybody
- How to Investigate By Computer
- How To Find Anyone Anywhere
- Cellular Telephone Modification Handbook
- Eavesdrop on PCs
- How To Determine Undisclosed Financial Assets
- A Practical Guide to Photographic Intelligence
- The Latest In Cellular Monitoring Equipment
- Business Intelligence Investigations
- Don't Bug Me: The Latest High-Tech Spy Methods
- Fax Interception
- The Psychological Subversion of Information Systems
- Super Picking (locks that is)
- Don't Expose Yourself When You Use Your Phone

- Privacy Poachers (What 'they' do with information on you)
- Video Surveillance Recorders
- Finder's Fee: The Skip Tracer's Text
- SpyCam—A miniature ⅓" CCD camera

And let's not forget the half-page ad for Spy World, a surveillance and countersurveillance retail and mail order operation, which bills itself as "New York's Leading Supplier of Professional Spy Equipment."

All the tools needed to wage Class 1 Information War on individuals are available from catalogs, magazines, and books. Consumertronics, a group in New Mexico, publishes techniques for ripping off credit card companies, cracking into ATM machines, beating the phone company, and just about any other scheme you could imagine. For example, one of their publications details how to cheat the electric companies by slowing down power meters. All of their publications are labeled "For Educational Purposes Only," because they don't want to be accused of encouraging illegal behavior. Next time you're at the supermarket, check out an issue of *Soldier of Fortune* magazine. The small classified ads in the back offer everything from weapons that would make any small country's army proud, to survivalism supplies, to ideas on how to protect yourself from the WOG (World Government) and the Communism that dominates the hills of Washington, D.C. The point is, of course, that almost any kind of information on just about anything is available, and the tools to get it are a phone call away. The amazing thing is that most of this is legal, and in some circles, encouraged as a legitimate means of investigation—privacy be damned.

Joe Apter is president of Telephonic Info, Inc., a databanker based in St. Petersburg, Florida which finds information on people and their assets. Telephonic Info offers a shopping list detailing the company's services. Looking for bad debtors or deadbeat husbands? Need to prescreen a possible employee, check out a possible mate or business partner, or find out if someone is a good credit risk? Joe's firm will do it all, and he does it totally within the law. But Joe's company is not alone; there are dozens if not hundreds of databanking firms around the country who offer similar services, but who might not be quite as ethical as Joe.

Imagine that someone wanted to put together a dossier on you, your spouse, or your parents. Here is what Telephonic Info or other data bankers can legally dig up: Address and length of residence; phone number (even if unpublished); social security number; date of birth; names of household members; maiden name; married name; previous marriages, divorces, dates, final decrees; age at death and amount of death benefits; creditors, credit inquiries, and credit reports. They can find out about your driving record, including any infractions and restrictions; real property owned, including sales prices, taxes, and property descriptions; IRS or contractor liens; mortgages; judgments; bankruptcies; equity value of assets. They can get info on your current employer, length of employment, wages, previous employers, and previous earnings history; your banking affiliations, bank account numbers, and balances; uniform commercial code filings; recorded financial transactions such as loans; your medical history, including hospitalizations, emergency room services, and doctors, treatment facilities, dates of service, description of medical care; and any past lawsuits, criminal offenses, misdemeanors, felonies, arrests, and convictions. Federal court, Superior Court, District Court, worker's compensation claims, payments, disputes, hearings; corporate affiliations, business type, names of corporate officers. All these—and more—are legal to obtain.[3]

How many of us would honestly want all of that information printed in the newspaper, open to inspection by our family, friends, and business associates? But the worst part of this is not so much that the records are spread all across the Global Network, but that the information may be wrong, and no one takes responsibility for the accuracy or the integrity of it. You can spend a lifetime and a fortune attempting to repaint the correct digital picture with no assurance of success.

Now, if we want to reach out to less scrupulous databankers, we can get an even more complete picture of our target. We can find, for a price, social security account balances, tax records, military records, video rentals, hotel stays, past and pending air and rail reservations, car rentals, passport number, immigration files, Medicare and Medicaid files, psychiatric records, prescription drug use, drug or alcohol rehabilitation, credit card balances, credit card statements, credit applications, education, grades, youthful offenses, telephone bills, current police investigations, allegations, law enforcement surveillance, insinuating affiliations, NCIC records, Department of Justice files, and just about any other bit of private information that you have generated during your life.

Such a complete electronic picture of an individual gives the Information Warrior unbelievable power over his victim, especially when the composite information is edited to paint an unflattering image. Despite the frightening potential for abuse, Congress has thus far done little to promise personal electronic privacy. But I would guess that if an enterprising databank customer had the wherewithal to assemble a complete data record of every member of Congress, we might see some action.

The Government Accounting Office has urged Congress to criminalize the abuse of medical records, at least. With Clinton's universal health plan coming to reality, the problem of abuse of NCIC and credit databases becomes even clearer. As Congressman Gary A. Condit said, "How will we be able to protect health records in a computerized environment if we can't adequately protect criminal history records or credit records?"[4]

The American people agree. In a 1992 Harris poll, 89% of those surveyed agreed that "computers have made it much easier for someone to obtain confidential personal information about individuals."[5] We should all be concerned because the Information Warrior, as usual, is way ahead of the good guys. The Class 1 Information Warrior armed with a complete profile of an individual with a skeleton in his closet, has the leverage to induce his victim to do his bidding by means no more subtle than pure extortion or blackmail.

Once armed with a complete picture of the digital you, the Class 1 Information Warrior can do a lot.

1. He can edit the information to paint the picture he wishes to paint. Selective truth is as good as a lie, and trying to repair a damaged reputation is often futile. Suppose someone accused you of renting adult videos, but didn't mention that of the 176 tapes you rented, only two were adult in nature. The picture is skewed in favor of accuser. (This intense, unfair investigation into one's personal life is sometimes known as getting Borked, after Congress's treatment of Supreme Court nominee Robert Bork.)

2. The Information Warrior can find your Achilles' Heel and exploit it to his advantage. Your position or access to further information might make you of value to him; in exchange for his silence, you might be persuaded to assist him in future endeavors rather than suffer embarrassment, family strife, financial loss, or criminal prosecution.

3. The Class 1 Information Warrior can send your dossier to people whom you would rather not have it. For example, if you committed a minor legal transgression in the past and omitted it from a job application, your job might be history. If your digital picture is different than the one you provided to get life insurance, Poof! you could lose it all. If you lied on a credit application and the Information Warrior finds the discrepancies, you could lose your assets and face Federal criminal mail fraud charges.

Yes, the Information Warrior can do a lot when he has your picture. But I find another capability of the Class 1 Information Warrior a thousand-fold more disturbing than the mere accumulation of a floppy disk full of data on an individual.What if the Information Warrior intentionally modifies or alters the digital picture of his victim? Let's put the pieces together.

- Thousands of databases hold together the digital pieces of our lives.
- Computers constantly trade information about each of us.
- Low-paid data clerks enter that information into the computers.
- Getting erroneous information corrected is a painstakingly difficult challenge.

I will paint a few scenarios, and let you consider the ramifications:

- An envious coworker with a friend who works for the local police arranges to have you listed as a car thief wanted in three states. You are stopped for a missing taillight.
- An insurance company clerk has been given two weeks notice. In a misguided attempt to strike back at her employer, she alters hundreds of random records, including yours, with a code saying you've died. Your social security checks stop coming, the public records confirm your death, and your obituary is printed. Try proving you're alive.
- The credit card receipts of a dozen Congressmen are given to the *Washington Post*. The receipts say they all had dinner at La Vielle Femme, which is actually a cover for a call girl agency. A reporter calls the agency to confirm Congressional "dining" preferences. What do they say?
- Racist right wingers alter the medical records of all state politicians who support minority causes to reflect a serious history of alcoholism. Then they tip off the media.

- Right-to-Lifers arrange to include child abuse charges in the police records of doctors who perform abortions.

Moreover, an Information Warrior will not rely upon only *one* method to strike out at his targets, especially with so many available to him. He may use a series of electronic weapons to achieve his goals or to be more assured of success.

In an astounding case of alleged Class 1 Information Warfare, Gilles Guilbault of Montreal claims that the Canadian government has waged an Information War against him for over a decade. In a letter dated September 20, 1993, he claims that his University credentials were erased, his career was shattered, he was forced into bankruptcy, and his life was all but destroyed by the government because he himself had too much information. M. Guilbault alleges that when he was an upper-echelon stockbroker and a member of several elite and exclusive private clubs, he learned of a sophisticated conspiracy to commit high level financial fraud. The plot, which included a kidnapping and the political assassination of Quebec minister Pierre Laporte, occurred during the Trudeau reign. He says that this case is the Canadian equivalent of the Kennedy assassination, and full disclosure would implicate many people in power. He further alleges that a number of prominent figures conspired to turn him into an electronic nonentity, so discredited that he would never be believed.[6]

Remember our very important businessman who got bumped off his flight to Vegas? What if a company vying for a huge contract needed to get its primary business competitor, our very important friend, out of the way for a few days? What could that company do if it had the services of an Information Warrior at its disposal?

You are the only person can pull this deal off. The *only* one. The whole deal rests on your ability to convince the brass that your company is the right one for the job. Your company is depending upon you but you're prepared. You arrive at the counter to pick up your first class tickets to D.C., the last flight that will get you there on time for the morning meeting.

"Excuse me, sir, there doesn't seem to be a reservation in your name. Could it be under another name?" Pretty smile.

"No, no, I made it myself. It has to be there."

"I'm sorry, sir, but it's not here. Would you like a seat?"

"Of course I would. That's why I made the reservation in the first place." Indignant.

"Yessir." The smile is gone. "That'll be $1,252. How will you be paying for that?"

You throw out the Platinum American Express card, looking at the clock. The boarding has already begun.

"Excuse me, sir. There seems to be a problem with your credit card."

"What problem?" you demand.

"It refused the charge." What she didn't tell you is that the little readout on the credit card machine said "STOLEN CARD: CALL POLICE."

"That's impossible . . . oh, all right, use this one." You hand over a VISA card which is also refused by the computer for the same reason, but as per her training, the ticket agent proceeds as if nothing is wrong, waiting for the police to arrive.

You suddenly feel a strong arm grasp yours. "Would you mind stepping over this way, sir?" You turn and two policemen—*not* the airport rent-a-cop types—are giving you the once-over.

"What's the problem, officers?"

"Would you mind stepping over this way, sir," the really big one repeats while not so gently pushing you to the side of the ticketing area. You have no choice, but panic sets in. "Do you have any identification, sir?"

"Of course I do. What the hell is the problem?"

"Your identification, please."

You make a sudden move to your inside breast pocket and both officers react as they were trained. The unholstered guns cause you to stop. You smile sheepishly. "My wallet . . . it's in here. . . .

"Slowly, please, sir."

You give them your driver's license. One cop takes it, steps away about ten yards, and speaks into his cellular phone. The other one just watches you. As the crackle of the speaker echoes through the hall you hear a couple of disconcerting words: wanted . . . Colorado . . . armed robbery. . . .

The cop returns. "You have the right to remain silent. . . ."

In less severe circumstances, harassment might be sufficient. One week, they might delete all funds from your checking account. The next week, they might add 114 calls to Zimbabwe to your phone bill. The next week your name is added to every X-rated mailing list in the country, and the next week your life insurance is cancelled. Good luck getting your life back.

One last technique that the Information Warrior might use in an assault against an individual is "spoofing," which takes many forms. Spoofing, or the intentional electronic masquerading of oneself as another person or electronic entity, is a powerful way to infect a victim's electronic life with misery.

Millions of people communicate across the Internet every day, discussing thousands of subjects in as many forums. One area of hot activity are the myriad sex boards, where people of kindred spirit from across the globe meet, trade stories, talk dirty, and exchange X-rated and pornographic materials. The following message appeared on a sex board in August 1993. (Names have been changed.)

FROM:tim@bigcompany.com
TO: everyone

Hey, does anybody know where I can get some good kiddy porn?
I love little boys and little girls.

Thanks

Within minutes, "tim" was derided from every corner of Cyberspace and his name sent to the police. Even within the anarchistic culture of the Internet sex-forums, there are self-imposed limits. The messages were explicit in their response. "You freak! You should be castrated . . . ," "The police are on their way . . . ," "We got a bunch of us coming over to beat the shit out of you. . . ." Those were the mild ones. Unfortunately, it wasn't "tim" who sent the message. A friend of his got his account and his passwords and thought it would be funny to play a little practical joke. If the boards can be believed, the "friend" quickly took a trip to the hospital.

As bad as Class 1 Information Warfare is, there are some goofballs out there in Cyberspace who think it's a big giggle. The demon dialer that hackers use to identify computers sitting on phone lines can also be used as a weapon of harassment. A demon dialer can be set to call a phone number every minute on the minute, or every ten minutes, ring once or twice, and then hang up. (Imagine being on the receiving end of that.) In one case, every time someone dialed a particular church, they were connected to a Dial-A-Porn 900 number. In juvenile days past, I was guilty of calling the local meat market, asking if they had pig's feet, and responding to an affirmative answer with "wear shoes and no one will notice." I fear that with profoundly sophisticated technology in the hands of the disenfranchised, the bored, the latch-key kids, and the downright malicious, our younger generations will learn the tricks of the Information Warriors without any help from us.

Class 1 might appear to be the kindergarten of Information Warfare, consisting only of isolated incidents and causing comparatively minor harm. Relatively speaking, that may in fact be true. But in more aggressive hands, Class 1 Information Warfare is employed as a means to an end, a preliminary tool, a diversion from the real task at hand. Let's not fool ourselves into thinking, "Ah, it's just a bunch of kids letting off some steam. Or maybe a few adults who never grew up, or would break the law no matter what the technology. That's nothing to worry about." Conventional wisdom forgets that the international cumulative effects of Class 1 Information Warfare, if properly organized, can lead to far more sinister acts, with far reaching consequences. Conventional wisdom has suggested that once the hackers are gone, all of our problems are over. Nothing could be farther from the truth. Because, sooner or later, we all graduate from kindergarten, and move on to learn and apply our knowledge with greater and greater skill.

Class 2: Corporate Information Warfare

"Business is War."

—JAPANESE ADAGE

"All's fair in love and war."

—CERVANTES, *DON QUIXOTE*

WE ARE AT WAR.

Michael Sekora of Technology Strategic Planning in Stewart, Florida, agrees with former President Richard Nixon that we are involved in World War III. Ex-master spy Count de Marenches calls it World War IV.

Whatever conflict number we assign Information Warfare, the New World Order is filled with tens of thousands of ex-spies, well practiced in the art of espionage, who are looking for work to feed their families. The world is filled with countries and economic interests that are no longer siding with either of the two erstwhile superpowers. The Haves want to keep their piece of the pie and expand it; the Have Nots want a piece of the pie they never had. And everyone is fending for himself and his future survival in the evolving global economy.

The words *industrial espionage* are spoken every day from the halls of Washington to the boardrooms of corporate America, and *global economic competitiveness* is now becoming as potent a national security buzz word as Reagan's *Evil Empire* once was. The theory behind industrial espionage is simple to the point of absurdity. If you invest five years and $1 billion in a new invention, either a product or process, you hope to make a profit on that investment. If, however, I can steal the knowledge to make that product, say for $10 million, I can sell the same item for substantially less and bring it to market in months instead of years. You invest the time and money, I steal the results, then we compete. Who's got the advantage?

While the United States was busily preparing to survive Armageddon by outspending the Soviets on military hardware, we ignored the fact that our entire industrial base was being raped and pillaged by economic competitors from around the world. We of course expected the Russians to do it; that was their job. Many of the educational attachés and trade delegations they sent to the United States were in reality KGB or intelligence operatives, with a mission to seek out our technology and our strategic plans for a possible military conflict. The FBI's CI-3 division on Half Street in Washington chased them hither and yon, trying to keep them honest, winning some and losing more. Today, the Russians still spy, but less for militaristic reasons. William Sessions, former director of the FBI, told a House subcommittee, "Russians do not have the currency to pay for advanced systems and designs, so they will steal them or obtain them through other illegitimate means."[1] They of course want to keep up, and they use the best means they have available to do so.

The Russian conundrum is simple: they have a minimal industrial base, a withering economy, no distribution system, a shaky political structure, and a couple of hundred thousand ex-spies. What is their best chance for moving into the world economy?

As we chased the Soviets and the Poles and the Czechs and the Bulgarians, our "allies" took us to the cleaners. In his 1993 book, *Friendly Spies,* Peter Schweizer examines in detail how our global allies pinched cookies from the American cookie jar while we protected them from the big bad Red Bear. The French, the Germans, the Israelis, the Koreans, the Japanese, the British, and the Canadians have all targeted the American industrial base and stolen as much as they could while our backs were turned. It just doesn't seem fair, yet we have only ourselves to blame. Foreigners see stealing information as a short cut to making costly and time consuming investments. If caught, the penalties are so low that most companies consider it a cost of doing business.

The U.S. Department of State can be surprisingly honest at times, as they were in a recent publication:

> Each day America becomes driven more and more by information. Proprietary information is our chief competitive asset, vital to both our industry and our society. Our livelihood and, indeed, our national strength depend on our ability to protect industrial and economic data.
>
> The struggle between capitalism and communism was decided essentially over two issues—the desire of humanity for freedom and the relative effectiveness of each system's economic competitiveness. While of utmost importance during the period of the Cold War, the need to protect economic information looms even larger in the coming years.
>
> Recent revelations in the media indicate strenuous efforts on the part of some foreign intelligence agencies to benefit their national industries. These efforts have included eavesdropping, hotel room burglaries, and introduction of "moles," as well as other sophisticated intelligence techniques. Our foreign competitor's interest in our information has never been more intense.[2]

Foreign companies have always recognized that the majority of the world's technology has come from the United States, and that since World War II we have been the technological king of the hill. So what were they to do? Thomas Hughes wrote in *American Genesis*, "Modern technology was made in America. Even the Germans who developed it so well acknowledged the United States as the prime source."[3] Not wanting to be overshadowed by America's commercial and military superiority, many countries went to extraordinary effort to steal our technology. More often than not, these foreign corporations in search of American intelligence or technology have received assistance from their cooperative governments. Spying is just another way of doing business in most parts of the world and we haven't been smart enough to realize that our secrets are worth protecting.

There is little suggestion that a paradigm shift of any appreciable size is on the horizon, but fortunately, a few voices have spoken up about the problem. Senator David Boren said, "An increasing share of espionage directed against the United States comes from spying by foreign governments against private American companies aimed at stealing commercial secrets to gain a national competitive advantage."[4] He warns that as we enter the next century, "it's going to really increase."[5]

During Congressional testimony on April 29, 1992, CIA Director Robert Gates said that foreign espionage is "assuming even greater importance than previously," and "is likely to assume . . . greater importance . . . in the future." Without giving away too many of the top spook shop's secrets, he went on to discuss the extent of industrial espionage that the U.S. is officially now acknowledging. As Gates points out, "There has been a proliferation of commercially available intelligence technology. . . . Some fifty Third World countries [are] now able to operate [espionage activities] and . . . there are large numbers of unemployed intelligence operatives from former Communist countries." So now not only do we have to worry about our allies, but the less highly developed nations who can also easily afford the technology and the staff to spy as well.

In 1989, Wayne Madson of Information Security Engineering published a list, entitled "Computer Communication Espionage Activities," that defined each of the world's countries' capabilities. He rated countries like Nepal and Yemen as "poor." Those countries with an "excellent" computer espionage capability included the U.S., Switzerland, the U.K., Taiwan,

South Africa, Sweden, Norway, the Netherlands, New Zealand, Israel, Japan, Finland, France, Germany, Canada, and Austra-lia. As one peruses the list, with hundreds of security and intelligence agencies listed, the sheer number who are "above average" or "improving" should lend credence to the assump-tion that the battle for Cyberspace is only now beginning.

The stakes are huge in Class 2 Information Warfare, as seen in the oil industry's immense global spy ring. In 1988, the University of Illinois published "A Study of Trade Secrets in High Technology Industries" and found that 48 percent of all companies surveyed admitted to being the victim of industrial espionage. In a real global economy of $26 trillion, properly serving only twenty-five percent of the planet's population, the motivation to open up new markets is too compelling to resist. Around the world, industrial spying is a national pastime.

Japanese spying against the United States is supported and coordinated by the national trade organization, MITI. MITI sets goals on behalf of hundreds of interlocking *keiretsu*, and determines which trade secrets to steal. The Japanese sponsor thousands upon thousands of students to come to the U.S. to study in our universities, but a little moonlighting is re-quested. Students are told where to keep their ears and eyes open, and they report information back to MITI on a regular basis. Nothing unscrupulous, just taking a few photos of technical facilities and noting seemingly innocuous off-handed comments. With MITI support, according to Herb Meyer, an intelligence expert, "the Mitsubishi intelligence staff takes up two entire floors of a Manhattan skyscraper."[6] I lay odds Americans don't have an equivalent operation in Tokyo, Paris, London, or Seoul.

According to author Peter Schweitzer, "IBM alone, accord-ing to internal company documents, was targeted twenty-five known times by foreign entities between 1975-1984. Japanese espionage in Silicon Valley nearly devastated the U.S. com-puter industry."[7] Hitachi, for instance, ponied up a reported $300 million in a settlement agreement after spying on a new generation of IBM computer equipment. The Hitachi plan was successful and the estimated losses to IBM could be in the billions. Not a bad investment on Hitachi's part.

Kodak lost a fortune when Fuji stole their top-secret plans to build disposable cameras. In response, Kodak hired their own Information Warriors, ex-CIA operatives, and beat Fuji to market with a new camera.[8] Nippon Telephone regularly records calls made by Japan-based U.S. companies and the Government requires that all encryption keys be given to them for safekeeping.

But we cannot accuse the Japanese alone. The French have come out of the closet and made their position clear: "militarily we're allies, but economically, we're competitors." And they have proved that over the years. Count de Marenches, whose tenure as head of French Intelligence lasted over a decade, hobnobbed with international powerbrokers from Churchill to Gorbachev to Reagan. He had unlimited control over the French intelligence community, and ultimately went public with the details of his cadre of hundreds of professional agents' espionage against the United States in the interest of French international competitiveness.

The airline industry has been of keen interest to the French for decades. Since industry and government are almost synonymous in France, it should come as no surprise that their cooperation could spell problems for our airline industry. To help out Airbus in 1988, French intelligence targeted Boeing—specifically a new generation of plane, the 747-400. In order to learn what Boeing was doing, the intelligence folks used communications receivers designed to pick up test flight data beamed down from the planes to Boeing technicians. The data was simply transmitted over radio, and the signals were unencrypted. All that the French needed was a portable dish, a receiver and two computers. The very same information that Boeing would never voluntarily give to an American competitor was being broadcast right into French hands.[9] One would hope that Boeing learned its lesson, but apparently not.

According to an official who left the company in 1993, Boeing is practically giving its new design secrets to the French on a silver platter.

Designing airplanes today is a long, expensive, and incredibly technical process. To save costs in building and testing a series of prototype planes, highly specialized software is used to electronically simulate how the plane will fly. This automated process makes it easier to build the plane and cuts the time from drawing board to runway by months or years, which can mean substantial profits for the company. Boeing uses such software, a million dollar program named Catia, supplied by IBM. However, IBM didn't design Catia. They acquired the U.S. marketing rights from Dassault Systems, the U.S. arm of French-based Dassault Aviation, a major supplier of aircraft to the French military. Dassault has offices in Los Angeles, Chicago, and Detroit which serve other aerospace and automotive customers, but the development of Catia software is done outside of Paris and so, unfortunately, is the customer support and product upgrades.[10]

The ex-Boeing expert claims that Dassault engineers are inside Boeing's facility on a regular basis—without security or supervision. He fears that Boeing's latest and greatest designs for the planned 777 airplane are Fed-Ex'd straight over to France on a regular basis. Is Boeing permitting itself to be a victim of Class 2 Information Warfare by inviting a known foreign competitor into their labs? Is it in fact providing costly design and research information to Aero-Spatiale and the European Airbus Consortium? Boeing's only response to these charges was that they were "comfortable" with the security of their 777 development program.

The French are notorious for national economic espionage endeavors, such as breaking into hotel rooms, rifling briefcases, stealing laptop computers, eavesdropping on international business telephone calls, and intercepting faxes and telexes. And if that isn't enough, they even use Air France stewardesses to listen in on the conversations of first class travelers.[11] They stole U.S. trade negotiation position papers

from Undersecretary of State George Ball in 1964,[12] and had a
bug put into H.R. Haldeman's overcoat during President
Nixon's first trip to France.[13] Service-Seven of the French
intelligence agencies bounced laser beams off President Reagan's
hotel room windows to eavesdrop on sensitive conversations.[14] These French efforts come from the top of their
government; in October 1981, a special department was created within French intelligence to increase the yield of industrial and economic secrets.[15]

One tried and true method for getting close to industrial
secrets is the use of company moles, who are actually loyal to
or in the pay of another country. During his confirmation
hearing in the fall of 1991, Robert Gates said, "We know that
foreign intelligence services plant moles in our high tech
companies."[16]

Technological Information Weapons will be used more and
more when physical access to the targets of Class 2 Information Warfare becomes difficult, and as employers screen out
potential moles and spies with greater efficiency. But again,
we may have to look in the mirror for a scapegoat. "The
intelligence agencies of Germany, Japan, South Korea, and
France, for example, were all developed with the assistance of
the U.S. intelligence community. Their methods, even their
eavesdropping equipment, came from the United States. Many
of these assets are now being used against the United States in
the name of economic competitiveness."[17]

While the U.S. media and law enforcement decried the
activities of our homegrown hackers, the Germans have been
using theirs to spy on other countries. One of the goals of the
German federal intelligence service, the *Bundesnachrichten-
dienst* (BND), was the monitoring of foreign technological
developments. In addition to performing "regular eavesdrops
on transatlantic business conversation with the full cooperation of the German national telephone company,"[18] and conventional spying techniques, computer hacking was a full time
occupation.

On the outskirts of Frankfurt, writes Schweizer, "approximately thirty-six computer specialists and senior intelligence officials are working on a top secret project to bring computer hacking into the realm of spying and intelligence. They hope that through the use of sophisticated computers and specially trained personnel, German intelligence agents will be able to enter computer databases of corporations and foreign governments around the world, and the access could be achieved while agents remained thousands of miles away."[19] The idea, called Project Rahab, was conceived in 1985 and formalized in 1988. Since only the West had any appreciable number of computers—there were next to none in Russia—the targets were obvious.

Success was theirs, according to CIA officials. In typically fastidious Germanic fashion, Rahab hackers plotted out the roadways and network connections across the Global Network to those computers and systems of interest. "In March 1991, Rahab employees hacked their way into . . . SWIFT . . . in order to establish a roadway to ensure easy access for when such access is deemed necessary." BND will be able, at will, to monitor or interfere with global financial transactions.

Computer viruses were also of great interest to the BND folks working on Project Rahab. A German hacker, Bernard Fix, created a virus that was particularly powerful, and in April 1989, Rahab began a duplication effort. "It was capable of destroying all the information in a large mainframe computer in a matter of minutes. If widely used, it could render national computer systems useless in the course of a few hours."[20]

Thanking the young American hacker for illuminating foreign capabilities may be a bit much for some people, but the lesson should be heeded. Schweizer sums up the publicized German Rahab activities thusly: ". . . In all likelihood [Rahab-styled techniques] will augur an era in which state-sponsored computer hacking becomes every bit the intelligence tool that spy satellites have been for the past thirty years. It offers the benefit of an agent on the inside without the costs inherent in his potential unmasking. German intelligence has seen the future, and it lies with Rahab."[21] We can no longer assume that the Germans are alone in their awareness that hacking is a tool of immense competitive value.

Class 2 Information Warfare is more than just industrial espionage. It can also involve economic espionage, the study and analysis of financial trends which are often available from nonclassified, open sources such as newspapers and television. Count de Marenches maintains that the French knew for a fact America would devalue the dollar in 1971—before it was announced. That move was of intense interest to our allies, and such knowledge can be turned into enormous profits if used correctly on the currency exchange markets.

Economic espionage is typically focused on large economic spheres instead of on a single company or technology. Advance knowledge of a quarter- or half-point change on the part of the Federal Reserve System is worth a fortune. If a major currency trader is preparing to shift his holdings, there is immense value in that data.

How many people became stinking filthy rich in the '80s? A lot. Of course a lot lost their shirts as result of fiscal overindulgence, but boats full of money were made—more than at any time in history. When we look back on many of the extraordinarily profitable ventures that were launched in those heady days, some of us may experience twenty-twenty hindsight envy. If only we had known about that computer deal, we would have made millions. Or if we had known They were going to build That Contraption, we would have bought in early. None of us can deny wishing, at least once, that we had been in on The Big One. At one time or another every one of us has said, "If only I was a fly on the wall. . . ."

Tens of billions of dollars went through the hands of KKR, the merger-maniacal New York investment firm who put together the RJR Nabisco deal immortalized in the book and movie *Barbarians At The Gate*. When companies merge or are targets of a takeover bid, their stock price is likely to rise appreciably in a small amount of time. The merger of Time Inc. and Warner Bros., the AT&T-McCaw cellular deal—think of any of the big headling-grabbing deals and we wistfully regret that we didn't know about it in advance.

In the Eddie Murphy movie *Trading Places*, advance knowledge of the price of orange juice futures made insiders a fortune in minutes. Advance insider information is time-sensitive; it only has value prior to the time when it becomes public knowledge. Once everyone knows it, the information's value plummets to about zero. The government publishes numbers every day, and some of those numbers can make or break fortunes by depressing or increasing the value of industries, stocks, and Treasury bonds. Many investors consider Federally-released employment statistics to be the most important monthly statistics. Advance knowledge of that information and ability to interpret it is worth a fortune, if acted upon prior to its general release.

Apparently this happened at least once. On October 8, 1993, the price of Treasury bonds surged about one-half point, just moments before the monthly employment numbers were announced. To make the bond prices move that much requires substantial capital, and the profits made are enormous. The Labor Department and the Chicago Board of Trade consider leaks as the likely culprit.[22]

But the Information Warrior, with the right tools and weapons at his disposal, will always be able to know which way the market is going. If he is clever, he can regularly make impressive profits without alerting the official overseers of the markets that he is trading with illegally-acquired insider information.

On a global scale, a big move by any major economy will create ripples throughout the world's markets in microseconds as automatic trading programs takeover. In *The Death of Money*, Joel Kurtzman says, "Today's world is very different from the world of the past. Economic success in this world, especially in the financial sector but increasingly in other sectors as well, is dependent on assimilating large quantities of information very rapidly."[23]

The increased amount of information and need to make

rapid decisions to exploit a particular opportunity or stay out of trouble often means that decisions are made on the fly. There is no time for reasoned thought.[24] The more time that one has to study the information and make a decision, the better off he is. The financial manager and his traders are the air traffic controllers of cybermoney; the pressures are enormous and mistakes can be unimaginably costly. There is strong motivation to go to extreme lengths to acquire economic information before it's officially announced.

Class 2 Information Warfare, however, is about more than the acquisition of information; it's also about the use of information—real or ersatz. Imagine the fallout if the following article appeared in the Paris dailies. "According to well-placed officials, the French government has launched a secret study that will definitively prove that the American drug Fix-It-All, manufactured by Drugco, Inc., causes severe liver damage. Sources say that the results of the study will be published in the next few months, but in the meantime, doctors are advised not to prescribe Fix-It-All to any of their patients." The study could be a fake, the findings totally manufactured as part of a well-constructed campaign of disinformation, but the results will be just the same. Drugco, Inc., won't sell much Fix-It-All and the company's image will suffer. Drugco, Inc. will have to go into defensive mode and expend considerable time and resources in damage control. Disinformation is as dangerous a weapon in the hands of an Information Warrior as it was in the hands of the Soviets.

The uncontrolled release of even legitimate information from a company can be just as devastating. Perhaps an Information Warrior is not profit oriented; he just wants to damage the reputation of the company in question. He could, for example, intercept the company's E-mail and identify any incriminating documents—or, if need be, create and disseminate them to the media, competitors, and the public.

Sowing distrust electronically has the appearance of authority and integrity. A bank could be hurt by having its customers' records suddenly distributed on street corners or plastered up as posters on construction sites. The mere appearance of impropriety could easily devastate a financial institution, despite their claims of being victimized themselves by the activities of an Information Warrior.

An investment house's strategies and formulas are among their most valued assets. Their open publication on Wall Street would not only be an embarrassment and a PR disaster, but a sure way to empty the company of customers. Knowing a competitor's exact investment methods would cause the most staid investment banker to shout in glee.

Politically, the power of information has been and will continue to be used as a weapon. The Bonn government was given a list of two thousand West Germans who spied for the notorious East German state police, the Stasi, during the Cold War. In 1974, West German Chancellor Willy Brandt resigned over the identification of just one spy in his government's midst.[25] What could happen if the names of two thousand more traitors are suddenly made public? Or more important, what careers are made and broken to keep the list secret?

Car magazines pay husky prices for photos of new car models months prior to their release. Computer-aided design terminals display three-dimensional pictures of these car designs years before they are made. An Information Warrior armed with quality van Eck detection equipment can keep car magazines happy for years. Imagine that Ford, GM, and Chrysler all are hit and their plans are published, years before release, in glowing color for millions of hungry eyes.

Make a valuable secret public, and all of a sudden it becomes next to worthless. The U.S. pharmaceutical industry loses about $5 billion per year, and the U.S. chemical industry between $3-6 billion, to overseas counterfeiters.[26] If the formulas and techniques for these and other industries were openly disseminated instead of stolen for profit, the losses could be much greater. The companies affected would see nothing in return for their multi-billion dollar investment.

Again, the Information Warrior has options, depending upon his motives.

Class 2 Information Warfare can also mean putting a company's information systems out of commission. In security parlance we call this "denial of service." What it means is that an Information Warrior may not elect to steal your secrets, or even seek to discredit you; he may merely want to see you suffer or go out of business. Accomplishing this requires some investment of time, money, and manpower (Motivation) but American business is so reliant upon their Computers Everywhere and their pieces of the Global Network that it is possible (Capability).

First of all the Information Warrior needs to pick his victim. It should be one that relies heavily upon computers and communications to carry on its day to day business activities. Without its computers, it would essentially be out of business, or so impacted that its customer base immediately defects to other companies. In either case, the results are the same. Obvious candidates for such an assault might be a small airline, a bank, an automated distributor, a private courier like Federal Express, an accounting firm, a payroll company, or any of thousands of other organizations. Even a hospital would come to a halt without computers these days. Although they wouldn't "go out of business," portions of local, state, or federal government operations would come to a grinding halt without their information systems.

Information Weapons will be chosen based upon the desired aim, but first things first: we must scout out and learn about our target. From publicly available sources we can learn about its finances, its products, and its market position. Find out its strengths and its weaknesses. Competitors will emphasize the weaknesses of our target from their perspective; for a few hundred dollars we can begin to construct a mosaic of the company's alliances, business relationships, its history, failures, and successes. In a large conglomerate, it might be necessary to first identify each of the smaller operating divisions to weigh the various importance of each to the whole before picking a specific target. Which division is the most profitable? Where can the most damage be done? It will not take long to draw a complete picture of our target and figure out where he is most vulnerable.

(Thus far, the Information Warrior can work entirely within the law. He can employ a competitive intelligence organization to learn everything about a company that it doesn't want made public—open secrets that are buried, but not dead.)

Then there is the element of timing. When is the best time for the Information Warrior to strike? What about tax time— would a systems collapse create trouble with the IRS? Is there a big deal pending? Would a massive system failure jeopardize a public offering, a bond issue, or a billion dollar merger? Timing is everything; just like the military landing on Normandy beach, or sending cruise missiles into Iraq, all of the elements of the assault force must be in place and prepared to strike in a coordinated manner. It is no different with Class 2 Information Warfare aimed at disabling any company or organization.

If the goal is to stop a big deal, the enemy must be engaged at the most propitious point, i.e., not after the fact but not so early that damage control can be implemented. Take the case of Gennifer Flowers. If her accusations against Bill Clinton had been made the day before the Democratic National Convention instead of months earlier, history might well have been different. The Information Warrior must be astutely aware that timing is absolutely crucial to the success of his endeavors.

Depending upon his target and his aims, the Information Warrior may elect to break into a computer system in order to get in information about a company now, or to have a future entry point when desired. Any and all information is of value, as is a surreptitious means of accessing the computers at will. But the Information Warrior may want closer contact; a means of physical access to his target. One way is to get one of his people hired at the company as an insider, another is to find a friend of a friend with access who is not above taking a bribe, and another is to compromise a current worker.

Poking through internal computer systems is one method of identifying potential accomplices, as is dumpster diving for lists of employees and their phone extensions. Finding a likely candidate for compromise, bribery, or blackmail is no more difficult than running names through the same databankers who profiled the company in the first place. Does a certain employee owe too much money? Have an extra apartment on the side? Is there an incriminating file in their college records? What skeletons do they have that may prove embarrassing to the target and therefore valuable to the Information Warrior? Getting the cooperation of unwilling participants is not all that difficult, as recent history has shown.

So how will the Information Warrior achieve his aims? The most efficient way is through what might be called the double whammy. Companies prepare for "single-event" disasters if they prepare for them at all. *The* flood, *the* power outage, even *the* hacker. But what about if more than one disaster strikes at once? Early 1993 showed us what happens. The World Trade Center bombing forced computer-reliant companies into emergency action, and for those firms with foresightedness, into their Hot Sites. Many firms though handicapped, were able to continue functioning by moving the critical portions of their operations into these bunker-like facilities across the Hudson River in New Jersey. Hot Sites are operated as a business by companies who offer an effective insurance policy to keep backup telecommunications lines and computer facilities running in the event of disaster.

But right after the bombing, the Great No-Name Storm of 1993 knocked out banking and ATM networks throughout the Northeast. Hot Sites, already overburdened by Trade Center customers, had no more room; some companies found they had to relocate essential services anywhere in the country they could. As a result, millions of banking customers were without ATM service for as long as a month. The Information Warrior is probably going to use the double whammy as a tactic against a major target just because it is so effective. The double whammy could actually be three or more congruent attacks, all centrally coordinated for maximum effect.

Let's hypothesize for the moment that an Information Warrior wants to totally disrupt the operations of a financial institution. Maybe he wants it out of business because they have the wrong political affiliations, or there is a perceived wrong to be avenged. Maybe our warrior is an international competitor who seeks to embarrass the bank out of business, or maybe he's just a complete nut-case running amok in Cyberspace. Through the assistance of an accomplice who works inside the bank, a piece of malicious software will be released into the central computers on, say, a Monday morning. By day's end, the accounts won't balance, error-filled customer account statements will be issued, or maybe the bank's credit card division will find an extraordinary number of deadbeats who aren't paying their monthly obligations.

If the Information Warrior has associates who are especially skilled with bank's software, he may elect to have one piece of malicious code detonate on Monday, and then another on Wednesday, but never on a Friday—that would give the bank plenty of time for damage control and repair. Banking computer software is complicated, so each and every error intentionally introduced into the system will have to be methodically sought out and repaired. Maybe the same error is reproduced several times in the code, so that when they think they have found the problem, an identical incident will crop up in a day or a week. Customers become very unhappy in the process.

If the software errors are reported to the media, or creep up day after day, the reputation of the institution will immediately begin to suffer. Who wants to have his money in a bank whose computers can't add two and two?

But the Information Warrior is only using malicious software as a ruse, a decoy for his real attack with the real Information Weapon he chose to debilitate the bank. The primary Information Weapon will be a portable HERF Gun, mounted in a bland, unmarked van. The planned assault is a simple one. After several days or weeks of constantly failing software, system collapses, miscounted money, federal investigations, media scrutiny, and customers abandoning the ship in droves, tensions will be extremely high throughout the entire organization. Employees *expect* the computers to fail. All trust in the system is gone. Are the print-outs right or wrong? Does every one of millions of daily calculations have to be rechecked by hand or by abacus to insure accuracy? Binary Schizophrenia is running at full tilt.

At 9:00 AM, the van will drive in front of the bank computer facilities, located and identified by the insider-accomplice. When the bank opens it's business as usual, despite mass defections of employees and customers. Inside the van, the HERF Gun (a modified radar system), is powered by a souped-up generator; one Information Warrior has his finger on the button. At the right moment, he pushes "shoot" and several megawatts of high frequency power enter into the bank's computers for a few milliseconds. The van turns the corner and drives off. Inside the bank, computer circuits are overloaded; network wiring carries a massive energy surge to the gateways, bridges, routers, and communications links that connect hundreds of branches and terminals; and the system crashes. If the bank has other computer centers, maybe HERF Guns will be used there as well.

The system is down, and what is the culprit? The software of course. Dozens of technicians spring into action, fearful that management will put their heads on the chopping block. In several minutes the system is back up and everything seems to be working, but still, why did the system crash? When they were repairing the software glitches they found, they had to make changes that might have caused other problems. But at least the system is up.

Until the van comes around the corner again at 9:24 AM and lets loose with another volley of electromagnetic disruption— blam!—and the systems go down again. The repair process is repeated, and ATMs and tellers are at work again in minutes.

Until 10:06 AM, when the van drives down the street and—
ready-aim-shoot—it bombards the computers with another
round of digital death. The engineers feel that there's hope,
though, and they tell the bank president and the media that
because the problem is occurring more often, they should be
able to isolate it more quickly. 10:29 AM, 11:00 AM, 11:46 AM,
High Noon, and so on throughout the day until 3:00 PM, when
the bank closes. Thank heavens. Throughout the rest of the
day, into the evening, and for the entire night, hoards of
technicians attempt to duplicate every condition that the
system experienced. They think they have found a couple
more lines of code that might be responsible. They hesitantly
reassure management.

Tuesday morning, the bank opens again, and at 9:15 AM, the
van comes wheeling down the street and. . . .

The question is, how long can our fictitious bank survive
such an onslaught? If the bank's security officers have read this
book or come to my sessions, they might suspect early on that
some fool rigged up a HERF Gun, but then there's still the
matter of figuring out which car or truck or van is the culprit.
And by then, the Information Warrior will have won the battle.
A big bank or Fortune 500 Company has its own army of
technicians, and sooner or later, someone will remember
reading or hearing about HERF Guns and begin the complex
and tedious process of triangulating the source. Small companies do not have the same deep pockets to keep themselves in
business.

For small battles against smaller adversaries, the Information Warrior will probably not be able to get inside the target;
he might have to rely on other methods to create a diversion-
ary distraction. Small companies can be hacked into with
amazing ease, and malicious software might be inserted from
afar. Creating dissension within the ranks works well in
smaller companies. The theft of proprietary information can
be selectively leaked to the right people within the company,
as an indictment of others. Stir up the Binary Schizophrenia

by making sure that the right people are already suspected as "industrial traitors." Then, when tensions are high, blast 'em with a dose of HERF.

Small accounting firms will come to a halt instantly if their PCs die. Local area network-reliant operations will come to a halt with the proper prescription of HERF. NBC headquarters in New York uses LANs for its on-air programming, and staff has been so cut back that a return to the old way of working by-hand would be a scramble at best. Sales and distribution operations must have computers up at all times, as must hospitals, power companies, manufacturers, and the local K-Mart—and none of them are in a position to recognize or react to such an assault. In many ways it would be easier for them to have a murderer walk in the front door with a semiautomatic and spray bullets at the workers—they can then get back to business—than it would be for them to deal with constant computer and communications failures that they do not fully understand.

Class 2 Information Warfare is creative, relatively inexpensive, and if well-planned, terribly effective. The myriad of double whammy scenarios is endless, yet most companies don't plan for one, much less two, disasters at a time. And that is a mistake.

The Information Warrior is not as rare as a flood, or as benign as an ice storm. The Information Warrior is not a natural catastrophe, an act of God, or Mother Nature getting even with man. The Information Warrior creates well-planned man-made disasters with all contingencies considered, all alternatives explored, and all escape plans evaluated.

Class 2 Information Warfare is more than just industrial or economic espionage; it's more than stealing secrets, eavesdropping on faxes, or reading computer screens via a sewer pipe. It's more than a HERF Gun in a back pack or bad code with a purpose. It's *all* of these things.

And with all that knowledge, power, and capability, a few Information Warriors will develop the means to wage Class 3 Information Warfare.

16

Class 3: Global Information Warfare

> *"History does not teach that better technology necessarily leads to victory. Rather victory goes to the commander who uses technology better, or who can deny the enemy his technology."*
>
> —OFFICER OF THE CHIEF OF NAVAL OPERATIONS.[1]

CLASS 3 INFORMATION WARFARE IS WAGED AGAINST INDUSTRIES, political spheres of influence, global economic forces, or even against entire countries. It is the use of technology against technology; it is about secrets and the theft of secrets; it is about turning information against its owners; it is about denying an enemy the ability to use both his technology and his information. Class 3 Information Warfare is the ultimate form of conflict in Cyberspace, waged across the Global Network by Computers Everywhere against Computers Everywhere. Class 3 Information Warfare is *very* bad news.

It is an invisible but very real war, where Information Weapons of mass destruction are let loose, either in a focused way, to achieve specific results, or indiscriminately, to have the widest possible impact. The victims are not only the targeted computers, companies, or economies, but the tens of millions of people who depend upon those information systems for their very survival. Take the power of Class 1 and Class 2 Information Warfare, multiply it tenfold, and you will begin to get a sense of the kind of damage that can be done. Class 3 Information Warfare creates chaos.

By now the reader should have a clear idea of the havoc that can be raised in Cyberspace by anyone—a preteen, a vengeful mother-in-law, a military man, a madman, or a terrorist. We know that anyone with the desire can acquire the same power that a mere two decades ago was only in the hands of the information elite. We also understand what sort of motivations might drive a person or group to take advantage of those capabilities.

Class 3 Information Warfare is bigger, and more widespread than the capability of even a hundred hackers. It is bigger than the FBI or the LAPD. It is bigger than the biggest company willing to spend a few million dollars for their competitor's secrets. Not everyone has the wherewithal to wage Information Warfare at this intensity, but there are powerful and rich individuals and institutions in the world who have, or will soon have, the capability and the motivation.

When teaching about Class 3 Information Warfare, I have found it useful to reinforce one thought: From both a competitive and combative perspective, it would be stupid for a well-financed and motivated group *not* to attack the technical infrastructure of an adversary. The vulnerabilities are clear, the risk so low, and the rewards so great. In fact, if someone wants to take on a technologically sophisticated society, the real question we should ask is not "why would they attack the computers?" but "why wouldn't they?"

Along this line of reasoning, it is evident that portions of the U.S. econotechnical infrastructure would be inviting objectives. In fact, we are already being targeted, but thus far, thankfully, in limited doses. We have not yet had to face the all-out devastation that Class 3 intensity brings with it. But that means we haven't had the opportunity to prepare for an inevitable assault in Cyberspace. We can, and must, begin to heed the warnings. The military understands their enemies; they plan for all eventualities in conflict. So we should understand what a Class 3 conflict might entail, and how we will react.

All of the stops are pulled out when one wages Information

Warfare at the Class 3 level. This level is waged by only the most elite of the Information Warriors, those very few individuals or groups who meet a number of select criteria.

Class 3 Information Warriors must have

- extensive financial resources
- sufficient motivation
- the ability to organize and control a large number of people
- a target with substantial reliance upon information processing capability
- a technical target
- patience

1. The Information Warriors must be well funded to be effective on the scale envisioned. The United States spends about $250 billion per year for bombs, bullets, and invisible airplanes. About $30 billion of that is spent on intelligence organizations (such as the NSA) for our own militarily focused Information Warfare. That annual investment makes America militarily impervious to attack, localized terrorist attacks notwithstanding. But our computers are another story, as we have learned.

   Even if the Information Warrior only spends millions of dollars (as opposed to billions) to launch an attack, say $100 million or so over two to three years, the results would be unimaginable. When compared to the cost and effectiveness of a well-armed militia, that means that almost anyone can play. When we think that drug cartels spend billions of dollars annually to protect themselves, an additional investment in an offensive information strategy would be a relatively minor expense. And that's scary.

2. The motivation of the Information Warriors must be strong. On a Class 3 level, the hope of becoming wealthy beyond imagination, richer even than Microsoft founder Bill Gates, might be enough. With money comes power, and megalomania is a millennia-old motivation. Re-

venge for real or imagined wrongs is also a pretty good motivator, too, and Information Warfare offers a fine way to extract retribution. Class 3 Information Warfare offers those nation-states unfriendly to the U.S. an alternative to conventional warfare. Iran, Iraq, Libya, Islamic fanatics, drug cartels, old-regime Stalinists, and Red Brigade-style terrorists head the long list of those antagonistic towards the U.S. It also offers the Have Not nation-states a means of becoming competitive quickly at our expense. Any list of candidates would be incomplete without mentioning the isolated fanatic or lunatic whose motivations are well beyond sound rationale. It is not inconceivable for small groups of individuals in positions of power, as suggested by Oliver Stone in his film *JFK*, to have the ability and motivation to finance such an invasion.

3. Manpower must be available. Waging Class 3 Information Warfare is not a one-man show. It will necessarily involve hundreds of people, probably located all over the globe, each with little knowledge of the ultimate purpose of their task, and with even less knowledge of their fellow warriors. These rank-and-file Information Warriors must be willing to work without questioning superiors. There are copious and willing populations worldwide from which to recruit assistance. In 1992 when presidential also-ran Pat Buchanan spoke critically about American immigration policies, he emphasized that with millions of foreigners in the United States, not all of them will have the best interests of this country at heart.

   As Count de Marenches points out, taxi drivers would make ideal operatives in an Information War. The majority of Washington, D.C., taxi drivers are immigrants who, de Marenches claims, could represent a security threat. The Count told ex-FBI director William Webster in March 1987, "A cab is quite simply an automobile with a big trunk that can transport people, papers, ideas, explosives, weapons—plus it has a radio. It's perfect. If I had to organize terrorists in Washington, I'd recruit a couple of cabbies. They're terrific. They're everywhere. And totally invisible."[2]

The Information Army must be disciplined. In a conventional military conflict, generals expect 100 percent compliance with orders, but a nation's military has certain powers that a private army doesn't have. Fear of the brig, treason charges, and court martial keep most soldiers in line. Likewise, in an Information Army, discipline must be maintained, even though the Warriors function in Cyberspace. Fear of death by murder is a pretty good start. The Mafia has historically maintained excellent discipline employing just such methods. Drug barons have little fear of reprisal for torturing and killing their own who are, or appear to be, disloyal. Radical political and religious factions use didactics or spiritual teaching to rationalize such extreme measures.

Information Warriors occasionally have to act ruthlessly. They should be willing and able to quickly and quietly eliminate those individuals within their own organization who may jeopardize their overall plans. Similarly, it may be necessary to eliminate innocent civilians who accidentally occasion upon illicit activities. On the other hand, the leaders might choose to sacrifice members of their Information Army as pawns in order to create a sense of discipline or push their plans forward.

4. The target must be an advanced post-industrial technical society. Shooting HERF Guns at sub-Saharan fruit vendors is not the way to disrupt a barter-based economy. If communications are accomplished with smoke signals, drums, or tin cans connected by strings, you can forget about malicious software as a viable weapon. Attacking a neolithic community with twenty-first century weapons is beyond useless; it's downright crazy.

But the Information Warrior who is planning to wage a Class 3 conflict in Cyberspace already knows that.

The target must heavily rely upon his technical infrastructure for its continued good health. Even a primarily industrial society such as Eastern Europe is not an ideal target. If the Information Warrior's target can continue to thrive without its information infrastructure intact, it does not become an attractive prey.

5. Patience is absolutely necessary to wage effective Information Warfare. Sure, we'll see the occasional goofball who attacks Cyberspace with an impulsive vengeance, only to effect limited and isolated damage. Like the Hinkleys of the world, he's just an amateur. The professional Information Warrior is willing to commit the funds, the personnel, and the energy to a Class 3 assault; he will bide his time, plan out every detail, develop contingencies, design redundancies, have backsups and backups of backups, spy on his own troops, and rehearse as many of the field operations as possible before the actual attack commences. He will make sure that only a small handful of his Army knows the big picture, with everyone else working on a need-to-know basis. With the right warriors at the head of the Information Army, patience becomes another effective weapon. Timing and patience go hand in hand. Strike too soon or too late, and all is lost.

The Information Army

For a Class 3 operation to work, an organization must be developed and in place prior to an effective assault. Everyone should know his or her job, where to be, and how to communicate. There are countless small operations to carry out beforehand, and they must be done efficiently and professionally.

For a cyberconflict of this magnitude, the money must be in

place, free to be drawn upon without first having to wade through a cumbersome vertical bureaucracy. For purposes of this discussion, we are assuming that the financial resources behind our imaginary Information Army are substantial, and that it has the means to distribute the monies and the influence to keep a large group happy and loyal for the duration. Financial experts who know how to manipulate large amounts of money undetected are available around the world. (The amount of cash that is laundered within the U.S. every year, $100 billion or more, is a thousand times more than the monies to be spent by our hypothetical Information Warriors.)

For the sake of secrecy, our Information Army will be a horizontal organization; unlike in most big companies or in the military, most of the divisions or groups will report to the top. Middle management won't cut it in the Information Army since the extra layers cut down on effective and timely communications, allow for power bases independent of the leader, and create opportunities for security leaks. The organization of the Information Army will be simple. Think of it as having one president, about a dozen vice presidents, each with his own specialty, and then several dozen terrorist-like cells reporting directly to each vice president. Our Information Army will not be so unlike a large multinational conglomerate, except that it will be run more militaristically.

C3I

At the pinnacle of the Information Army is what the military calls C3I—Command, Control, Communications, and Intelligence (some military planners now call it C4I, adding computers into the equation)—and what business calls the board of directors. This is where strategic plans are made and directives for tactical support are calculated. C3I motivates and finances the Information Army; it is its raison d'être. Decisions are made here. All monies come through C3I. The power over life and death sits with these very few individuals who will ultimately exert extraordinary influence over the lives of millions.

There may only be a couple of generals in the Information Army who can see the whole picture. Terrorist groups are often organized in this way. Thus, if one member is captured, he can't tell what he doesn't know, regardless of the interrogation methods used. A leader, very possibly the financial sponsor, will be the single voice guiding the entire effort. A trustworthy technical general will sit at his side, to design and oversee the technical operations. He will need to know the big picture, and will actively contribute to the planning. An internal security chief will set the policies and guidelines for loyalty. Financial management will have to know almost everything, and internal legal counsel will have to know as little as possible, yet still be able to serve the client. The more ruthless the leadership, the greater the allegiance.

C3I will be as small as possible since publicity and fame are the last things the Information Army wants, at least at this point. The smaller the core group, the better the secret. It would also make sense for the leaders of the Information Army to headquarter themselves somewhere other than in the United States. There is no compelling need to be here physically and if they are positioned on our shores, the potential legal problems are vast.

The Information Army reporting to C3I will consist of divisions, each of which has a specialty necessary to the overall goal.

COMMUNICATIONS GROUP

One of the most critical tasks is the creation of a system to fill the many communications needs of the Information Army. While planning will be required, there is nothing new to invent here. Run by the Communications Group, or "C Group," most communications can be done over the Global Network itself. Using the public phone networks for voice, fax, and data communications is inexpensive, reliable, and portable. The Information Warriors will supply the security and privacy with strong encryption and key management schemes available from tens of security products manufacturers. They may even build some of their own products to maintain as low a profile as possible.

The Information Warriors can even use the Global Network to achieve anonymity and privacy. They will be able to communicate just as tens of millions do every day, but with encrypted messages. Unless encryption is made illegal, such messaging techniques will be invisible. The use of secure private bulletin boards scattered among different locations will provide yet another method for communications, and will not raise anyone's suspicions.

Redundancy will be necessary; multiple communications routes will be made available in the event one is compromised or lost due to systems failures. Ham radio offers a portable means of backup communications in the event that the phones or the Global Network itself are the ultimate targets or if there is reason to suspect a security compromise. Headquarters will always need to be able to communicate with its troops. By the time the operation commences, the Information Army will have built its own virtual network, perhaps even using its target's communication systems as the initial underpinnings. C-Group will take advantage of Global Positioning Satellites (GPS) to track the locations and activities of the Information Warriors as a means of further control.

C-Group is intrinsically involved with the strategic planning that occurs within C3I Headquarters. Almost all members of C-Group must be trusted beyond reproach, as they must have a degree of understanding of the scope of their activities. To make interception and traffic analysis of their activities much more difficult, convoluted routing of communications paths all over the country and the world will require C-Group to be multinational. From the Information Warrior's standpoint, it's worth the extra effort: better safe than sorry.

MAPPERS

I call the mappers the navigators of Cyberspace. They will calculate and draw pictures of the Global Network to show how things are connected, graphically depicting how the telephone systems connect to each other and to the cellular networks and the satellite links. Some members will concentrate on how banks move money—the Federal Reserve System, the SWIFT network, the ATM networks. Other mappers will concentrate on the hundreds and hundreds of civilian and military networks that permit government to function. The mappers will organize a Rand McNally of Cyberspace, including insets and details, with the capability for zooming into areas of particular interest. They will map out how the Global Network connects to hospitals, doctors, insurance companies, and pharmacies through the medical databases. They will map out how Corporate America communicates with itself and with the rest of the world by navigating through the internal private networks of the country's biggest companies.

One of the mappers' most important functions is to designate, by location and type, the entrances and exits of each digital highway system. Not only will the mappers need to provide directions to a particular electronic neighborhood for other Information Warriors, but they will point out exactly where the doors are and where the escape routes lie. It's like having a street map with the addresses of each house, the names of each resident, and the kind of lock that each house uses to protect its assets.

Much of the information needed to build these maps will come from open source materials available to anyone for the asking. The telephone companies publish entirely too much private information for anyone's own good. The government, to support competition, openly publishes the designs for future networks. A mapper's job is never done.

CRACKERS

Once the mappers provide the addresses of the target, these guys will be responsible for breaking the locks on the electronic doors. The crackers will use a set of software tools for deciphering passwords, breaching operating system security, and building trap doors for future use. This group will not officially know that the mappers exist, but will rely upon their directions for Global Network navigation. They are to be as quiet and invisible as possible.

Once they gain entry into a system, they will want to install a door via a Trojan Horse program so that they can have access in the future, as occurred in the 1994 Internet security breaches. This is to be done as quickly as possible as the crackers want to raise no suspicion at all—if they do, the doors will be closed. In some cases, they may be given passwords or access codes to certain addresses, but they will not know that they came from their highly organized brethren, the sniffers.

SNIFFERS

Sniffers working in the Information Army will be broken into three groups. One group will concentrate on "sniffing the switch," looking for passwords, access methods, and security-related information that can then be provided to the crackers. They will gain access into the phone systems using information provided by the mappers and the crackers, then eavesdrop upon data traffic in search of even more access information.

The second group of sniffers will, from their terminals located anywhere in the world, travel the Global Network and capture as much sensitive and proprietary information as they can. Following the directions of the mappers and using the tools the cracker left behind, the sniffers will search for any information of value. They will sniff away on the LANs, WANs, MANs and every other network they can penetrate. They will capture and store satellite or microwave communications containing hundreds of conversations. They will accumulate, categorize, and store vast amounts of information that they themselves will probably never look at, much less analyze. That is left to another group altogether.

The third set of sniffers will function more like a military or paramilitary unit. They may need to install physical taps or eavesdropping equipment on selected targets where electronic access is insufficient. They may need to tap a phone or a fax, or use laser beams to read the vibrations on a window pane from a mile away. In conventional parlance, these guys would be regarded as the "black bag" sniffers, used where physical access to the targets is required.

READERS

The readers have a most interesting task. Their job is to listen to the emanations coming from computers and computer screens. Using the best van Eck detection equipment available, including real-time fast Fourier transform hardware chips, they will target businesses and industries in search of secrets. Since most people don't know their computers are transmitting information through the air, they are ripe to be plucked by the readers. Readers will also search powerlines and water lines for information that is proprietary, sensitive, and valuable.

SOFTWARE DEVELOPMENT GROUP

This team of engineers could come from former Iron Curtain countries, since there are plenty from whom to choose, and they could telecommute from home. Wherever they are based in the world, their task is to develop the software tools that the mappers and crackers use and that make the lives of the readers and the sniffers easier.

Some engineers will be experts in mainframes, some in minis, some in PCs, and others in communications. Their labs will be equipped with everything they need to get the job done. They will be able to duplicate a field condition as reported by the mapper or cracker, develop a reliable means to compromise it, and then deploy that software to their comrades. One group of engineers will develop malicious software—the

Trojan horses and worms and spoofing software that will be used by other divisions of the Information Army. A "virus factory" will develop self-replicating viral software. Others will develop software that can crash systems almost undetectably. This group's only goal will be to efficiently turn software-based technology against its owners.

MOLES

During the Cold War, the Russians placed their moles in England and the U.S., while we had our moles inside of Russian organizations. Industrial spies place moles within target companies. And so the Information Warrior will use moles as key agents in his master plan.

Moles are the inside agents of the Information Warrior. As insiders, they can deploy malicious software, garner confidential information from the target, or provide invaluable inside information in time of conflict to C3I. Some moles may only be security guards or delivery men who are given physical access to their bosses' confidential information. Moles are occasionally expandable, but in a well-run operation, they disappear at the right moment.

ANALYSTS

With endless streams of information pouring into headquarters, the top Information Warriors are going to need to have a method of organizing it into a useful form. As in any intelligence operation, the collected data is essentially useless until it is cataloged and cross-referenced. This is the analyst's job.

Information of immediate value—security information of worth to the crackers or the sniffers—will need to be quickly processed and distributed. Information to be used later, as a weapon, will need to be easily located and retrieved. The Information Warriors will want to have all this data at their fingertips.

The analysts will constantly massage the databases they create, probably using heuristic artificial intelligence techniques, and allow their team and C3I to examine it from different perspectives. They may identify the data by location, industry, or financial benefit. The information they analyze may force changes in the overall plans of the assault, but that is to be expected. None of the Information Warrior's plans are in concrete for Cyberspace is a breathing, dynamic place. Thus, they will make constant adjustments to meet their overall goals.

MANUFACTURING GROUP

The Information Warriors will need to build some of their own equipment in addition to buying what is available from retail sources. Quality van Eck radiation detectors will be manufactured in-house, to avoid raising suspicion by purchasing too many on the open market. Illegal cracker tools, if unattainable by scrounging through hacker bulletin boards, will also be built from scratch. If the plan calls for custom integrated chips built, they will be designed by chippers, in cooperation with the software development group. Chip manufacturing can be done by a silicon foundry in the Far East, where few questions are asked when cash is on the table.

SOFTWARE DISTRIBUTION GROUP

If C3I decides that massive PC and LAN failures are required, this can be accomplished by wide-spread distribution of malicious software. The Information Army will have sufficient resources to buy a legitimate software company with a reasonable market penetration for its products. Given the patience of the Information Warrior, he could take the time to build up the company by offering quality products at a low price and selling as many copies of the software as possible. Alternatively or in combination, a shareware company might be organized or purchased that would extensively distribute software through an apparently legitimate operation. What customers will not know, however, is that the software upon which they have come to rely has a ticking time bomb inside.

SHOOTERS

Shooters are the infantrymen of the Information Army. They are the ones who will use the HERF Guns to disable their adversary's systems. (Or, if the technology becomes more widely available, they may strategically place EMP/T Bombs for even greater damage.) Vans carrying HERF Guns can be rendered invisible with proper urban and suburban camouflage: people will not notice a repair truck that happens to have an antenna on its roof. The shooters will also have additional gear in their vehicle, perhaps legitimate broadcast or repair equipment in case of a casual look-see by law enforcement if stopped for a traffic violation. Since HERF Guns often look like a normal transmission setup, identification of their purpose would be most difficult. EMP/T bombs will be a bit more difficult to position but as the technology improves in quality and shrinks in size, a good sized canister of electronic equipment is pretty innocuous in appearance.

The shooters might use the same electromagnetic weapons against satellite communications systems, which would require more power and larger facilities, but the transmitting equipment could be located anywhere from the desert of the American West to the jungles of South America to tiny islands in the Caribbean.

Depending upon the ruthlessness of those at C3I, the shooters may or may not be told of the potential for collateral biological damage; a dose of electromagnetic energy might take out the shooter as well as his victim's information processing systems. The EMP/T bomb might be built to physically destroy itself with a conventional explosive after its initial detonation. The explosive is assumed to be the sole source of damage until the real effects are discovered. Forensics is a well-developed science and sooner or later the FBI will find out the bomb's real function, but the shooters will be long gone by then.

PUBLIC RELATIONS GROUP

I use this term loosely, for the Information Warriors do not have the best interests of the public at heart. For example, one PR effort might be to "turn" key employees at selected companies or agencies. If they need a mole or an insider, they may use embarrassing information as a weapon to accomplish that task. The fear of disclosure to one's company or family, to law enforcement, or even to the general public is plenty of motivation for an otherwise innocent individual to assist the Information Warriors. A cash incentive can be used if blackmail fails.

The disclosure of supposedly confidential information to the public is a very effective weapon for the Class 3 Information Warrior. If the private financial records of a high roller at an investment firm or bank is given to the *National Enquirer* or the *Wall Street Journal*, his entire company will certainly suffer. Imagine the effects of such a leak if used as a component of Class 3 Information Warfare. Alan Greenspan has stated that the private meetings of the Federal Reserve Board should not be made public; such disclosure could severely hurt the economy. That is just the sort of information that the Class 3 Information Warrior would like to use.

The PR crew will feed information to the press on a selective basis. After a few serious cyberevents, our experts might decide they should make an announcement to the media that our computers are being targeted and there's nothing we can do in defense. The widespread dissemination of such threats is a useful tool for the Information Warrior, especially if he can back up his claims with solid evidence or predictions of future events.

Public pronouncements will be tightly controlled by the Information Warriors. Perhaps they want to sway opinion against the banks, the government, or an entire industry. They will disseminate half-truths and distortions throughout the business world to further their goals. The Information Warriors will have collected substantial information, some of it very negative. If that data is released on company or agency letterhead, it will carry extra weight. Since they will be working by remote control over secured communications channels, detection will be most difficult, and the threats near anonymous. If the blackmail operation is carried out against a hundred or more private groups simultaneously, the Information Warrior might well succeed in tying up law enforcement resources for a very long time. There are only so many agents to go around and sooner or later they will be unable to address, much less solve, so many cases. The results might be considered humorous by the top dog Information Warriors at C3I. Law enforcement will have to pick and choose those cases for which they have the manpower, and ignore the others.

This is exactly the situation faced by the police in New York city when it comes to street crime. Mugged in Central Park? Fill out this form, but don't count on us finding the guy. Robbed of $100 at gunpoint? It's a waste of time, but here's the complaint form. The FBI does take blackmail and computer crime seriously, but in Cyberspace there will be little they can do to fight them if carried out on a wholesale level. For most victimized organizations, they will probably face the embarrassing likelihood of disclosure and have to live with the consequences, especially if the motives are not profit driven.

We have hypothesized an organization whose sole aim is to act as malevolently as possible towards its adversaries. In the case of Class 3 Information Warfare, the biggest adversary that they can come up against is the United States itself, by attacking our econotechnical information infrastructure.

At one point or another, the Information Warrior is going to have to land on the so-called beaches of Cyberspace and attack. When he attacks and in what manner is, of course, decided by C3I. Since we are addressing the vulnerability of the American econotechnical information infrastructure, let's take a bird's eye view of the possibilities. Remember, we are looking at the Big Picture.

DAY ONE

Day One will been preceded by lengthy planning and coordination. The moles will be in place. Substantial information will have been collected, organized, and distributed. The clandestine software will have been designed and distributed; the front companies will be in place and operational; the tools and weapons designed, built, tested, and deployed. The military goes through this exercise daily, and large companies adhere to a similarly well-thought out business plan. Class 3 Information Warriors are no different.

To have the greatest impact on the American economy and society, very specific targets will have been selected and their vulnerabilities found.

The three biggest financial targets in the United States are the Federal Reserve System, the Internal Revenue Service, and Wall Street. If any one of them suffers substantial damage, the effects will be felt in milliseconds, nationally and internationally. Individually, each of these could represent a computer Chernobyl. If all three are severely disrupted, the effects would be unlike any disaster we have never seen.

If *only* these institutions are hit, the impact would have immediate repercussions on our populace, and cause an instant decline in confidence in the financial underpinnings of our society. A run on the banks? Maybe. Will our international loans be called in? What will happen to interest rates? What about the International Monetary Fund?

For maximum effect, the Information Warrior will want to use the double (or triple) whammy. The moles will unleash the malicious software; the shooters will fire HERF Guns. The more widely the attack is distributed, against multiple locations, the more effective the results. The same double whammy will be applied to the other quarry of the Information Warriors. Our communications systems are so intertwined that bringing them all down at once is not likely, but strategic communications systems failures associated with the primary targets will further confuse any efforts at disaster control and recovery. By this time, every news network will have broken into the afternoon soap operas with a report and CNN will be covering events live. All we will know for sure is that something is terribly, terribly, wrong.

If the chippers have been able, for example, to place defective chips in late-model Chryslers, programming them to fail upon the reception of a specific radio frequencies, the electronic ignitions of hundreds of thousands of cars could all fail in a matter of hours. To add insult to injury, moles within the traffic control departments of major cities could instigate a major system-wide failure, turning every light green at the same time. Airports connected by ground-based communications systems would be crippled, in any case, the computer reservation systems for the big airlines would also be set to fail.

At this point, panic is spreading and Binary Schizophrenia is raging. The Information Warriors have struck the money, the communications, and the transportation industries. What's left of Wall Street is reeling, and the London and Tokyo markets have no idea how to react. Computers are failing everywhere. What next?

Bringing down the power companies' computers would further the Information Warrior's goal of fueling public panic and further shrouding his identity in mystery. If a nuclear plant were disrupted, our natural paranoia would be heightened, contributing to the feeling of helplessness. The broadcast networks who have been covering these events then find their feeds cut, their satellites jammed or non-functional. The "man in the street" loses his source of news, the comfort of being informed, the sense of community he gains from sitting in front of his global village hearth. Sitting in a veritable electronic black-out, he looks for those radio and cable stations that still can transmit.

Among the confusion, less noticeable victims are also under attack but with potentially deadly results. A few local hospitals lose power and computer controlled life-support systems fail. Software-driven 911 emergency systems are overloaded by an invisible enemy.

The experts are baffled and shaken, no one seems to know what to do, so survivalist adrenalin kicks in, tempers flare, and the fear of the unknown dominates the collective psyche. Stores are emptied as families stock up on the necessities for an emergency of unknown origin and indeterminate duration. It's every man for himself, except in New York where the bars are full of revelers remembering the last blackout or trying to relive Saint Patrick's Day.

Then comes the announcement.

The Information Warriors break into the communications networks that are still functioning. They spread their message all across the Global Network, via fax, and E-mail to every cybernaut in the world. They provide the media, the White House, and the Pentagon with their statement.

They announce that this is an attack against the United States of America—for reasons to be enunciated at their convenience—and this is only the beginning. They warn us that from now on, our computers are under attack. They can never again be trusted to work as expected. Baby Boomers will recall the television show "The Outer Limits:" "Your television is under our control. Do not attempt to adjust the dial. . . ."

From locations far away from the chaos, the Information Warriors will spell out what America can expect in the next week, month, or year. "Forget life as you know it. Things are going to be different for a while. We are in control." Their message will be clear and unmistakable. They are not going to let up their assault. They will continue until a) their demands are met, b) they feel like stopping, or c) every last one of them is dead. Not the kind of warm and fuzzy message we Americans want to hear.

When we repair the damage in one area, they will have

already struck somewhere else, and then they'll return to the first and strike again. They'll make perfectly clear that no person, no company, no government function is off limits. They'll tell us that we'll never know where or when or how the next victim will be hit, but rest assured it will happen. And, with appropriate arrogance, they'll deny that they can ever be caught. After all, they are hiding within the infinitely complex fabric of Cyberspace.

The big question will be, how do we respond?

17

Defense Before Defeat

"Why do today what you can put off till tomorrow."

—PROCRASTINATOR'S PLEDGE

"If we really, really, try, maybe we can ignore it."

—CUSTOMER SERVICE MOTTO

IF I'VE MADE IT sound like the Information Warrior has already won the war . . . well, that was not the intent. He hasn't won. Not yet. But he still *could* if our complacency remains as entrenched as it has been over the last decade and a half. The Information Warrior can be defeated if—and only if—we put our minds to it, and that will require a national effort like we have not seen in years.

We can defeat the Information Warrior. We can render his anti-social, anti-business, and anti-American endeavors futile, but it will take a serious effort on our part. The Information Warrior uses information as a weapon to further erode our personal privacy, and to gain competitive advantage. He uses our information infrastructure as a vehicle for and a target of his Information Weapons. But he can still be defeated.

Like any criminal, the Information Warrior is generally looking for an easy target. If he runs up against roadblocks, he will try to find another weakness until he gets what he wants. The Information Warrior will concentrate his efforts to find the one single weakness in our privacy or our information infra-structure that will permit him to widen the crack in the dike of

312

our defenses. We should expect no less from him because it is in his best interests to do so. He will not pummel his head against the protected walls of Cyberspace when he knows that another open entryway is beckoning him.

The technology, the techniques, and the tools exist to defend against and defeat the Information Warrior. A myriad of companies offer products to protect against viruses, hackers, modem attacks, HERF Guns, and all the other tools in the arsenal of the Information Warrior. Given that the technology exists to protect ourselves on a personal, corporate, and national level, we should try to understand why we remain defenseless. Why has so little been done, and why have the available defensive technologies not been deployed to the extent they should have?

Two reasons—apathy and arrogance.

There is no escaping this fact. After World War II a policy on military defense of the United States and Western Europe was created to reflect the New World Order of 1945. We established that policy to prepare for our adversaries' capabilities *not their presumed intentions*, and today, we must establish a policy to defend our Cyberspace against our adversaries' capabilities, both in the immediate future and for the long term. But both apathy and arrogance stand in the way. I fear that as a result, we will wait until a computer Chernobyl befalls us before we take the threat of Information Warfare seriously.

On a corporate and national level, the danger of procrastination is potentially very dangerous. Thurow writes, "In crisis (Pearl Harbor) or in situations which can be made to look like crisis (Sputnik), Americans respond magnificently. Clear problems (Sputnik, Iraq's invasion of Kuwait) get clear, clean, well managed solutions. America is capable of claiming the twenty-first century for itself. The American problem is not winning—but forcing itself to notice that the game has changed—that it will have to play a new game by new rules with new strategies."[1]

Historians claim that the devastation at Pearl Harbor in

1941 need never have occurred. They maintain that we received two warnings about an impending attack—one from the activities of the Japanese at their embassies and from radio interceptions of their military machine, the second from an experimental radar system that was being tested in the Pacific. The radar operator reported what appeared to him to be a number of aircraft coming our way. Somewhere in the command structure, though, the belief was that the new fangled radar contraption was not reliable. The brass assumed that the signals were caused by faulty equipment and chose to ignore the second warning.

The rest is history. But we're still not listening.

Procrastination is an addictive drug in which all but the Felix Ungers of the world indulge at one time or another. Incessant postponement catches up with us sooner or later, generally at a much higher personal or financial cost. Procrastination is not healthy for this country. Consider the costs:

- Environmental messes—land fills, nuclear waste dumps, a disappearing ozone layer—get messier every day
- Failing or weak S&Ls dig themselves deeper and deeper holes
- The national deficit is skyrocketing

Each problem we choose to ignore only ends up costing us more in the long run. We must not allow chaos in Cyberspace to be added to the list, not when we have before us a way to avoid the dangers and expenses of moving into Cyberspace unprepared.

Adequate defenses against every cyberthreat are available. Just as the technology for the offensive Information Warrior is cheap and readily available, so the defensive techniques are well known and available for the asking. Technology alone, however, will not solve the underlying ailments affecting our culture. Technology alone does not solve the issue of personal privacy; technology alone does not solve the problems and costs to this country caused by international industrial espionage; technology alone does not protect us from a malicious attack against the American economic infrastructure. What is needed, what is absolutely necessary is a national policy which acknowledges the threat to all of us—individually and as a nation—while mapping out a plan for action.

As the Clinton administration prepares to launch us further into the Information Age, with their proposed National Information Infrastructure, one key ingredient is missing: an understanding that such easy access to information can be either good *or* bad. When he was a Tennessee senator, Vice President Albert Gore advocated an electronic superhighway which would tie together more and more computers through faster and denser electronic networks. Those highways are fraught with risks, specifically those of security and privacy.

Having said that, I still believe the National Information Infrastructure is a good idea. We need to walk into Cyberspace with our eyes open. We need to balance pragmatism with our utopian visions. What we need, more than anything, is a National Information Policy, one that will offer America the chance to lead the world into the next century. A policy that will allow us to design our future, not be blindsided by it.

18

Outline of a National Information Policy: A Constitution for Cyberspace and an Electronic Bill of Rights

"in order to form a more perfect Union . . ."

—THE CONSTITUTION OF THE UNITED STATES OF AMERICA

"We remain unwilling to impose any discipline upon ourselves that demands a change in lifestyle."

—DAVID HALBERSTAM[1]

ON MAY 14, 1787, George Washington, James Madison, and Benjamin Franklin joined fifty-two other men representing twelve of the thirteen states to, in the words of Alexander Hamilton, "render the Constitution of the Federal Government." The Constitutional Convention met through September of that year, writing the instruction manual on how to run the United States of America.

Two hundred years ago, the world was a very different place. The war with England was over and the United States (plural) were preparing for peace. They needed to forge unity amongst themselves, establish the new country as a viable international partner, and build a strong defense for a secure future.

316

Weaknesses in the original Constitution (the Articles of Confederation) prompted the new nation's leaders to come to Philadelphia for four months of emotional debate. Their ultimate goal was a Constitution which would reflect a balance between monarchy and democracy. Despite vast differences among the participants and their views on how to fashion a new nation, they succeeded at their task. Signed by only thirty-nine of the original fifty-five delegates, the Constitution of the United States became the supreme law of the land on June 21, 1788, with its ratification by nine of the thirteen states. Due to deficiencies in state and individual rights, the First Congress submitted twelve amendments to the Constitution to the states in 1789. The ten surviving amendments, known as the Bill of Rights, are viewed as the ultimate safeguards of our personal freedom and liberty, perhaps even more so than the original body of the Constitution itself.

These two documents, The Constitution and the Bill of Rights, have carried this nation forward for over two hundred years and have suffered only seventeen changes. Today, however, we see that our national migration into Cyberspace represents such a fundamental change in our national character that the existing tentacles of laws and legislation are not automatically sufficient. The United States again finds itself at a crossroads.

The Constitution was written for and by an agrarian society that relied upon oil for lamps, manual looms for clothes, and horses and sails for transportation. It was written at a time when loading a musket took the better part of a minute and communications could take days or weeks, not fractions of a second. The Constitution was written to establish a new nation on Earth (a physical place that can be found on a map), not in Cyberspace (a virtual intangible place, the borders of which defy conventional cartography). The framers provided the means to amend the Constitution as needed, but they could never have imagined the technolgocial advancements of today's world.

Thomas Jefferson wisely recognized that fact. He wrote,

I am not an advocate for frequent changes in laws and constitutions, but law and institutions must go hand in hand with the progress of the human mind. As that becomes more developed, more enlightened, as new discoveries are made, new truths discovered, and manners and opinons change, with the advance of circumstances, institutions must advance also to keep pace with the times. We might as well require a man to wear still the coat that fitted him when a boy as civilized society to remain under the regimen of their barbarous ancestors.[2]

In Jefferson's day, the Constitution provided a workable alternative to anarchy, but as every day passes, we find that we are outgrowing our country's overcoat as we become the first nation to move into Cyberspace. The world is a very different place from the one in which this country was founded over two hundred years ago.

The fundamental concepts of a real place versus a virtual place are profoundly different. Two hundred years ago people lived in a tangible world, where they could touch and feel their property and money. Today, we trust that the computer has got it all straight. Two hundred years ago ownership meant physical possession: a man's property could be measured between sticks in the ground. Today, possession of financial wealth is determined by reliable electron excitation, ownership has become a quantum uncertainty, and place is as untouchable as Alice's netherworld. You will never be able to drive a car down the information highway!

Cyberspace just doesn't accommodate many of the existing models we have generated to run modern society for two centuries. Can the traffic rules from horse and buggy days be applied to a high speed interstate system or to urban congestion? Do the procedures of the old Pony Express have any real applicability to a modern postal service that delivers nearly 200 billion pieces of mail each year? Can the rules of a preindustrial agrarian society be reasonably expected to fill the needs of a postindustrial society in which information is the prime commodity of value? Stretching existing laws and judicial interpretation through awkward convolutions hasn't worked. Some fundamental changes are called for.

We find ourselves in a position similar to our ancestors, who wanted to create a model for the future success of the newly established country. It is now time to build a policy for *our* time in history; to establish rules and guidelines that are congruous with the fabric of Cyberspace. The United States has always met the challenges before it, and we are today presented with unprecedented opportunity, to, as Richard Nixon might say, "seize the moment." Standing before us is the opportunity to lead our nation, and perhaps the world, into an era of success, achievement, benevolence, and greater prosperity than civilization has ever seen.

Our ancestors brought harmony and cohesion to peoples whose only unifying bonds may have been their hatred for England, but they succeeded. Just as they found the courage and farsightedness to negotiate and compromise and balance issues of their day, we must find it within ourselves to recognize that we have a tiger of unprecedented size by the tail and that it needs taming. We must identify and concentrate upon our common interests while minimizing our dissimilarities. We are all in this together. This book has already outlined the risks of standing on the sidelines and permitting unbridled electronic anarchy. The foundation for our rapidly evolving information-based society must be a framework of precepts, concepts, and guidelines by which we will define our mores, our behavior, and our life in Cyberspace.

That framework is a National Information Policy.

A National Information Policy must provide the ground rules for living in Cyberspace, and how we plan on dealing with other peoples and countries when we meet them there. It must outline the reasons for its own existence and establish our identity as constructive members of the global community. It must be as flexible as our Constitution, so that it can guide us through this country's second two hundred years—and beyond.

A National Information Policy must be able to tell us why we are building a National Information Infrastructure and how we will operate it. Today the motto of those building the NII is, "It we build it, they will come." We cannot afford to allow the future of our country to remain a field of unsubstantial dreams.

The following outline of a National Information Policy is not a proposed legislative document; it is not to be construed as a contract, a law, or a set of specific rules. It is meant to call attention to a set of critical issues that must be resolved and agreed upon to provide freedom, growth, reward, security, and privacy for those who choose to live and work in Cyberspace. With luck, the following outline will be a call to action for citizens, industry, and government to jointly tackle critical national issues, strip away partisanism, and implement a shared vision of a bright American future. The task ahead of us is difficult, but it is a task we cannot shirk, for if we do nothing, the United States will stagnate into a second class nation and we will have only ourselves to blame.

Outline of a National Information Policy

None of the issues that must be considered in the formulation of a National Information Policy stands alone. Each is intertwined with the others; the Hindus would say they are "karmically related." We begin with some fundamental questions now being discussed on the Global Network, within the government, throughout the business world and, more and more, in our homes. There are no right answers—not yet. But as you think about these topics, you will soon have a better understanding of just how interrelated Cyberspace and our society really are.

WHAT IS INFORMATION?

When I ask this question in a room of a hundred people, I usually receive two hundred different answers! This simple question, more than any other, underscores the need for a workable definition by which we can begin to construct a National Information Policy.

We tend to make distinctions between *data, information,* and *knowledge. Data* are individual facts or statistics in a raw and uncorrelated state. Data require organization for them to have value, at which time they become *information.* The telephone book represents a huge amount of data that have been organized in such a way that information is conveyed to the reader. Endless streams of letters and numbers represent data, but properly organized, they become words and sentences that convey information, even knowledge. *Knowledge* is the smarts behind the information. Knowledge requires the assimilation of information by the human mind: only then can it be put to use.

For purposes of a National Information Policy, no clear lines of demarcation exist between data, information, and knowledge. What are useless data to you may be invaluable information to me. For the purposes of this discussion, we can ignore any of the subjective values and limits that we might place upon these nomenclature. We will use the term "information" to refer to any sort of data, regardless of any real or perceived appraisal.

In the physical world, information is communicated by hard copy (stone, papyrus, Bic pen on paper, the printing press), or word of mouth. (Granted, some cultures use drums or horns to communicate and others rely on smoke signals, but these have never been a viable alternative for an advanced society.) We have come to respect information in written form, or in the broadcast media. The phrase "put it in writing" still carries undeniable strength. We are conditioned to prefer information that is stored and transported in physical form. As humans, we like to flip through the *TV Guide* or *Cosmo* or newspapers and clip out items of interest. We like word-of-mouth transmissions. We like rumor and innuendo and contributing to the flow of information; these attributes are . . . so human.

Before Cyberspace, word-of-mouth communication limited the size of your audience and was determined by how loud you could yell. Before the radio, the telephone, and the phonograph, word-of-mouth was a slow process. Information was transferred primarily by physical exchanges between people. Either they spoke to each other in person or exchanged physical objects such as letters or photographs that stored the information in a people-friendly way. With the introduction of Cyberspace, this limitation disappeared.

If I copy information from your computer or eavesdrop upon your electronic conversations, have I actually stolen something from you? You still have the information, don't you? Haven't I just borrowed it? Information doesn't have the luxury of being measured in pounds and ounces, or feet and inches; its very nature—intangibility—lends its existence an abstract quality.

Intangible information assets maintain an awkward legal status, if we use concrete assets as the only point of reference. Prosecutors may charge a suspect with interstate theft, thus making it a Federal offense, although the stolen items were only strings of 1s and 0s from a distant computer. On appeal, Federal judges may overturn the conviction due to confusion over the legal status of information; prosecutors having based their cases on ill-fitting laws. Without a working definition of information as it exists and behaves in Cyberspace, progress is constrained by eighteenth-century paradigms.

Information must be defined for it to exist independently within the constructs of the legislative and judicial systems. People have a defined legal status, and so do corporations, sole proprietorships, limited partnerships, and street vendors. Cars have a legal status, as do houses, boats, television sets, furniture, and other concrete, tangible assets. You can mortgage a house or repossess a car—you can't do that with information. Information, as a raw commodity, has no agreed-upon legal status.

One of the first goals of National Information Policy is to

establish information as a distinct, definable construct by which we can start to quantize our life in Cyberspace.

INFORMATION EVALUATION

Information Is drastically different from conventional physical assets in two ways:

1. Information is the only asset that can exist in two places at once. If I had a quarter and gave it to you, I would no longer have it. If I had information, though, and then gave it to you, we would both have it. Does that double its value? Or is it worth only half of its original value? In Cyberspace, the answer is yes to both.
2. The value of information is not predictable in time. Information is entropic: that which is of incredible value today may shrivel to worthlessness overnight. Or information may only be of value as long as few people have it, and as soon as it's widely available, its value sinks. That's why secrets cost so much. Information is also antientropic. It can grow in value independent of any additional input; an idea "before its time" my be worth a fortune a year or decade hence, but that value cannot be predicted.

Information has intrinsic value, otherwise there's no point in having it; measuring the value of information against other assets is the problem. Information tends to fit into the barter system quite well, where the laws of supply and demand fluctuate as much with the individual as with real-world events. If I know something I don't care about and you'd give your eye-teeth to know, the value of the information is high for you and low for me. Likewise if you knew something that I desperately needed to know, we might have reason to trade— thus creating value. To each of us alone there was no value in the information we possessed. The value only became real when we recognized each other's needs.

These complexities make information valuation a cumbersome guessercise, but recent advances have refined the process. By making reasonable assumptions, a baseline of information worth can be established and then plotted over time. One of the measures used in appraising information is the cost of acquiring the information. A research and development or engineering facility will properly evaluate its proprietary information—the result of extensive, costly, and time consuming research—to be of higher worth than simple data compiled and entered into a computer by a clerk.

Another measure is the cost to the company or individual if the information is lost. If previously private information is suddenly made generally available, how much loss would be incurred in terms of sales, profits, negotiation, or—in the worst case—lives? When one car company had its new designs stolen, its loss was internally estimated at $500 million. Is that a real number that can be proved, or it an ersatz claim based upon unreal assumptions? Bell South claimed that Craig Neidorf, hacker and underground publisher of *Phrack*, released internal company documents worth tens of thousands of dollars. It was later discovered that Bell South had sold the same information for only a few dollars. Needless to say, the Federal prosecutors had egg on their faces when they dropped the charges against Neidorf.

Have you ever seen a balance sheet or a financial statement that included a line item called "information assets?" The depreciated value of real estate, computers, and furniture is accounted for, but information is still an intangible hidden asset. Does the information have value? Of course it does. The success of companies and the government is largely dependent upon the existence, availability, integrity, and privacy of that information. But how do we quantify its value?

In more and more companies, information has become its single greatest asset. Software companies and financial organizations are typically information-asset-intensive based firms. What happens, then, if a company included information assets as a line item in their ledgers? Does the value of the company suddenly skyrocket because they changed their accounting methods? Or would adding information assets cause other assets to suddenly depreciate because the company's value must be constant from one system of evaluation to the other?

According to Peter Drucker, "we need an economic theory that puts knowledge into the center of the wealth-producing process."[3] Maybe we've been measuring modern information-based companies' values with a system incapable of fitting the new business models. We now need an alternative model for an evolved form of our particular brand of capitalism; one that would prove superior to our current model and that of our competitors.

The downside to itemizing information assets would mean an increasing number of lawyers laying in wait. Corporate assets must be carefully protected, and those include information assets. But unlike physical assets that can be protected with walls, fences, and locks, protecting information assets can be as frustrating as nailing Jello to the wall. So if information assets are accounted for separately, any breakdown in the information infrastructure of that company is like a holding up a "lawsuit" magnet and pointing it at the courthouse.

The idea of information insurance is not new, but it's a very complicated issue. Limited types of Cyberspace insurance are available: a simple example is the long-distance carriers, which offer insurance against phone fraud and telabuse. Insurance is occasionally available against computer viruses, but the payoffs are minimal, assuming that the lost information can be recreated. This approach evaluates information's worth only in terms of the cost of data entry.

A National Information Policy should encourage the development of a method by which information can be quantitatively measured. No one technique will fill all private, business, and governmental needs, but in lieu of the present arbitrary capriciousness, we must at least agree upon a minimum baseline for reference, while leaving plenty of room for sub-jective flexibility.

WHO OWNS INFORMATION?

When I asked this question of a group of lawyers, there were a lot of coughs and stammering attempts to answers, but there was little confidence behind their theories. The argu-ment "possession is nine-tenths of the law" suddenly has no real meaning if a hundred people can possess the exact same information.

A useful parallel can be drawn to copyright law. The Software Publishers Association vigorously pursues copyright infringements and software piracy violations based upon intellectual property ownership, as established by copyright and patent laws. On one hand, copyright law in the United States and other technical societies is clear and reasonably enforceable; one of the biggest issues we face is bringing the international community into conformance with our standard. On the other hand, we are culturally trained to look the other way with copyrights; software, music, television programs, and movies can be copied at the push of a button. Copyright laws were written before even the xerox machine was in-vented. What changes must we make to protect information authorship and ownership in the Information Age?

The ownership of information is a tricky issue, dependent upon the rules we choose to follow. Consider:

1. Who owns the electronic mail you generate at the office? Courts have ruled that Government E-mail is owned by the American people, even if it's personal. Does or should this argument hold true to the private sector?
2. If I post an electronic message on a BBS, does the message go into the public domain or do I still own that information? Can someone else copy and distribute it without consulting or possibly paying me?

3. Can information ownership be established with an electronic copyright for Cyberspace?
4. How do we distinguish between raw data available in the public domain and "value added" information, organized into a usable, useful form? Who owns that information?
5. What does "public domain" *mean* on the Global Network? Does public domain apply to America only, or does it have significance around the world, too?
6. Who owns your name, address, and social security number?

Understanding the nature of information ownership will be a necessary cornerstone of a National Information Policy. The goal is to develop a consistent set of guidelines that our social, political, and legal systems can interpret and apply consistently throughout Cyberspace.

AMERICAN CYBERSPACE

When we speak of the Global Network, a picture may come to mind of a globe whose surface is blanketed with gossamer threads connecting every city and village. Techno-purists feel that Cyberspace is borderless; there are no national or regional boundaries to inhibit anyone from communicating with anyone by phone, across the network, or across the universe. And from one perspective we must agree: If Cyberspace is "that place in between" the phones or the computers, then there are no borders. As we electronically project our essences across the network, we become temporary citizens of Cyberspace, just like our fellow cybernauts. By exclusively accepting this view, however, we limit our ability to create effective national information policies and to define the economic security interests of our country.

Think of Cyberspace for a moment as being divided into groups of local or regional cyberspace—hundreds and millions of smaller cyberspaces all over the world. These smaller cyberspaces are capable of functioning independently of one another. A small office LAN or a huge company's telephone and communications network are simply smaller independent cyberspaces.

Let's conjecture. If there were only two computers in the whole world, Cyberspace would consist entirely and solely within the connection between those two machines. If there were only one computer network in the universe that network would actually *be* Cyberspace. So we could say that there is an IBM cyberspace, a Hughes cyberspace, and an undoubtedly huge Microsoft cyberspace each connected to millions of other cyberspaces through the Global Network. Taken one step further, when we use our PC, we could be said to be entering our personal cyberspace. It's not about size or distance; it's about an essence. Following this line of reasoning, Cyberspace becomes a bit easier to visualize and manage.

Connecting the countless local and personal cyberspaces are the world's communications networks: think of the wires, fibers, and microwave and satellite transmissions as information highways with off-ramps leading to lots of little towns, cities, and neighborhoods. Connecting one cyberspace to another cyberspace is no more complicated than opening a door, and that concept can help us establish the borders of smaller cyberspaces when we begin formulating a National Information Policy.

If my computer calls yours, then I am electronically knocking on the door of your personal cyberspace. You may not answer the door, you might tell me you're busy and ask me come back later, or you might let me in. In that case, you and I are now in *our* cyberspace—the amalgam of our two computers and their connections. If we meet on the Internet, our discourse might be seen as the modern equivalent of an eighteenth-century town meeting in a public square—the Speaker's Corner of Cyberspace. Taking this somewhat simplistic approach gives us an advantage that we otherwise might have missed: we can assign familiar physical concepts to cyberspaces. Cyberspaces have doors that will either open or remain closed when electronically approached from afar; or the doors are unlocked from within providing an open invitation for discourse. One could argue that the same paradigm will work on a larger scale. Big companies have big networks with doors that regulate entry to big "C" Cyberspace.

On a bigger scale yet, our model suggests that American cyberspace can be distinguished from French cyberspace, which can be distinguished from Russian cyberspace. The doors to American cyberspace can be said to be located on those information systems physically located on U.S. soil. The German with whom I correspond enters American cyberspace when he and I converse, just as I enter German cyberspace because his personal cyberspace is located in that country.

The two major constituents of Cyberspace are:

1. Personal, corporate, or organizational ("small-c") cyberspaces. The doors to these cyberspaces are the electronic borders by which we can specify the location of an individual cyberspace. The doors of these cyberspaces open up onto the information highways.
2. The information highways and communications systems, including the National Information Infrastructure. These are the threads that, tied together, make ("big-C"). Cyberspace. The service providers—those who hang the wires, lay the cables, and launch the satellites—do not contribute to the content of messages or affect the value of the information as it moves down the road. They're not supposed to; their job is get information accurately moved from a door in one cyberspace to a door in another cyberspace, with no changes.

These definitions are not intended to detract from the perception of Cyberspace as a nonphysical place where one can find freedom and escape. I believe that both views can successfully co-exist much as the same glass can be half full and half empty at the same time. It just depends what we're looking for and how we look at it.

By working with this approach and being able to localize and identify the components of Cyberspace, a National Information Policy becomes a more accessible goal.

FEDERAL VERSUS STATE CYBERSPACE

A National Information Policy must be national in scope and applicability. Any other approach is insane.

When the Constitution was framed during the summer of 1787, the most heated debates involved "States' rights." The Federalists favored a strong central government while their Anti-Federalist opponents argued for greater state autonomy. This fundamental question—to what extent do the states have the right to govern themselves without Federal interference?—also brought us the Civil War. We still see this debate raised again and again, most visibly in the last decade with the hotly contested question of abortion. Typically if a law is broken within the borders of a state, that individual state has jurisdiction: its law enforcement will investigate and make arrests, and then its court system will try the case.

However, if a crime involves crossing state lines, federal laws come into play and the FBI or other appropriate agencies step in. Some cooperation may exist between the state and federal levels, but efficiency is often sacrificed to overlapping authority and competition among law enforcement agencies. In other cases, the federal government has reserved jurisdiction over certain crimes—such as kidnapping and counterfeiting—for itself.

Cyberspace makes jurisdictional distinction all the more difficult. If a computer crime or phone fraud occurs entirely within one state, the situation is clear: local laws and procedures are followed. But let's say that my computer invades your cyberspace without invitation, and that damage occurs as a result. If I connected to your cyberspace through the National Information Infrastructure, my connections might have taken me through six other states. If I steal information from your company's computers, who has jurisdiction?

Conventional wisdom says that because the stolen information crossed state lines it becomes a Federal case. But the local state prosecutors on both ends might also want control. The issue of jurisdiction becomes a tangled political mess, all because we don't yet have rules that apply to Cyberspace.

The National Information Policy must address the confusions and ineffectual processes of the existing system. All fifty states have their own computer crime laws—fifty different sets of rules applied to American Cyberspace. A centralized set of computer crime laws must establish guidelines for jurisdiction and have the authority to work across state lines or within the states themselves. States now have the right to adapt certain federal laws and prosecute locally; the National Information Policy must provide the federal and state governments the ability to enforce whatever rules are decided upon in an egalitarian manner.

The rules of behavior for Cyberspace must be fair, but more importantly, they must be evenly enforced because of the very nature of the medium. Otherwise, when I travel with my computer I am subject to one set of rules in New York, another in Florida, yet another in California, and so it goes forty-seven more states. "Ignorance of the law is no excuse" is the awkward legal precept governing a motley-ruled Cyberspace: no one can follow dozens and dozens of interrelating and contradictory laws—including lawyers and prosecutors.

Let's look at another example: If I have a telephone conversation with someone from another state, do I have the right to record that conversation? In many states, there is a provision called the one-party consent rule which says that as long as one person is privy to the taping (in this case, me), then it's OK. The intent here is to keep third parties from taping or eavesdropping upon conversations to which they are not a party. When I called my local state attorney and asked my question, he didn't know the answer even after a couple of days of research. "Too complicated," his office said. I then called the U.S. Attorney in my area and asked him the same question, and he, too, had no certain answer. He said, "That's what the courts are for." I spoke to a friend in the Justice Department in Washington and he wasn't sure if *anyone* really knew the rules.

So I then called a telecommunications lawyer. He began to spout off a series of state and federal statutes, but even as he explained them, he realized that they just didn't make sense. He referred me to a law firm in Washington, D.C. specializing in the area of communications law. One of the partners in this law firm described to me the confusing maze of old laws, conflicting new laws, contradictory state laws, and more amended laws, some criminal statutes, and some civil. Even he admitted, "I agree this makes no sense."

I further complicated the original question with others:

1. If I tape a phone conversation in a state with a one-party consent rule and both parties are physically located within that state at the time, but the connection between us is routed through a central switch in another state without the consent rule, which rules apply?

2. What happens if I replace the telephone with a computer, and I am having a real-time electronic conversation with another cybernaut. I save the entire conversation to disk. Do the same telephone-instrument rules apply? Is such recording only legal if we meet in a designated electronic town forum? From the Justice Department and from the lawyers, the answer was the same: we need new laws to meet the needs of Cyberspace. Jim Settles, an FBI agent with the National Computer Crime Squad, was surprisingly honest when he said, "The judicial system is in the dark ages when it comes to the information age."[4] We know how to handle a thief who steals a piece of paper with valuable information. We have a reasonable idea of how to deal with a stolen diskette with information on it. But we start getting vague when we have to figure out the implications for the theft of transitory data traveling down a wire or through the air.

This piece of the National Information Policy should be easy to construct. It requires a common sense approach—there is no magic here—and the establishment of rules that facilitate the goals of the National Information Infrastructure. We need the consensus of all parties—individuals, businesses, and government—who are willing to put aside old values and preconceptions and replace them with the realities of a virtual world.

WHO OUGHT TO BE RUNNING CYBERSPACE—IF ANYONE?

One answer of course is to leave well enough alone and hope for the best; to hope that, over time, the needed policies, rules, guidelines, and mores will somehow successfully assemble themselves into a workable solution, while we suffer minimal disruption or damage in the process. I think not—too much is at stake.

Cyberspace offers an infinite amount of opportunities, and the desire for control over the new highways is measured in the hundreds of billions of dollars. The U.S. information industries are, more than ever before, expanding into Third World countries with an eye towards the huge profits that will come from dominating markets with billions of potential customers. Domestically, the cable companies, phone companies, and entertainment industries are forging unprecedented alliances to build competing spheres of influence and control over their pieces of Cyberspace.

But the government has a word in all of this, too. The Federal Communications Commission sits at the heart of the debates when the Regional Bell Operating Companies fight the cable companies for control of the high-speed information highway off-ramps that will enter your home and business. Ostensibly they represent government control over the airwaves and communications networks, but as the myriad issues overlap into undecipherably complicated consequences and unanswered questions, a centralized government-only authority can be called into question.

The government is moving into Cyberspace in a big way and has legitimate concerns—from national security to import/export to insuring that sheer chaos won't reign on the information highways. Federal, state, and local governing agencies need to have a voice in settling and inhabiting Cyberspace. Historically, however, government and business are at odds, each looking at the other as a hindrance rather than a partner.

With no National Information Policy in place, everyone is scrambling for economic and political gain instead of considering the good of the country, its security, and best interest of its citizens. That shortsightedness and greed needs to be replaced with a national consensus. I do not believe, however, that the care and feeding of the National Information Infrastructure (NII) and control over its socioeconomic ramifications should sit exclusively with either the Federal government or the business community. It just won't work that way any more.

It has been suggested by Washington insiders that the Vice President or other high-level official be named the country's Chief Information Officer to oversee the NII. What they don't see is that business will simply not tolerate a politically-based scheme. There needs to be a much broader-based representation of interests for any effort to be successful. Look what happened when the administration dropped the Clipper Chip bomb on an unsuspecting American information industry.

The answer may lie in the creation of a policy making and advisory organization that more closely resembles the function and form of the Federal Reserve Board. Therein the government and major banking concerns work in concert to manage U.S. monetary policy, consult with the international financial community, and try to keep our fiscal affairs in order. Surely, we can achieve similar compromises between government and business in the management of Cyberspace. A National Information Policy Board would exist to manage the formulation and enforcement of the National Information Policy, as well as the growth of the National Information Infrastructure. We have only scratched the surface of what a

National Information Policy should include to guide and protect us as we enter this brave new world.

IS INFORMATION A STRATEGIC ASSET OF THE UNITED STATES?

If we say, "No, information has no value," then this discussion is over. But, as we all realize, information is of critical importance to this country, as it is to other advanced industrial/information-based societies and even to emerging countries in the Third World. At the core of the National Information Policy must be a recognition of the importance of information to our political and economic future.

We must ask ourselves some tough questions. Our answers will be instrumental in determining the destiny of this country.

Is a U.S. industrial secret (e.g., a chemical formula, a new core technology, new software) today's equivalent of a military secret? I suggest that, yes, major industrial advances are national economic security assets that, if lost, would negatively impact the growth of the United States, its economy, it's global competitiveness, and the interests of its citizens and workers. If 3M invents a new barnacle glue worth a couple of billion in sales and the manufacturing details are stolen, the return on 3M's investment is diminished. They will earn less in profits, pay less in taxes, and possibly need to layoff workers or initiate a hiring freeze. Such a theft is an attack against the interests of the United States and we need to build our National Information Policy to reflect this truism in the Age of Information.

In days bygone, the Federal government was mostly interested in keeping atomic and related military technology out of foreign hands. The loss of commercial, nonmilitary information has been ignored at the federal level for fifty years, but times have changed. The concept of "federal interest" computers (à la the phone company and banking systems) has entered the lexicon of modern law. For each billion dollars in lost sales or revenues, thirty thousand fewer people can go to work each day and support their families, suggesting that every job lost due to foreign economic espionage is indeed an attack against American interests. For example, as previously shown, the French government, in its pursuit of economic intelligence to enhance their economy, has engaged in industrial espionage for years. Under a new model encompassing Cyberspace, would a French-sponsored attack against our national economic interests—in this case via Cyberspace—be considered an act of aggression? Not in the military sense, but certainly if they take a vital piece of information from us that act should be considered aggressive. The question that follows then is, "What is or should our reaction be?"

"Oh, that's OK guys. We know your economy needed a boost; the information's on us." Not in my way of thinking. Despite the fact that we are military allies of the French, does that give them the right to take what they please? Does it mean we should close our eyes, or wink, calmly ignoring our losses?

Since the fall of the Berlin Wall and the end of Soviet Empire, the United Nations has turned to economic sanctions as a method of coercing belligerent or non-compliant members into behaving. If the French, Israelis, Germans, or Japanese attack our national economic security via information-based interests, a National Information Policy should provide us with a range of possible responses. Economic sanctions? Information isolation? Or perhaps we should deploy an elite, rapid-response SWAT team to extract equal economic/information benefits in response? After all, cheating is par for the course in international economic competition.

Whatever response we choose, will we treat all infractions the same? And what if the attack or theft was not sponsored by a recognized country, but by a political faction or a terrorist group?

Would we react differently if the foreign country, instead of stealing information, disabled our information services? Perhaps a terrorist group, for whatever reason, shuts down a piece of American Cyberspace: a metropolitan telephone switch, an airline's computers, a nuclear power plant's control systems, or even part of the Federal Reserve System. How do we define nonmilitary aggression in the New World Order? Is *this* the price of freedom?

The National Information Policy will need to recognize information as a strategic national asset and we must have clear-cut mechanisms on the local, state, and federal levels by which we can protect ourselves from aggression by Information Warriors. Government and business must develop bonds, based upon their common interests. Anything other than a proactive approach is sheer folly, and a recipe for failure.

SHOULD WE SPY ON THE WORLD?

After all, they're doing it to us. Incidents of foreign-sponsored proprietary business information theft are up 400% since 1985. Shouldn't we try to level the playing field and do a little industrial and economic spying of our own? There are plenty of good secrets inside Japan and Germany and France which would help our industries become globally competitive. What designs for next generation chips will the *keiretsu* spring on the world? How about pharmaceutical formulas from Europe. Or maybe we want to know in advance what the Bundesbank is thinking and planning to do about fiscal policy? It's only fair . . . or is it?

One school of thought says, absolutely! It's spy versus spy versus spy and we ought to play harder. The post-Cold War U.S. intelligence community has the ability and our country should receive additional value from the $30 billion we give them every year in black budgets. We should employ the intelligence expertise and highly-advanced technology we used against the Soviets and apply it to U.S. global economic competitiveness. The extraordinary eavesdropping capabilities of the NSA and CIA could provide American industry with blow-by-blow accounts of every business development, political whisper, or economic ripple anywhere on the planet. Perhaps we might choose to turn the ears of the American intelligence apparatus towards our global trading partners and competitors to enhance our negotiating position. Whoever the object of interest, we would have special access to their secrets.

But, wait! That's cheating, and we can't announce to the world that we're resorting to their tactics. This school of thought suggests that the American image as "good guy" would suffer if we announced that we planned on cheating, too. "We're the good guys, and we have to play by the rules." The question is, which rules?

The international political fall-out from such an openly contentious position might interfere with the military and economic influence we now wield on the world stage. Besides, this group argues, how are we going to divvy up the information to industry when it's collected? Sell it? Publish it? Give it to big companies? Defense companies? Politically correct companies? Today, no one answer is right.

The CIA and their brethren are reluctant to supply information outside of their top-secret cliques. Their rationale is that the very nature of the gathered information would give away how it was acquired in the first place, and that might interrupt an operation or endanger a man's life. So they classify the heck out of everything that comes across their desks. No one ever went to jail for overclassifying information, but underclassification could be viewed as treason.

And then we have to recognize a potential dealbreaker: Spies are prepared to put their lives on the line for their country, but they may not be willing to risk it all for IBM or General Motors. Perhaps information gathered in the normal course of spying could be given to industry; or only information with military value. In February 1992, CIA Director James Woolsey put forth such possibilities to Congress during his confirmation hearings.[6] In a world where the theft of information is regarded as an investment, how can we balance the scales, and still be the good guys?

So, it sounds like it's OK for the little guys to pick on the big guys with industrial espionage and similar high-tech hi-jinx, but it's not cricket to spy back. Under this line of reasoning, that's the handicap we choose to suffer.

But a third school of thought finds answers within the very fabric and existence of Cyberspace itself. Its propenents point out that information is an almost inexhaustible resource and that the Global Network if properly tapped, can provide our intelligence services and industry with most of what they need to make decisions.

Robert Steele spent eighteen years in intelligence, including service as deputy director of the U.S. Marine Corps Intelligence Center. As president of Open Source Solutions, a nonprofit educational clearinghouse, he argues for a realignment of the intelligence community to better meet America's military and economic needs. Steele maintains, with highly visible support, that nearly 80 percent of the information the government considers classified is available to anyone for the asking. Why should the DEA have to contact the Defense Mapping Agency or the National Reconnaissance Office for a highly-classified, satellite-imaged map of Cali, Colombia when they can get a perfectly good map from the tourist board? Or why run to the NSA for information on Tempest busting, when a publicly available BBC tape or hacker magazine tells all? Steele argues that the intelligence community could do a much better job for less money, and with less danger, if it spent its energies on collecting open-source information and turning that information into knowledge.

His concept of a National Knowledge Strategy promotes an open cooperativeness—a virtual national intelligence organization—involving industry and the intelligence community. This noncentral intelligence agency would focus on open-source data collection, storage, organization, and dissemination to industry—all without political risk. Steele says the first nation to implement an intelligence mechanism of this type "will achieve enormous competitive advantage as we enter the Age of Information."[7] Japan has already started down this road and the U.S. is going to have to play catch up.

The intelligence community can be of enormous benefit to

the economic national security of the United States, and a National Information Policy should outline their new role. Their expertise, advice, and methods can help protect our U.S. industrial and economic secrets from the Information Warriors as well as assist the private sector in establishing its own private spy organizations.

THE MILITARY IN CYBERSPACE

The military has the budget, manpower, and technology to do just about anything it wants. The Pentagon has spent hand-somely to develop information weapons for use in military conflicts. Are there other nonmilitary uses for these weapons, uses that can benefit our economic national security?

As an alternative to actual conflict with an adversary, could we lob EMP/T bombs at them? We could render electronically-detonated weapons impotent in mere microseconds, disrupt their communications networks. What about knocking out a satellite's transponders? Perhaps sufficiently disrupting an adversary's ability to run a war would obviate the need for bloodshed.

The military could make an adversary wake up and pay attention by shutting down their military or industrial infra-structure as an alternative to, or in combination with, block-ades and embargoes. Whether or not a cyberassault on a foreign country is an act of war will be considered on the international stage. In the meantime, in the formation of a National Information Policy, we should keep our options open.

What should the penalties be for domestic spying on economic national security interests? Is the current slap on the wrist enough to deter theft as a low-cost high-return means of investment, or should the penalties be stern enough to abate espionage? Or don't we have the political will to decide?

Should foreign countries and citizens have access to tax-payers-subsidized U.S. trademark, patent, and FOIA informa-tion, or should nationalistic restrictions apply?

AN ELECTRONIC BILL OF RIGHTS

The United States is unique in the amount of civil rights and protections given to its citizens. Even countries like Canada and the United Kingdom reserve the authority to violate what we would consider one of our most basic rights—freedom of speech—when they deem it appropriate. Thanks to the first Congress back in 1789, though, Americans enjoy more freedoms than any other citizenry on the planet. Today, we must ask ourselves what rights and privileges an individual has in Cyberspace.

Today those rights are nebulous at best. Polls taken over the last few years show that a majority of Americans feel that our rights have been slowly eroding as we increasingly share our lives with computers. Some of us worry about Big Brother, evolving with technology but regulated by pre-Information Age laws. Our challenge is in protecting our privacy from governmental intrusion.

A.E. Dick Howard, Professor of Law, echoes this sentiment.

It's now possible for government to snoop, pry, find out about people in a way that wasn't technologically feasible fifty years ago. It does raise the question of whether people want to live in a society in which they may suspect that every moment of what they're saying, what they're doing, what they're hearing—even their innermost thoughts—are somehow going to be tapped or be overheard.[8]

Anyone even peripherally involved with the Global Network strongly supports minimum interference with what they consider their basic Constitutional rights. "Give me Internet, or give me death," will be a rallying cry of cybernauts in the debates on the National Information Infrastructure. Cyber-civil disobedience has become a real possibility in the 1990s. Under the aegis of a so-called Constitution for Cyberspace, individual rights must be clearly spelled out, just as the first ten amendments did for the citizens of our fledgling nation. One of our first tasks is to comprehensively define the paradigm of individual rights in Cyberspace. Only then will we be able to establish a meaningful Electronic Bill of Rights. The framers of the Constitution had to come back for a second pass to establish and protect the rights of the individual citizen. Let's see if we can get it right the first time.

No subject is more complex—on land or in Cyberspace— then the First Amendment. We like to think that, as Americans, we have absolute freedom of speech, but I was corrected on that point by an Englishman. We cannot threaten the President (even in jest) without the Secret Service taking us downtown for a serious talk. Yell "I got a bomb" at an airport security checkpoint or "Fire!" in a crowded theater, and see how far freedom of speech gets you. Freedom of speech has some limitations that don't really disturb too many people; we don't take kindly to extortion, or threats of bodily harm, or inciting a riot. But on the other hand, we have to tolerate hate groups spewing racial slurs down the Main Streets of our towns. It's a compromise between censorship and total freedom to expression—whether we like what is being expressed or not.

So, as we move into Cyberspace we must decide on the limits—if any— of freedom of electronic speech. Is freedom of speech in Cyberspace absolute, or are there certain instances in which, for the good of society, a limited and specific form of censorship makes sense? It will be difficult to resist the temptation to make exceptions to the First Amendment, but each exception allowed will lead to a loss of freedom—a very valuable commodity in Cyberspace.

An issue very closely related to freedom of speech, and just as essential, is freedom of the press. When the National Information Infrastructure is complete, each of us will have the capability to be our own news service. Instant news from anywhere on the planet will be available to anyone with a multimedia PC or personal communications device. Will anybody and everybody be competitive with CNN? Not if news services think ahead and plan to take advantage of the technology. Instantly they will have 250,000,000 potential reporters who can bring new meaning to on-the-spot coverage. Someone will bring you "News From the Net," probably both by computer and on channel 451. ABC's "America's Funniest Home Videos" will go the way of eight-track tapes as dozens of new multimedia "Funniest Home Video" BBSs appear—and some enterprising chap figures out how to capitalize on it. With a veritable infinity of possible connections and geographically unlimited audiences, will media conglomerates be restricted to a limited number of cyberchannels? Alvin Toffler said, "If you control the media, you destroy democracy. If you don't control them, they will destroy it."[9]

Everyone is a potential publisher in the Information Age, and we all have two distinct methods from which to choose: passive publishing and active publishing. The difference is crucial when coming up with common sense solutions to the complexities of electronic freedom of speech and press. The active publisher transmits information from his electronic address to yours. Some of it may be solicited, such as electronic newsletters, and some of it will be unsolicited—electronic junk-mail. Unsolicited advertising is usually as unwelcome in our cyberspace as it is in our mailbox, partly because the receipt of those ads takes up valuable computer resources; some people call it an invasion of their space. Making a formal distinction is necessary to accommodate any guidelines we may wish to establish. Perhaps active publishers will face the same rules as paper-based publications, and passive publishers will have to adhere to some as yet undefined restrictions.

The passive publisher is unique to Cyberspace, although he resembles a library. The passive publisher compiles his information and stores it on his computers; for you to have a copy, you have to go get it. You might even have to enter a password or security code to get to in the door. Passive publishers may publish their information for free, to anyone who wants it, or they may charge a fee—by the minute or by the amount of information received. The distinction between passive and active publishing is essential when we try to decide what, if any, kind of censorship we might want to allow. If television's "seven dirty words" or the movie industry's letter rating system are going to be adopted in Cyberspace, should it make a difference whether the material in question was actively or passively published?

If Cyberspace were rated like the movies, a lot of the material on the network would rate at least an R, with copious amounts NC-17 and XXX material. Parents are understandably upset; though they may have HBO blocked at home, their children can still travel around the seedier corners of Cyberspace and get an education far more explicit than anything you'd see in Times Square. X-rated material, normally only available to those over eighteen, is plentiful on the Global Network. How can we control "adult" or contraband material in Cyberspace? What reasonable standard can we apply to determine if the transmission or storage of information meets contemporary legally enforced standards? Here, the question of active versus passive publishing again comes into play. If I am sent without request, obscene or illegal electronic materials (child pornography, stolen credit card numbers), should I be held liable for possession? Or is there a basis for prosecution only if I electronically solicit and receive it? How does one make a provable legal distinction?

Assuming some information is deemed illegal or contraband, how does one confiscate it? We will have to decide, for example, if the Fourth Amendment's concept of, "secure in house, papers, and effects" covers information that may be temporarily stored on a disk, or information in transit along the information highways. According to Ira Glasser, executive director of the American Civil Liberties Union, "Because of the Supreme Court rulings, the Fourth Amendment has become a relic of formalism: it protects the places where private information used to be, but not the places where it is today."[10]

How is search and seizure applied in Cyberspace? If a computer cop has cracked the password system on a BBS and found information contraband, was that a legal search and can he use what he found as the basis for court-approved warrants? Or would that information be referred to as "from a confidential source" and then used as the basis for future legal prosecutorial maneuvering? Can the police indiscriminately listen to the airwaves, eavesdrop upon data networks, or poke around Cyberspace in search of incriminating evidence, or should we draw a legal line delineating what is acceptable versus unacceptable behavior on the part of law enforcement?

How do we handle BBSs? Can the owners and operators of the boards be liable for their contents? Could Compuserve be held responsible if a plot to blow up the Washington Monument were stored within their databases and was planned by using their E-mail? Would a small, home-based BBS be judged by the same criteria? Or perhaps to allay legal culpability, electronic bulletin boards and electronic service providers will be expected to act as informants by scanning their contents or transmissions for illicit materials.

Freedom of speech in Cyberspace will also need to speak to the issue of malicious software. Portions of the computer community would like to make virus writing illegal. Others believe the First Amendment gives them the right to write any software they want. Both factions vehemently argue, but they tend to agree that the law has to step in if a virus or malicious software actually causes damage. What about the computer programmer who makes a mistake; could he be prosecuted if his error causes damage? Intent will ultimately have to be proved.

National security proponents want to have their say about freedom of speech, as well, and nowhere do they speak louder than when it comes to encryption. The NSA and their pals restrict the export of good cryptography, but the Global Network may require a new definition of "export." When Phil Zimmerman wrote PGP and placed it in Cyberspace, he gave the world community unlimited access to a sophisticated and powerful encryption and privacy program. Can the private publishing of software be considered a violation of export restrictions intended to control the flow of militarily sensitive devices to unfriendly foreign countries? This one example clearly demonstrates how intertwined national security and the rights of the individual, including the right to freedom of speech, have become. Today's complexities will be viewed with fondness in five years, unless we find the means to reconcile these myriad interests so we can all comfortably coexist in Cyberspace.

The fine art of spoofing presents other ethical and legal problems. It's easier to mask one's behavior by building fake electronic identification than it is for a teenager to acquire a fake driver's license to buy beer. If I am able to adopt your electronic identity, you could be in big trouble. I could send a message in your name to PRESIDENT@WHITEHOUSE.GOV that will guarantee you a visit by some very displeased federal agents. Using your name I could say anything I wanted to anyone I wanted.

We will also have to determine if eavesdropping with Van Eck devices upon information unintentionally broadcasting from our computers or communications equipment is legal. Should its use be relegated to law enforcement only? Will the ownership of HERF Guns be outlawed in a Cyberspace version of the Brady Bill? A National Information Policy should provide us with the answers, if we design the policy with clear goals in mind.

How will our Constitutional rights be affected as we are confronted with situations unique to Cyberspace? The problems mentioned above are only the tip of the iceberg—new issues will present themselves as technology develops. Any National Information Policy worth the name must provide the basis for an electronic Bill of Rights as we move into the next century.

DATA BANKING

In Cyberspace, you are guilty until proven innocent.

Personal credit is issued or denied based upon the contents of computer files. Tax liens are enforced based upon information supplied by a computer. If the phone company computer says you owe money, then you must be a deadbeat. You can't get on an airplane unless you have your name in the computer.

Regardless of claims to the contrary, we as individuals are treated as though the information stored within computers is sacrosanct and correct. It is incumbent upon *us* to prove the computers wrong if we disagree. They, the computers, are given the benefit of the doubt and assumed to be right. We humans are fallible and therefore must be wrong. Guilty until proven innocent.

I don't believe that the framers of the Constitution would have written such assumptions into their Bill of Rights, so, in our efforts, we must arrest the creeping control of computers over our lives. The original wording from the Fifth Amendment states that "No person shall be . . . deprived of life, liberty, or property without due process of law." How does this apply in Cyberspace, if at all? Americans fought to the death over principles like "innocent until proven guilty." In Cyberspace we have it all backward. The prevailing assumption is that the computer is right, and we're lying.

The problem is compounded by the fact that our personal data—correct or not—are shared by computers throughout the Global Network. Although an error is corrected in one computer, that same erroneous information will likely have already been spread to countless other computers. What means of recourse exist if the pictures of our digital selves are wrong? What can we do if we find an error? Until specific laws were written, we had little recourse with the credit reporting agencies, and to this day, it takes a resourceful, intelligent, and determined person—with plenty of time—to take on the credit bureaucracy. (What about our medical files? I've asked to see mine and been told "No, you can't have them. They're not yours.")

Americans must have the means to know and to challenge, if necessary, what is written and said about them in Cyberspace, especially those items that directly affect our lives. The courts say we have a right to face our accusers, but if our digital profile is wrong, who do we challenge? What mechanism do we have to rectify the errors? We can sue those who slander us, but isn't an inaccurate electronic portrayal of my credit or medical history defamation of character as well? What standards can we apply that will balance the right to conduct business with our right to electronic privacy?

One of the most fundamental questions we have to ask ourselves is, "To what degree do we want to provide individual privacy in the Information Age?" Are we going to permit technology to strip away the foundations of freedom upon which this country was founded, or do we have the collective wisdom and will to ask questions that have no simple answers:

Who owns your name? Do you have some control over how it is used? Should your name automatically be included in a database just because you may have had a transaction with a person or company? Can they or should they be allowed to sell your name, and information about you, without your approval? Maybe each time your name is sold or used, you should receive a royalty check.

When a purchase is made at the supermarket, should they be permitted to associate your name with those purchases, and then sell that information to other marketers in search of the perfect customer?

Banks, insurance companies, accounting firms, and hundreds of other companies maintain extensive files in their computers, detailing our every transaction. Should these companies have an obligation to protect that information, and if they fail to, should we have legal recourse? If our entire personal financial picture—good or bad—is exposed, should we be able to hold the offending organization liable, or will we just chalk up such occurrences as an unavoidable byproduct of life in Cyberspace? I hope we don't slough off these tough questions just because the answers aren't immediately evident, or because a special interest group objects to losing a source of income, or because we can't bring ourselves to shift our perceptions to the new paradigm of Cyberspace.

Perhaps the concept of mandated privacy has a place in our

Electronic Bill of Rights. Under this premise, information on individuals enjoys a special status, and its protection must meet certain ethical and legal guidelines. Corporate personnel information might have to be electronically segregated from the accounting or manufacturing systems; financial or medical records might have to meet higher security standards to ensure privacy. We might insist that all personal information is processed on computers immune to van Eck eavesdropping. All fax and electronic communications might be required to use encryption in order to protect the individual. Perhaps passwords alone will be considered a useless deterrent when personal privacy is the yardstick, and stronger identification methods will be demanded. If a violation results in an illegal electronic disclosure; who is liable and what penalties are appropriate?

The concept of "public records" has dramatically shifted since the paper-driven small-town governments of the eighteenth century. The premise behind public records was that any of us could walk down the dirt road to the wooden courthouse and get information on community activities. I doubt the Constitutional Convention would have permitted wholesale distribution and dissemination of "public records" by third parties for profit. We need to redefine what we mean by public records and how they are to be used in the twenty-first century.

Whether from public records or private databases, anyone with the desire can assemble a composite electronic picture of who and what we are. What is done with the acquired information is anyone's guess, since we are not protected by current law. A specially constructed judicial forum tailored to the peculiarities of Cyberspace might prove necessary. "Cyber-court" might have technically literate juries and judges, and offer a streamlined process to adjudicate cybercrimes. (How can a computer criminal be judged by a jury of his peers if none of the twelve members of the jury have ever touched a keyboard?) Cybercrimes could be prosecuted by degree. We can choose, if we like, to make distinctions between first

degree and third degree eavesdropping. Attempted interception would probably be no more significant than a misde-
meanor, but a HERF Gun hold-up is serious.

Sentencing might be fairly creative, too, because the courts
would want to weigh the severity of the crime against the
sophistication of execution and its purpose. Is it appropriate to
send computer hackers to jail? Should the keyboard criminal
be treated the same as a gun-in-your-face criminal? Is the
convicted industrial spy to be classed with the serial killer, or
does he belong in a category of his own? Should an attack
against the "economic national security interests" of the
United States be judged more harshly than domestic espionage
or strenuous hacking? There is simply no off-the-shelf answer.

We will need to establish the authenticity of information
used in a legal proceeding. If the police have confiscated
computer information to be used as evidence, how can we be
sure that the information hasn't been altered to strengthen
their case? Falsifying hard-copy documents or artifacts is
cumbersome and usually easy to detect, but altering electronic
data is a key-stroke away. In the not-too-distant future we may
find that an authenticity stamp, an electronic signature or a
nonrepudiation mechanism, must be placed on all digital
evidence.

For all of the freedom Cyberspace presents to law enforcement as an investigative tool, with it must come responsibility
and accountability. In the physical world, law enforcement is
often viewed as being above the law. Beating a suspect half to
death might be called "over-zealousness"; a SWAT team who
breaks down the wrong doors and assaults innocent people in
their home "acted with the best of intentions"; a street cop
who accidentally shoots and kills a bystander is "officially
reprimanded". These are excuses that merely attempt to place
law enforcement above the law, free from the legal reigns of
accountability. Cyberspace will offer renegade cops even more
opportunities for mischief.

On the international front, import and export policies are
going to be directly and forever impacted, as Cyberspace takes

on more importance. How will the domestic privacy rules of one country complement or conflict with those of another? Will some countries view state-sponsored unauthorized entry into their Cyberspace as an act of war? The cyberequivelent of the GATT talks will take place in the not-too-distant future; the need has already presented itself. But until we set our internal policies and decide how we wish to conduct ourselves globally, we have little to say as a nation about how others behave.

Of all the goals of a National Information Policy, none are more important in building understanding and cooperation than education. A National Information Policy must provide vehicles for awareness, education, and training so that we are all playing from the same rule book.

Assume you are driving into a town or small city for the first time. On the outskirts you see a sign that says:

> WELCOME TO OUR TOWN. TO SAVE MONEY, THERE ARE NO TRAFFIC LIGHTS, SIGNS, OR OTHER STREET MARKINGS. THE RULES OF THE ROAD ARE AVAILABLE FROM CITY HALL, THREE BLOCKS ON THE RIGHT. PLEASE FAMILIARIZE YOURSELF WITH THEM.

This is the state of the art in Cyberspace. The rules are few, and discovering them takes a concerted effort. We are bringing up a new generation who will use computers from the day they can sit at a keyboard, but too many adults let their kids wander the Global Network without any lessons about right and wrong. We teach our kids that it's wrong to steal from K-Mart, but not that it's just as wrong and illegal to copy software.

A National Information Policy must also prod the public and private educational systems into providing instruction not only in the use of computers but also in the ethos of Cyberspace. Learning how to push the buttons is a far cry from knowing whether pushing the button is pushing the bounds of acceptable behavior.

Corporations and the government must also provide education and awareness training to their employees. Employees should explicity know the difference between right and wrong, legal and illegal; they should understand what kinds of Cyberspace activities could jeopardize their companies, their jobs, or the security of their country. A National Information Policy should strongly encourage such support from every corner of industry, government, and the educational system.

A National Information Policy must provide an umbrella over our personal, business, and national lives in Cyberspace. Anything short of that will be shortchanging this country's destiny.

Not all fifty-five of the men who came to Philadelphia in 1787 signed the Constitution. Of the thirty-nine who did, some signed it reluctantly. Everybody made compromises—some more than others—but in the end, they created a work that has endured for thirteen generations. They knew that unless they found answers, there could be no country, certainly not the one they envisioned. Despite seemingly endless conflict, despite professional, political, and personal discord, they found strength in what united them, not what made them different. They stayed the course and they met the challenge.

Today, our challenge is similar: to set up housekeeping in Cyberspace before the guests arrive. We have to define our future role in the global village, not let those stronger and better prepared dictate our limitations or cause us to be victimized. Building a National Information Infrastructure without a National Information Policy is like trying to build a skyscraper without an architect, without blueprints, without engineers, without a foundation. That is a clearly backwards approach.

A National Information Policy shouldn't be thrown together piecemeal or be allowed to evolve from political, technical, or special-interest whims. It must be comprehensive and as all-inclusive as possible. Patchworking short-term answers leaves us in the position of eternally catching up when we should be leading. The opportunity is to define our destiny.

We have to come to agreement on the following fundamental questions before we can proceed:

- Do we recognize that information is the cornerstone of a knowledge-based society and its economy?
- Is the American economy a national security asset?
- Are we willing to behave and react accordingly?
- Do we want to level the playing field of international competitiveness?
- Do our citizens deserve electronic privacy such as might be established by an Electronic Bill of Rights?
- Do we want to lead the world into the twenty-first century rather than follow on the heels of others?

If our answer is yes, then let the debate begin!

19

The Future of Information Warfare

THE FUTURE IS PROBABLY THE MOST EXCITING PLACE I'll ever visit. Can't wait to get there.

Decades from now, the changes we have seen occur to our econotechnical society over the last few years will be viewed as baby steps into the Information Age. The old adage, today's magic is tomorrow's science, is a truism. We ain't seen nothing yet.

Information technology is going to change, and those changes will deeply affect every segment of society because, as we have seen, the technology has become personal; it creeps into our lives and we have adapted and will continue to adapt to its ever more powerful influence.

There is no reason to assume that each leap in technology will result in purely benign application. No matter what we do, as information technology evolves, there will always be some way to screw things up, either by accident or intentionally. Our job is to predict and minimize the damage. The future of Information Warfare will be largely determined by two factors:

1. New technology. As suggested, a National Information Policy should be able to accommodate as much future

354

information technology as it possibly can. We know where we are going technically, but there will always be surprises. The future as it appears in the minds' eyes of our gurus and in the research labs of the government and industry will be in our homes tomorrow. We should be prepared.

2. The world is getting wired. Europe and other knowledge-based economies will be following our lead and moving their peoples and cultures into Cyberspace. Information Warfare has largely been an Americocentric phenomenon, but just as we face risks, challenges, and opportunities, so do the countries of the European economic community.

Future Information Technologies

Popular science magazines, the science sections of the general press, and techie television shows peer into their crystal balls in an attempt to divine how life will be lived in five, ten, or fifty years. What we will do, however, is examine future technology from the Information Warrior's standpoint.

The most obvious evolution will be that computers and information systems will get smaller and smaller, faster and faster, more portable, and easier to use. If the current trends in development occur, computer systems ten years from now will be 128 times as powerful as they are today. A mainframe on a desk will be seen as quaint antiquity, and we will even have the power of several mainframes on our person or in our homes. Our personal communicators, or PDAs will have real-time interactive multi-media connections to anyone who has a similar device. Universal translators will spark a revolution in travel and tourism because language will no longer be a barrier.

The future digital storage capacity of computers will make 600 megabyte CD-ROMs look like a thimble of information. IBM has demonstrated the ability to manipulate single electrons and the development of quantum computers is not far behind. Memory density will increase by a factor of 1,000 in the foreseeable future where a nonvolatile memory device the size of a sugar cube could store a good portion of the Library of Congress. In a few years, 100 gigabytes (that's 100,000 megabytes) will be a bare bones necessity for any computer system worthy of the name.

And money. What about money? People who still use cash will do so for only the most pedestrian activities.

National databases will continue to be a sore spot to privacy activists and libertarians. The NCIC database will be expanded to include regional and local criminal databases, making it even more difficult for a lawbreaker to escape detection. The fears of a centralized medical database and centralized banking transactions database and insurance claim database make a National Information Policy all the more urgent—because they are coming.

Colleges and universities will be replaced with a higher educational database that provides personally tailored interactive instruction and testing. They will prove to be attractive playgrounds for those who think that modifying curriculum, morphing a professor during a lecture, or switching all classes to the Advanced Swahili channel is fun.

These are all fairly predictable outcomes from technological progress and the risks will be similar to those we face today. But as truly new technology comes about, do we have anything to worry about?

It has been suggested that the ultimate in personal identification is right around the corner. Instead of relying upon easily forged social security cards or medical-history smart cards; or instead of counting upon photographic identification where the face can be customized to match the picture; or rather than requiring voice identification which can be spoofed by the technically literate; why not use our unique DNA strings as the means of absolute identification. At birth, every member of society will have a DNA sample taken, and will be issued a DNA card. If there is a question of identity, scrape a little skin from under a fingernail, shake it up in a portable DNA analyzer and in less than two minutes, positive identification can be established.

But is this a good thing? With data bankers now looking for the ideal customers, or the IRS looking for likely tax cheats, or illegal money-laundering schemes, can DNA mating be far behind? The onging international genome project is mapping the gene structure of man—a mammoth scientific endeavor. We will know which genes carry which diseases, which genes suggest predilections for certain behavior and which others correspond to anticipated appearances for the newborn. If we are each DNAed at birth or DNAed to get a new social security card, not only does the National DNA Identification database know who we are, but also what we are. Insurance computers will ask the DNA computers if we should be insured or if an operation is likely to succeed; they will be able to build DNA-based actuarial tables—kind of takes the fun out of living. Employers will know our genetic dispositions, and future DNA engineers will be able to automatically pair up ideal mates for ideal offspring. The genetically impoverished may be subject to DNA discrimination. It's going to happen, unless we just say no.

Virtual Reality

All of this increased computing power will permit us to build more and more realistic artificial realities in which we may immerse ourselves for business, relaxation, recreation, and education. Mail order and mall stores will offer thousands of Virtual Reality software programs to run virtual reality computers in every home and office. Companies like Nintendo and Sega will own the gaming VR markets with home versions of *Star Trek*'s holodeck. New industries will develop interactive virtual realities for training, education, real-life simulations, an alternative to travel, and perhaps even for cyber-sex, also known as teledildonics.

But the question will be, how much virtual reality is too much? Excessive muscle stimulation can trigger temporary atrophy; what will stimulating all the senses in exaggerated simulations of stress due to the mind? It is said that multimedia accelerates learning; what are the limits of total mental stimulation for extended periods? Will there be a reality endorsed by the AMA and the FDA called Virtual Valium?

In other words, how much information is too much information? VR will likely become an escape vehicle for the economically depressed because it will be an affordable electronic drug. *Fantasy Island* is only a quarter away. Soap operas will never be the same. People addicted to virtual realities—whichever ones they choose—will seek treatment. Sudden religious revelations will increase; so will mental breakdowns. Too much forced virtual reality could be construed as abuse or torture. Virtual reality will cut down on cigarette smoking but can also be used for indoctrination. How much is too much? Will a software company be liable for murder if their virtual reality software overtaxes a weak heart or scares someone to death? Subliminal advertising was eliminated decades ago, but how about subliminal software?

Virtual reality is all about perception, and as technology improves ten or hundred fold, how will we be able to tell what is real and what is not real? Morphing—the visual blending technique made so popular by movies like *Terminator II*—makes the impossible come to life. Finely honed digital visual effects will be indistinguishable from reality. Manipulation of part-real and part-synthesized images will lend confusion to the veracity of multimedia communications. The news media receives a videotape of a massacre or disaster or momentous event. How do they know its real? Today a videotape is pretty good documentary evidence; in the future a Rodney King video might not be believed when image and data fabrication become as easy as using a word processor. Advanced technology covers up a fictional crime in just this way in Michael Crighton's *Rising Sun*.

"I'm from Missouri" will take on new meaning when a

digital identity can be assumed to be no more reliable than are the stories of Elvis sightings in supermarket tabloids. Ersatz information distribution takes on greater importance when we are genetically biased to the axiom, seeing is believing. Given the amount of data required, the security implications of multi-media are immense. Hidden information may be secreted within complex audio and video transmissions, making the modulation of a group of pixels or audio signals to contain secondary codes a favorite technique for future Information Warriors.

The question "Where are you?" will be answered at the push of a button. Global positioning satellites will know, to within a few feet, your exact location. Lives will be saved as personal digital assistants broadcast the location of lost or injured or kidnapped people. But what about employees? Will their every step be tracked to enhance security or to evaluate their performances for promotions? To the dismay of the unions who say the practice is an invasion of privacy, we already track the routes and times of trucks to increase shipping efficiency. Computers already know almost everything about us; will we also decide to add our every location to this list?

Nanomachines are tiny, tiny machines, so small, dozens of them would fit on the head of a pin. Nanoengineers come up with designs for nanomachines to do microminiature jobs. The medical community is exploring nanomachines that will be injected into the body to make repairs on a vein or a muscle or organ. The electronics industry envisions the day when nanomachines will construct other nanomachines to build superminiscule circuits. But ultimately software will drive these Lilliputian cogs and gears, and will be subject to the same deficiencies software suffers today. Nanomachines will be designed to enter environments hostile to humans, and be required to walk to work. Six-legged silicon bugs can already propel themselves today, but to what purposes can such devices be put by the imaginative Information Warrior? What a way to march unseen right into an adversary's electronic infrastructure and do damage at the microscopic level.

Futurists in the bioelectronic industry are looking at ways of merging conventional electronics with living systems to increase speed and density, and reduce power and heat in a new generation of information systems. Widespread commercial applications are not likely to come about for twenty years, but we inch towards such goals with pacemakers and remote triggered electrical stimulation for behavior control. This is about as personal as an information system can get. As information systems are embedded within the human body, the ethical and legal perplexities are only compounded. Will they make us think better and remember more? Or perhaps they will help postpone the aging process by optimizing the body's functions the way yogis alter theirs by slowing down their heartbeat? Or can they be used to manipulate and control the unwilling? Both.

While bio-chips are on the horizon, direct man–computer communications is here now. The military calls them SQUIDs, or Super Quantum Interference Devices. SQUIDs are placed on or near a subject's head to detect brainwave pattern activity. The SQUID and the subject learn from each other, so that when, say the pilot of a jet fighter thinks about arming and firing an air-to-air missile, it arms and fires. In the coming years SQUIDs will evolve and will be able to electronically read minds as Hollywood imagined in the Natalie Wood movie *Brainstorm*. When SQUIDs become reversible and can communicate thoughts and information right into the brain, that's when we really have to watch out.

In the future, the ultimate form of Information Warfare may prove to be the direct insertion of information into an adversary's brain from afar. Also known as psychic warfare, the CIA has been studying remote viewing and how it can be used to identify people or objects from the other side of the globe. Parapsychology, including extrasensory perception, far from a science, is seen by the military as a potential means of "soft kill" against enemy soldiers. In the future, will thoughts be read from a distance? Can minds be forced to act in one manner or another or even to shut down by remote devices targeted at specific individuals? We're already examining the possibilities in research on nonlethal weaponry.

But perhaps one of the greatest concerns that we should have is what happens when there are no more secrets. In the world of Information Warfare, that thought makes one group cringe in horror while another views it as the Holy Grail. The movie *Sneakers* proposed the ultimate hacking and intelligence device that made all encryption schemes worthless. Any information, encrypted or not, was no longer a secret.

When surveillance technology reaches the point at which defensive privacy and security mechanisms are no longer effective, there are no more secrets. The satellites will know where you are, what you are doing, what you were saying and to whom. When there are no more secrets, if someone wants to get the electronic goods on you, there will be nothing you can do about it. When there are no more secrets between competing companies, proprietary information will mean less and marketing successes will have to be based upon new criteria. Perhaps we will even see a return to the most ancient computer of all, pen and paper. When there are no more secrets between countries and governments, when we know their every thought and they know ours, the global contest for influence, power, and superiority will be fought on a playing field for which there is no historical precedent.

The World is getting wired. When there are no more secrets, all we will have left is our honor and our integrity.

The other inevitable step in the future of Information Warfare is the increasing globalization of Cyberspace. It is now being populated with the unconnected billions from every continent. Europe is the closest behind the United States in building information superhighways having proposed a $150 billion pan-European project that rivals or exceeds our own NII. As their economic union strengthens, their computing and telecommunications needs will increase. As world trade barriers collapse, extensive communications capabilities will permit even the smallest of companies to trade their wares across the world. When this occurs, European companies and governments will also become targets of Information Warriors.

Europe's history is dramatically different than that of America. Over the centuries their lands have seen seemingly endless political and religious conflicts. Unlike the U.S., each country has had to defend its own soil. History has shown that ethnocentricism and political diversity have been a constant breeding ground for conflict. Economic jealousy founded in accidents of history fuels competition between culturally, politically, and militarily unique nation-states. As the Eastern European countries and former Soviet republics enter the world community, the potential for discord will increase. Packed into a space slightly larger than the United States, over 600 million people occupying almost three dozen countries must peacefully coexist.

European countries have felt the influx of economic and political refugees from the Mideast and Africa, and some political groups are rebelling with stronger nationalistic stances. Many Third World countries view certain European countries with distrust and disdain for former colonialism and the perceived mistreatment of immigrants. These are the very people, who in time, might well act as Information Warriors on behalf of their respective native lands.

Although Information Warfare is somewhat Americocentric today, what holds true for one Information Age society also holds true for others. All will become attractive targets. We see some European cultures making the jump from the early stages of industrialism to the Information Age, bypassing the painful learning curves of behavior and survival in advanced industrial societies. In the search of longterm identity and success, the more technically primitive countries should be expected to make every possible attempt at making the greatest possible progress in the shortest possible time. Information Warfare provides one means to that end.

Europe has been the victim of terrorism for decades. While

technology and information systems have been targets of some terrorist groups, as Europe gets wired, the effect of large scale attacks will increase profoundly. England has already felt the effects. In the terrorist campaign the IRA wages against the British, bombs have been a principal weapon. But one set of bombings in London's financial district shattered windows for blocks and effectively shut down the stock exchange. Losses were estimated to be in the area of one billion dollars, which is a very effective use of a low-tech weapon against a high-tech infrastructure. Conjecture must lead one to the conclusion that direct systemic attacks against the British econotechnical infrastructure are not too distant a probability.

Because Europeans have been subject to terrorist attacks, and because wars have been fought on their home soil, as a people, they are more attuned to the need for security and the right to individual privacy. Seeing armed militia at major airports is not uncommon, and for good reason; security checkpoints make our airports look like an unguarded subway station. As Europe moves into Cyberspace, we can expect them to have a heightened sense of the risks that they face—much more so than Americans do—and be willing to impose the necessary controls as a matter of self-restraint.

The French, for example, are extremely restrictive about what kinds of encryption products are permitted within their borders, suggesting that their government wants to make domestic eavesdropping efforts as easy as possible. The Clipper Chip proposal met with nearly universal derision when we suggested that the same system might be used throughout Europe. The bottom line was, the U.S. was not going to dictate unilaterally a world-wide encryption scheme; especially one designed in a technical and political void by the National Security Agency. No way. One fear was that the U.S. had built in a back door that would allow our government to surreptitiously read international communications.

From a global standpoint, America's First Amendment and

Bill of Rights is a local ordinance. European law enforcement agencies do not have to follow the same rules that ours do. Citizens of many European countries much more accustomed to benevolent socialist policies tend to trust their governments and assume that they will not abuse their rights. On the other hand, child pornography is legal in some countries, but vocal criticism of some governments is subject to arbitrary censorship. The rules are different.

Moreover, Europeans have already voiced concern over the United States' lax handling of personal data. Threats have been voiced that unless protection of such data is enhanced to levels that meet European standards, multinational businesses will be reluctant to or prohibited from transporting data and information into American-based computer systems. That alone could be a blow to expanded trade and commercial activities across the Atlantic.

Nation-states will by necessity develop their own National Information Policies to further their own interests and to protect their assets and their citizens. Some countries have already implemented policies in the form of state-sponsored espionage, nationalistic electronic protectionism, and enhanced privacy rights for their peoples. But over time, conflicts over policies and practices in Cyberspace are bound to result, just as they do in all forms of business and political undertakings. As we develop our own National Information Policies, it will do us well to consult with our international trading partners to promote early discussions on global agreements.

In the United States, the National Security Agency sets the standards by which computer security is measured, and in Europe, a coalition of England, Germany, Belgium, and the Netherlands has established a corresponding set of criteria. The U.S., Canada, and Europe are attempting to find a compromise so that our respective pieces of Cyberspace can talk to each other in a manner that provides for the privacy and security each side desires. Japan has its own sets of specifications, and as we all meet in Cyberspace, a common global means of establishing privacy and security will be even more necessary.

As NAFTA has broken down trade barriers between the U.S., Canada, and Mexico, we should insure solidarity on the Global Network. Over the years GATT has helped to increase international trade from a few billion to trillions of dollars in annual trade. Similarly conceived cybertreaties will be constructed when we realize just how much sense they make.

If the United States, the countries of Europe, other knowledge-based societies, and emerging ones have their own best interests at heart, internationalizing Cyberspace should become a political priority.

Conscientious and creative use of the Global Network during the colonization of Cyberspace will be an economic windfall to the world's economy well into the twenty-first century. Cooperation and compromise will have to occur on many fronts by all participants. America can give our concepts of freedom of speech and freedom of the press to the global village. International standards of personal privacy might be based upon the European precedents to the ultimate benefit of new democratized societies. Surely we will find a common reason to outlaw industrial and economic espionage. Perhaps law enforcement agencies will be given the political ability to coordinate investigation and prosecution of computer crimes, espionage, and cybercrimes on the Global Network.

Given the vision and collective political wisdom of countries whose leaders have had to build entire economies from scratch, it is only a matter of time before they tackle the same issues we in the United States face today. The nations of Europe must look at their own migratory paths in the next decade as much as we should build our policies and practices based upon our national considerations.

In the coming years we will see amazing technology permeate every facet of our lives, some of which will be welcomed, some of which will be less well received, and some of which will be used against us. We will see personal empowerment increase in significance as technology and information become the media for influence. We will see the world shrink even more than it already has in the last two decades. This new virtual world we are building will be as real to our descendants as this physical one is to us.

The future is what we make it. Let's make it a good one.

Afterword:
Practical Proactive
Security and Privacy

EVEN A FEW defensive measures can reduce your chances of being victimized by an Information Warrior. Remember that the more barriers you raise—the harder you make their job—the greater the chance of them moving on and leaving you alone.

Defending the Digital You

With a little bit of effort, each of us can take a stand to protect our individual electronic privacy. As of today there is no absolute means to avoid prying eyes; public records are still legally available to anyone with an interest in the private details of your life. But you can at least make sure that what some of the computers say about you is accurate.

One of the first steps is to look into how the credit reporting bureaus portray your financial worthiness. The three big credit reporting agencies—TRW, Equifax, and Trans Union—are all required by the Fair Credit Reporting Act to provide you with a free copy of your own credit reports. Get them!

There are a number of books on the subject of how to interpret or repair what the credit reports say about you; they are worth the investment. Most cities now have credit repair businesses that claim to be able to fix your credit reports; be very, very careful. For every legitimate credit repair company, there are ten more than can actually cause more damage—and they charge husky fees for the opportunity. Fixing your own credit is difficult. The credit agencies have a firmly ensconced system that discourages complaints. They tend to act as though you are guilty until proven innocent, but you are protected by law and have very clear rights. Take advantage of those rights.

The first step is to write letters to TRW, Equifax, and Trans Union, requesting a copy of your report. Make sure you request your files from all three; they are competitors and sell their services to different banks and companies across the country. Just because you fix one credit report doesn't mean the others are fixed as well, so you have to go through the same steps with all three. Within about a month, you will receive copies of your credit reports. Each company uses a slightly different format. Analyze the reports and look for whatever discrepancies and errors you find. The next step is the tough one. You are going to have to prove the errors!

Write back to the credit agency and detail exactly why you think the credit report is wrong. Be as specific as possible. When I first went through this process a number of years ago I found on my report:

- Debts that were never mine. I challenged these, asking the companies claiming the debts for substantiation. If the credit agency receives no response from the company, the negative information is removed.
- Negatives from years and years ago. All negatives older than seven years (ten years for bankruptcies) can be deleted. Many companies don't keep active records for more than a couple of years, so if you dispute their

digital allegations, it may simply be too complicated for them to respond. In this case, you win, and the negative is pulled.

- Inaccurate late payments. These are almost impossible to defend if the credit issuer says you were late. When it's their word against yours, you lose. Substantiate as much as possible with canceled checks, old credit card statements, etc.

- A totally wrong accusation. Although I was able to back up my case with extensive documentation, the offending party still refused to admit their error. The credit agency changed my alleged debt from a negative to a neutral, but it was still there. I spent the better part of a year pressuring the credit agency to see the common sense of my argument that a satisfied debt that never *was* a debt still made me look like a deadbeat. Only after I spoke to people at the executive level did my credit report get fixed.

You may feel that the credit agency is not responding properly. Push them to live up to their legal responsibility. Perhaps the information they received by the credit grantor is wrong. Don't hesitate to go straight to the bank, the credit card company, or whomever you disagree with. They have the power and control to update your credit profile by directly reporting an error or resolution of a dispute to the credit reporting agency. Negotiate. Get everything in writing and double check with the credit agency that the error has been repaired.

Sometimes the negative is technically accurate, but there are mitigating circumstances. By law the credit bureaus have to let you add a one-hundred word explanation for each item on your report. Take advantage of your rights. When your credit file is pulled, at least your version of the story will be told as well.

If you don't get satisfaction from the front-line people at the credit agencies, insist on speaking to management. Supervisors are merely clerks with a title and they still don't have the authority to make things right. I asked one supervisor at Equifax, "Can't you see the problem here? It's just a matter of common sense." To which she replied, "We don't use any of that here." How right she was. It took a month to find a vice president authorized to use common sense.

Go to the bookstore, pick up a copy of a credit repair book, and then go for it. It will be frustrating. You might get writer's cramp and cauliflower ear, but you have to stick with it. In the end, it's the only mechanism you have to set this part of your digital profile right.

Make sure your medical files, which provide another detailed picture of your life and upon which insurance companies rely, are accurate. The Medical Information Bureau is the place to start. Privacy groups say that the MIB makes you jump through hoops to get results, but they too have to follow the Fair Credit Reporting Act.

FREEDOM OF INFORMATION ACT

The government keeps extensive records on each of us, and you have a legal right to see many of them. Under the Freedom Of Information Act, you can write to government agencies such as the FBI and request that they provide you with copies of your records and files. In the letter, identify yourself as completely as possible, including social security number, address, date and place of birth, and previous addresses. In the case of the FBI, mail your request to: FBI Headquarters, J. Edgar Hoover Building, Tenth and Pennsylvania Ave., Washington, D.C., 20535. Make sure that you also ask for any files which may be held by field offices in specific cities; you might want to send copies of your FOIA request to those offices as well. Make sure you have your letters notarized. You can also write to the CIA and the Justice Department in search of what the government has on you.

DATABASES

When you apply for credit, ask that your name be kept off mailing lists sold to other companies. In some cases you can make the request verbally; in others, a letter may be required. For your existing accounts, ask the company to delete your name from their marketed mailing lists. If enough companies comply, the volume of junk mail you receive will shrink by half in just a few months.

You can also have your name removed from direct marketing mailing lists. The Direct Marketing Association will tag your name with a "Don't Solicit" message—meaning no junk mail or junk phone calls—but that doesn't necessarily mean you will be erased from their computers.

Joe Apter, President of Telephonic Info, says that the best way to maintain privacy in the electronic world is to stay out of computers. Easier said than done. That would mean no checking accounts, no savings accounts, no credit cards, no charge accounts, no magazine subscriptions. If you drive, the DMV computer's got you; if you pay taxes, you're in the IRS and Social Security computers. Apter adds that today some banks will cooperate with their customers' desires to enhance their personal privacy. Ask your bank, Apter advises, if they will add a code to your account that will keep your files private from all except lawful governmental access.

Lastly, you can join any of the many personal privacy and advocacy groups dealing with these issues on both a social and political level. You can write your Congressperson expressing your concerns and how you think they should be dealt with. Let the White House know, too. These days, even the President has an E-mail address. Remember, you have a voice.

As we continue our migration into Cyberspace, the rules and laws will change, and it is our personal responsibility to stay on top of developments. Keep informed of your rights. Subscribing to a personal privacy journal will help you stay current on the latest developments. If enough people feel that their personal electronic privacy is important, if they make their voices heard by the political powers that be, and if the advocacy groups receive enough support, then there is room for hope that the current situation will improve. But it won't happen if we sit idly by, waiting for the other guy to take care of our problem.

A few more common sense steps will make it harder for you to become a victim:

- Guard your social security number with a vengeance—it may well be your most valuable piece of personal information. Even though it is often available from public sources, don't make a snoop's job any easier. If someone asks for it at a retail establishment, you don't have to give it to them! If someone calls and asks for your social security number—unless you know who it is, why they need it, and if they're entitled to know— don't give it out.
- Be careful of telephone scam artists who offer you a free prize if you'll just answer a few questions. The information they ask for can be exceedingly personal and you have no obligation to provide it.
- Check your bank statements carefully—especially ATM withdrawals—and make sure that no one can see you enter your PIN number at public bank machines.
- Be careful when using telephone credit cards. Shoulder surfers love nothing more than people who don't hide their access codes.
- Giving out credit card numbers on the phone should be done judiciously.
- Don't expect any privacy on the Internet unless you use encryption. PGP has become very popular for secure communications and several products are based upon it.
- The rule of thumb is, don't say anything on the telephone you wouldn't want seen in the newspaper. Encrypted mobile and home cellular phones will soon be priced for the mass market, if you want true privacy.

And watch out for those baby monitors: ours has picked up some great gossip from the neighbor's phones!
- Personal computer users should *always* practice safe computing.

Defending Against Class 2 Information Warfare

Corporate America has the ability to protect itself against the Information Warrior, if only it will take action. Many of the weaknesses that businesses experience are self-induced and easily fixed—any company can protect its information assets to reduce the chances of a successful attack and to minimize any damages.

When it comes to Information Warfare, there is no way to insure that a company is absolutely invulnerable to attack. Even the military, with all the money it spends on security efforts, has experienced severe breaches to its information infrastructure. The goal here is to build in enough proactive defenses to dissuade most, if not all, attacks.

Consider the conventional thief. Does he attempt to rob the house with the most security or the least? A house with no security is a much more inviting target than a house with a security system, a big dog, and locks on the windows. The bank with light security will be higher on the hit list than the bank with an armed guards and a vault that closes itself when a threat becomes apparent. So it goes with electronic information assets.

The first step any organization can take is to recognize that information is critical to its success. Some companies may decide at the board level that without adequate information asset protection, the company—or its board members—may be legally liable if they become a victim of Information Warfare. In a litigious society insufficient protection is inexcusable. Other companies may worry about a slump in customer confidence if customers' privacy or assets are compromised.

Whatever the motivation on the company's part, a high-level, management-mandated decision to protect information assets is the first step to corporate security in the Information Age. Any effort to protect information assets must include a corporate-wide policy which clearly spells out the importance of information—and access to that information—to the financial well-being of the company. Developing a corporate policy is a comprehensive effort requiring the mandate of top management, the support of middle management and the compliance of every employee. Without policy, there is no security.

Depending upon the organization, the actual methods for information asset protection will differ but all the following measures should be considered:

- Examine legal liabilities. A corporate counsel should provide input into the development of any security policy, since the law is constantly changing and many of the current legal cyberbattles are being fought on old legal footings. There is little case law in these areas, but examining the legal culpability of an organization is essential to determining its defensive postures.

- A comprehensive risk analysis should be performed by the audit and MIS departments on a regular basis. They should evaluate the risk to the company if computer systems fail, from either intentional or accidental forces. How long can the company function without computer services? What will the ultimate cost to the company be in real dollars? A risk analysis should examine everything from the effects of a virus attack to the severing of high speed communications.

- A Security Profile Analysis, an empirical technique I developed, examines the company's networks from the bad guys' perspective. An SPA looks at myriad components—from network systems to employee behavior—to determine how an Information Warrior might be able to penetrate your facility or compromise your information assets. This is a very enlightening exercise—most companies discover they don't know what they have or even what their networks look like.

- An employment screening process should be considered. It might be worth asking permission of your potential hires to examine their personal records—even though you could do so legally without their permission—to avoid falling into the trap of becoming a clandestine antipersonnel Information Warrior yourself. Any personnel databanking should be well thought out, have a specific purpose, be unbiased, and remain within the legal limits of state and federal statutes.
- Establish a clear set of ethical guidelines for your company and your employees. The rules by which you wish to operate your piece of Cyberspace should be understood by everyone under your company's aegis and will help set a positive example for your employees.
- Join several security organizations and participate in their annual conferences. Don't just send your technical staff: the highest level management should attend and become involved. The costs of attending these events are minimal and the opportunity they provide for social networking between companies and security practitioners is invaluable.
- Adhere to the copyright restrictions on all company software and applications. The penalties are severe for illicit copying of software, on both the personal and corporate level. The Software Publisher's Association is an excellent source for current policies and actions.
- Make security awareness, education, and training an ongoing part of all employee programs. The fundamentals of protecting company information should be covered and covered again through electronic and written communications, video support materials, and interactive computer training. Getting your employees on your side is worth every penny it costs.
- Examine how your garbage disposal is handled. Dumpster diving yields quick, inexpensive results for those on

the search for lazily discarded information. Shredders or a burn bag may be necessary to keep sensitive data truly private.

- Backup your system. Determine which files you can not live without and make sure that the hard disks on all PCs, networks, servers, and hosts are regularly backed up. If you don't, you will pay the price—sooner or later.
- Plan for natural disasters. Large companies use what are called Hot Sites. When the World Trade Center was bombed, floods raged through Chicago, Andrew leveled South Florida, and an earthquake struck San Francisco, major companies minimized their downtime by implementing their off-site disaster recovery plan.
- Plan for the Information Warrior. If your systems suddenly undergo attack from an unauthorized intruder, what should you do? If a breach of confidential information occurs, the company should have a plan to respond, including the possible notification of the authorities. Planned reactions can speed up recovery in the event of intentional system failures.
- Consider establishing a data classification system for your organization. Applying military-think with "unclassified," "secret," "top secret" and such isn't necessarily the way to go; there's an easier way. A company essentially has three kinds of information:

1. General company information—lists, designs, customers, and pricing.
2. Information on employees, including a fair amount of private information that cannot be legally released to third parties.
3. Information on customers and suppliers.

When considering information assets in this way, we can assign a degree of sensitivity to each category. Your information assets will fit into one of the following data sensitivity definitions:

1. Loss of this information can cause a near-fatal blow to the company. This information should be accessible to the fewest people possible.
2. Loss of this information would cause severe, though not irreparable, harm to the company. Take extra effort to protect it.
3. If this information gets out it would hurt, but no serious damage would occur.
4. This information is often already public and anyone's for the asking. Who cares?

Whatever system or definitions a company might choose, learning what information assets it controls, who uses them, and how well protected they are is an invaluable undertaking.

- Coordinate your physical and electronic security efforts. They are stronger working hand in hand and may be less expensive to implement. Teach guards that floppy disks are as valuable as calculators and computer hardware. For very sensitive facilities, consider installing bulk erasers into the entrance and exit paths to make sure no unauthorized electronic data goes in or out.
- Test the physical security of your plant from time to time.
- Test the electronic security of your systems with a penetration analysis. Security budgets often double after one of these!
- Take advantage of the wide variety of techical solutions for security problems covered in this book.

PRACTICE SAFE COMPUTING

- Using antiviral software to minimize the risk of infection. Using two or more competing software packages that utilize both scanning and heuristic or behavior-based detection mechanisms will greatly reduce the chances of being hit with a virus. Software applications such as word processing, databases, and graphics should only be permitted to enter a company's computers from specific places within the network. Users should be restricted from loading their own software into the networks without authorization.

- PC security software will help to control the importing and exporting of software applications and sensitive company data in and out of workstations. Determine what, if any, company data may go home with employees and effect the security controls to reflect those choices.

- Use access-control software and hardware controls to limit access to network resources or data. A clerk should not have access to financial or design information, but the CFO will need the ability to access accounting centers throughout the organization. With so much connectivity between offices, controlling access to vital corporate functions is an absolute must.

- Look for creeping modem growth—an ideal way to sneak company data out of your control. Use a demon dialer to identify any surreptitious modems that could be costing the company a fortune in lost information.

- Implement an audit system. Audit software monitors and records how employees or others are using information resources. If there is a compromise or attack, audit trails will help give a backwards road map to the source.

    Watch out, however, for overusing keystroke monitoring audits. Efficiency experts once considered using this method to see who got the most work done, but the Department of Justice strongly recommends against it as a possible invasion of privacy at the workplace. Let someone else be the test case.

    Be careful of E-mail monitoring. Some take the position that since the network is owned by the company, the company should be able to do anything it wants including reading personal employee E-mail. Others insist that employees must be given some degree of privacy at the workplace. Get legal advice before taking any steps.

The biggest conundrum is how to investigate the electronic files of an employee suspected of sabotage. Is breaking the law the only route to protecting your company? Make sure you document everything, and involve your lawyer.

- If you are connected as a host to the Internet, get a firewall. A firewall isolates you from the network, excepting those people you want admitted or want to let surf the 'net. This is one surefire way to protect the corporate jewels.

ENCRYPTION

- Encryption is the ultimate means of information asset protection. If properly implemented, encryption will foil almost any attack short of a nationally-sponsored effort. Encryption can be used to protect any information asset, whether stored on tape or disk, or while in transit on a communications link.

Generally, encryption should be seriously considered on all intercompany transmissions. If data are being sent across the Global Network, either by Internet or fax, encryption will thwart almost any attempt at illicit eavesdropping over telephone lines or leased lines. Even small companies (such as law firms that handle sensitive information) should seriously consider adding encryption to their communications.

Encrypting data on a local area network is becoming increasingly popular, as is encryption of data stored on hard disks, file servers, and bigger computers. Laptops are stolen at alarming rates, so adding encryption to them is an inexpensive alternative to losing sensitive information.

All international data and faxes with any sensitivity should be encrypted. Period. Assume all international voice communications to be public; someone is listening.

Picking an encryption method can be confusing, and there are as many opinions are there are choices. Many proprietary encryption algorithms claim both high strength and high performance, but selecting a reliable one is a difficult proposition. Keep in mind that stronger algorithms are slower in software and more expensive in hardware, while weaker algorithms can be implemented inexpensively with little impact on performance. DES is still a middle-of-the-road approach, but will be decertified by the government in 1997. Efforts are afoot to create a Triple-DES standard, which will save billions in replacing existing systems.

Whatever means of encryption is selected, make sure the key management system is both easy and strong. RSA's public key encryption has become an almost de facto standard because of its ease and its strength. Other key management schemes are automatic and require little or no human intervention. The Internet is embracing Phil Zimmerman's Pretty Good Privacy, or PGP. Dozens of products exist to solve just about any encryption problem you care to solve.

- Don't rely on passwords alone to protect the front door of your piece of Cyberspace. They are the weakest form of identification you can use. At a minimum, try to implement passphrases instead. The password KILA-BUNI or the PIN 1009188 is harder to remember than a longer passphrase such as "My blue dog is bright red," but passphrases are much harder to guess or discover. If you do use passwords and passphrases, changing them on a regular basis is one of the smartest things an individual or an organization can do. When someone leaves the company, make sure that one of the first things you do is delete his user ID and password from all systems.

  Stronger authentication is more expensive, but you get

what you pay for. Physical ID plus a password requires the user to identify him-or herself twice, once with something they know (the password) and once with something they own (a card or token). For high security applications consider using biometric identification based upon a fingerprint, a retinal scan, or facial infrared imaging.

- Display a warning screen that states company policy whenever someone signs onto a company computer. The Department of Justice has suggested wording that states that the use of company computers is restricted to those with specific approval, and all other access or use is prohibited. Using an on-screen warning for both onsite users and those calling in from a remote computer site puts the company in a better legal position if any breaches end up in court.
- *Never* use the default security specifications that come in products you buy and install. Always, always, always change them. The Information Warrior knows that most of us leave them in the factory default condition, making illicit entry or compromise all the easier.
- Configure security policy to your needs and coordinate those needs among all security people throughout the company. The mainframe people and the LAN people and the communications people all need to be working from the same play book.
- See if the internal phone system or PBX is connected to your computer networks. If it is, make sure that the security is strong. The boundary between phone fraud and computer crime is becoming increasingly fuzzy—in Cyberspace, everything connects to everything.

The bottom line is to put up enough barriers against the Information Warrior so that unless he is really after you, he'll go knocking on the next door and leave you alone. The casual 'net-surfing hacker looking to hone his skills on your MIPS will move on to his next victim if he runs up against tough security.

All these precautions can pay off in more ways than one. You may want to consider using the enhanced security of your company as a marketing tool. Depending upon the nature of a company's business, strong security or enhanced personal privacy guidelines can be attractive to potential customers.

This chapter offers only a small list of the security issues and options that an individual or company can consider when attempting to protect personal or institutional information assets. As technology improves for both sides in the Information Wars, and as the National Information Infrastructure grows and matures, the issues will change and relative risks will increase and decrease. Security and privacy issues will also change, and we must have a flexible enough mechanism and infrastructure to react rapidly to the risks and vulnerabilities.

Above all, we must remember that only when we as a country are successful in enacting a National Information Policy will our personal, professional, corporate, and national security needs be adequately and clearly addressed.

The resources section of this book provides a list of companies, publications, associations, government, and underground resources valuable to anyone interested in any facet of security and privacy. Some of these resources are for training and education, some are very technical, and some provide excellent product information. Everyone from the tenderfoot security beginner, to nontechnical management, to human resources, to the experienced professional should find resources that address their needs.

Perhaps the best resource of all is you. Use it wisely.

The Ten Commandments of Computer Ethics

1. Thou shalt not use a computer to harm other people.
2. Thou shalt not interfere with other people's computer work.
3. Thou shalt not snoop around in other people's computer files.
4. Thou shalt not use a computer to steal.
5. Thou shalt not use a computer to bear false witness.
6. Thou shalt not copy or use proprietary software for which you have not paid.
7. Thou shalt not use other people's computer resources without authorization or proper compensation.
8. Thou shalt not appropriate other people's intellectual output.
9. Thou shalt think about the social consequences of the program you are writing or the system you are designing.
10. Thou shalt always use a computer in ways that insure consideration and respect for your fellow human being.

SOURCE: Computer Ethics Institute, Washington, D.C.

Resources:
Who Ya Gonna Call?

Somewhere in this list you will find what you're looking for.

CREDIT REPORTING AGENCIES

Trans Union
Consumer Relations Center
208 South Market
Wichita, Kansas 67202
800-879-2674

TRW
National Consumer Assistance Center
PO Box 749029
Dallas, Texas 75374
800-392-1122

CBI Equifax Credit Information Services
PO Box 740256
Atlanta, Georgia 30374
800-879-4094

CBI Equifax Corporate
1501–1525 Winward Concourse
Alpharetta, Georgia 30202

You have clear rights under the Fair Credit Reporting Act. For credit repair, make sure you go to all three companies. Their computers don't talk to each other; they're competitors.

Medical Information Bureau
PO Box 105 Essex Station
Boston, Massachusetts 02112
617-426-3660

330 University Ave.
Toronto, Ontario
M5G 1R7, Canada
416-597-0590

Often used by data brokers, insurance companies, employers, and investigators, these agencies are also subject to the Fair Credit Reporting Act.

Privacy

Mail Preference Service
PO Box 3861
New York, New York 10163-3861

If you'd like your name removed from junk mail lists, write to these guys. Only those companies who are members of the Direct Marketing Association are said to honor your requests, thus the riff-raff of direct mail will still probably reach you.

Telephone Preference Service
PO Box 9014
Farmingdale, New York 11735-9014

As you might expect, this organization is supposed to tell direct marketing firms not to solicit you on the phone. The privacy groups say it helps to contact this group, but not a lot.

Security Organizations

National Computer Security Association
10 S. Courthouse Ave.
Carlisle, Pennsylvania 17013
717-258-1816

The NCSA covers the entire range of information security problems and offers training, education, conferences, and other resources for its members. The group works and lobbies in Washington to promote security related issues, and publishes a newsletter.

Computer Security Institute
600 Harrison St.
San Francisco, California 94107
415-905-2310

This fine organization has provided information security education for over twenty years. Their annual convention is the largest in the field.

Open Source Solutions
11005 Langton Arms Court
Oakton, Virginia 22124
703-242-1700

OSS, Inc., Robert Steele's nonprofit educational association, pursues cooperation between industry and government intelligence in the development of a National Knowledge Strategy. Its annual conferences are anything but conventional.

ISSA
401 N. Michigan Ave.
Chicago, Illinois 60611
312-644-6610

A national organization made up of regional groups in major cities, it holds monthly meetings and conferences.

MIS Training Institute
498 Concord St.
Farmingham, Massachussetts 01701
508-879-7999

Information management and security training and seminars.

Privacy International
666 Pennsylvania Ave.
Washington, D.C. 20003
202-544-9240

This is the U.S. office of a London-based nonprofit organization that concentrates on electronic privacy and data protection.

Skill Dynamics
One IBM Plaza
Chicago, Illinois 60611
800-IBM TEACH 426-8322

This subsidiary of IBM provides security training as well as courses on practical security implementation.

Computer Professionals for Social Responsibility
666 Pennsylvania Ave.
Washington, D.C. 20003
202-544-9240

The nonprofit CPSR has been at the forefront of the battle in using FOIA to get to the bottom of many government activities.

American Society for Industrial Security
1655 North Fort Meyer Drive
Arlington, Virginia 22209
703-522-5800

Physical surveillance and electronic security.

Open Systems Foundation, North America
11 Cambridge St.
Cambridge, Massachusetts 02142
617-621-8700

Open Systems Foundation, Europe
Excelsiorlaan, 32
1930 Zaventem
Belgium
011-32-27-239854

The OSF is a multinational effort involving major manufacturers who try to solve enterprise-wide security problems. They spawned DCE and DME.

Software Publishers Association
1730 M St. NW
Washington, D.C. 20036
202-452-1600

Sometimes affectionately called the "software police," the SPA monitors and assists in software copyright violations.

Electronic Frontier Foundation
666 Pennsylvania Ave.
Washington, D.C. 20003
202-544-9237

Founded by Mitch Kapor, the EFF depends and promotes freedom in Cyberspace.

Computer Ethics Institute
11 Dupont Circle NW
Washington, D.C. 20036
202-939-3707

What's right and what's wrong, morally speaking.

Security and Privacy Publications

Security Insider Report
11511 Pine St.
Seminole, Florida 34642
813-393-6600

Controversial and compelling monthly newsletter covering all aspects of information security, personal privacy, and related topics. Written by the author, Winn Schwartau.

Info Security News
498 Concord St.
Framingham, Massachusetts 01701
508-879-7999

The industry's primary bimonthly magazine for general information security topics. Heavy on product information. Great resource.

Telecom and Network Security Review
Telecommunications Advisors
722 SW 2nd Ave.
Portland, Oregon 97204
800-435-7878

The definitive source on telecommunications fraud and telabuse. They cover it all—from legal to technical to product solutions for PBXs, cellular, and most communications.

Security Technology News
1201 Seven Locks Road
Potomac, Maryland 20854
301-340-7788

Biweekly newsletter covering a wide range of security issues.

International Privacy Bulletin
666 Pennsylvania Ave.
Washington, D.C. 20003
202-544-9240

Quarterly put out by Privacy International.

Privacy Journal
PO Box 28577
Providence, Rhode Island 02908
401-274-7861

Up-to-date information on personal privacy and what we can do to protect it.

Virus Bulletin
21, The Quadrant
Abingdon Science Park
Abingdon, Oxfordshire
United Kingdom
OX14 3YS
011-44-235-555139

All you need to know about viruses.

Computers and Security
Mayfield House   562 Croydon Road
256 Banbury Road   Elmont, New York 11003
Oxford
United Kingdom
OX2 7DH
011-44-865-512242

Erudite and academic journal for advanced security practitioners.

The Computer Law and Security Report
Mayfield House   Elsevier Publications
256 Banbury Road   655 Avenue of the Americas
Oxford   New York, New York
United Kingdom   212-989-5800
OX2 7DH
011-44-865-512242

Down-to-earth British coverage of security and its ramifications on business and the law.

Security Book Catalog
Butterworth Heinemann
80 Montvale Ave.
Stoneham, Massachusetts 02180
800-366-2655

A wide assortment of books on information security.

Data Pro Research
600 Delran Parkway
Delran, New Jersey 08075
800-328-2772

The ultimate source book for security-related topics. Heavy on product analysis, applications, and product listings.

Security Management
1655 North Fort Myer Drive
Arlington, Virginia 22209
703-522-5800

A slick monthly with a lot of how-to security applications from the physical to the electronic.

PIN Magazine
PO Box 11018
Washington, D.C. 20008
301-652-9050

Personal Identification News focuses on means of identifying people: from passwords, to smart cards, to biometrics. Annual conference.

Cryptologia
17 Alfred Road West
Merrick, New York 11566
516-378-0263

Cryptography and more cryptography. Academic and technical.

Monitoring Times
PO Box 98
Brasstown, North Carolina 28902
704-837-9200

Everything about scanning the airwaves—radio and cellular.

Intelligence Solutions Newsletter
7035 Highway 6
Suite 120
Houston, Texas 77083
800-877-9138

Security issues from Jim Carter's unique perspective.

International Journal of Intelligence
PO Box 411
New York, New York 10021
212-737-7923

Occasionally has good articles about information security and intelligence concerns.

Ross Engineering Newsletter
44880 Falcon Place
Sterling, Virginia 22170
703-318-8600

Countersurveillance and bug detection.

EMC Technology
State Road 625
PO Box "D"
Gainesville, Virginia 22065
703-347-0030

These guys are the experts in electromagnetic control— from Tempest, to shielding, to HERF. Very technical.

Security Magazine
1350 E. Touhy
Des Plaines, Illinois 60018
708-635-8800

Heavy on physical security and video surveillance but also starting to cover information security.

Computer Security Digest
150 N. Main
Plymouth, Michigan 48170
313-459-8787

News briefs and topical odds-and-ends.

Full Disclosure
25819 W. Grass Lake Road
Antioch, Illinois 60002
708-395-6200

A strongly opinionated editorial view drives this irregularly published newsletter, but it is an interesting source of data.

Low Profile Newsletter
PO Box 84910
Phoenix, Arizona 85701
800-528-0559

Privacy-related issues and news.

Internet World
11 Ferry Lane West
Westport, Connecticut 06880
203-226-6967

'zine about living on the Internet. Great for beginners and 'net-surfers alike.

Wired
544 Second St.
San Francisco, California 94107
415-904-0660

A superflashy, high-gloss 'zine destined to become the upscale standard for cybernauts.

CCS
Counter Spy Shop
630 3rd Ave.
New York, New York 10017
212-557-3040

Countersurveillance and privacy-enhancement technologies and products for individuals and businesses.

Underground Resources

MAGAZINES

2600: The Hacker Quarterly
PO Box 99
Middle Island, New York 11953
516-751-2600

One of the hacker's bibles and the subject of debate on Capital Hill. Take a trip to the other side.

Gray Areas
P.O. Box 808
Bromall, Pennsylvania 19008-0808

Focuses on fringe topics of interest to hackers.

Mondo 2000
P.O. Box 10171
Berkeley, California 94709

The original cyberculture 'zine.

Hactic
Postbus 22953
1100 DL Amsterdam
The Netherlands
011-31-20-6001480
E-mail: heu@hacktic. nl

A leading international hacking magazine written in Dutch.

Axcess
4640 Cass St. #9309
San Diego, California 92169

Mondo-type style and information.

Black Ice
P.O. Box 1069
Brighton BN2 4YT
United Kingdom

Mondo-Wired style, with a British accent.

Boing Boing
11288 Ventura Blvd. #818
Studio City, California 91604

For do-it-yourself cyborgs.

FringeWare Review
P.O. Box 49921
Austin, Texas 78765

Articles with a cyberpunk bent, comes with a catalog of
FringeWare products.

Nuts & Volts
430 Princeland Court
Corona, California 91719

The best magazine available for hardware-oriented hackers.

Intertek
13 Daffodil Lane
San Carlos, California 94070

An informative and serious cyberpunk magazine.

Consumertronics
2011 Crescent Drive
PO Drawer 537
Alamogordo, New Mexico 88310
505-434-0234

How to rip off the electric company, computer phreaking, credit card scams, and assorted extremes of information.

American Eagle Publications
PO Box 41401
Tucson, Arizona 85717
602-888-4957

Highly controversial publications that discuss how to write computer viruses.

ELECTRONIC MAGAZINES

Phrack. The definitive hacker publication. For electronic copy by E-mail phrack@well.sf.ca.us and ask to be added to the list. For hard copy contact:

Phrack Magazine
603 W. 13th #1A-278
Austin, Texas 78701

Computer Underground Digest. A regularly published digest covering the computing underground. E-mail tk0ju2@ mvs.cso.niu.edu and ask to be added to the list.

HACKER MEETINGS

PumpCon. Philadelphia, October. Raided for two straight years. Information circulated on the 'net a few months prior.

SummerCon. The famous yearly private hacker gathering. Invitation only. Email summercon@stormking.com.

HoHoCon. Texas, December. The largest, wildest hacker con we've got. E-mail hohocon@zero.cypher.com.

DefCon. Las Vegas, Summer. More organized than the rest, but not quite as large . . . so far. E-mail dtangent@defcon.org

You owe it to yourself and your company to check these out. Outrageous, anarchistic, chock-full of information. See how the other side lives by getting one-on-one with the underground.

2600 Hacker Meetings.

First Friday of every month at the following locations. Everyone is invited—hackers to professionals to law enforcement to those without a clue.

2600 Enterprises
PO Box 99
Middle Island, New York 11953-0099
516-751-2600
E-mail 2600@well.sf.ca.us

| Ann Arbor, MI | Galleria on South University |
| Austin, TX | Northcross Mall Food Court |

Baton Rouge, LA	LSU Student Building, by Swensen's
Bloomington, MN	Mall of America Food Court
Boise, ID	Student Union at Boise State University
Boston, MA	Prudential Center Plaza, Terrace Food Court
Buffalo, NY	Eastern Hills Mall, near Food Court
Chicago, IL	Century Mall, in the 3rd Coast Cafe
Cincinnati, OH	City Center Mall, by Marshall Fields Lower Entrance
Danbury, CT	Danbury Fair Mall Food Court
Ft. Lauderdale, FL	West Hollywood Bowling Alley
Houston, TX	Galleria Mall, second story, overlooking skating rink
Kansas City, KS	Overland Park Mall Food Court
Los Angeles, CA	Union Station, inside main entrance by pay phones
Madison, WI	Union South, main level by pay phones
Memphis, TN	Hickory Ridge Mall Food Court
New York, NY	Citicorp Center Lobby, near pay phones
Philadelphia, PA	Thirtieth Street Amtrak Station, under stairwell seven sign
Pittsburgh, PA	Parkway Center Mall Food Court
Poughkeepsie, NY	South Hills Mall, near Food Court
Raleigh, NC	Crabtree Valley Mall Food Court
Rochester, NY	Marketplace Mall Food Court
St. Louis, MO	Galleria Food Court
San Francisco, CA	4 Embarcadero Plaza (inside)
Seattle, WA	Washington State Convention Center, first floor
Washington, DC	Pentagon City Mall Food Court
Granada, Spain	Kiwi Pub in Pedro Antonio de Alacore Street
London, England	Trocadero Shopping Center next to VR machines
Munich, Germany	Hauptbahnhof (Central Station), next to Burger King

2600 meetings are not terribly sinister and are often attended by "suit" security types. The most exciting was the one

at the Pentagon City Mall Food Court, when mall cops and the
Secret Service attempted to break up the meeting.

Movies

Tron. Disney's great virtual fantasy.

Prime Risk. The Federal Reserve under attack. Hard to find;
try late night television.

Wargames. Teens think it's just a game but the military
computer thinks World War III has begun.

Sneakers. Great entertainment. Pushes technology to the
limit.

The Lawnmower Man. The merger of man and Cyberspace.

U.S. Government Resources

National Institute of Standards and Technology
Computer Security Labs
Gaithersburg, Maryland 20899
301-975-2000

The NIST works closely with the NSA in information
security. Get their catalog of publications, including the Rain-
bow Series of computer security pamphlets. They have a free
BBS and newsletter, the *CSL Bulletin*. Their Computer Security Publications booklet is invaluable.

National Computer Security Center
9800 Savage Road
Fort Meade, Maryland 20755
301-859-4371

This relatively open section of the National Security Agency
sets security standards for the government. They evaluate and

certify computer and communications security products. Technical, exacting, and scholarly in nature, they also have an annual conference. Publishers of the *Orange Book* and *Red Book*, NCSC provides a BBS, Dockmaster, for qualified security folks.

Canadian Resources

Government Services Canada (GSC)
Industrial and Corporate Security Branch
Hull, Quebec
Canada

Supply and Services Canada
Industrial and Corporate Security Branch
Ottawa, Quebec
Canada

Royal Canadian Mounted Police (RCMP)
Ministry of Supply and Services Canada
Ottawa, Quebec
Canada

These organizations print a number of information security pamphlets. Write for their publications.

European Resources

British Embassy
3100 Massachusetts Ave. NW
Washington, D.C. 20008
202-462-1340

For up-to-date sources on British government security efforts. In the past they made the ITSEC (Information Technology Security Evaluation Criteria in coordination with Germany, Belgium and the Netherlands) available.

Computer Security Branch
Information Technology Division
Dept. of Trade and Industry
Room 847 Kingsdale House
66-74 Victoria St.
London SW1E 65W
United Kingdom

ITSEC and other government security documents.

Commission of the European Communities
Directorate-General XIII
Information Industries and Innovation
Directorate F
RACE Programme and Development of
Advanced Telematics Services
rue de la Loi 200
B-1049 Brussels
Belgium

Part of the ITSEC group.

European Computer Manufactures Association
114 Rue du Rhone
CH-1204 Geneva
Switzerland
011-41-22-735-3634

The ECMA is a standards group comprised of a wide range of security standards. Write for a catalog of their offerings.

Electronic Resources

The Global Network provides a wide range of services to those interested in these areas.

BULLETIN BOARDS

There's no way to make a complete and accurate list for these; they appear and disappear on a daily basis. Hacker boards aren't what they used to be—with the computer police busting hackers all over—but they're still worth a look-see. All you can do is ask around your local boards that are listed in regional computer magazines. After a while, you'll find that there are more than you can handle.

National Institute of Standards and Technology Bulletin Board
301-948-5717 (300, 1200, 2400 Baud)
301-948-5140 (9600 Baud)
Use N, 8, 1 or E, 7, 1

Government security publications, announcements news are available electronically. No charge.
The National Computer Security Association hosts security related discussions.

Computer Security BBS   303-962-9536
Computer Security Connection   703-756-8333
Compuserve: Type: GO NCSA
Comsec BBS 415-495-4642
Security issues discussed online.

The WELL in Sausalito, California is a particularly interesting site, with heated argument being the rule. Public access site with diverse discussion bases: WELL.com Whole Earth 'Lectronic Link.

The WELL
27 Gate Five Rd.
Sausalito, California 94965-1401
415-332-4335

Phantom.com Phantom Access Technologies. A more "hackerish" public access site, run by ex-LoD members.

Phantom Access Technologies, Inc.
175 Fifth Avenue, Suite 2614
New York, New York 10011
212-989-2418

THE PRESIDENT OF THE UNITED STATES

PRESIDENT@WHITEHOUSE.GOV
VICEPRESIDENT@WHITEHOUSE.GOV

Write to the White House from your computer. You probably won't get much of an answer, but they promise better response mechanisms in the future.

THE INTERNET

On the Internet, subscribe or ftp to:

comp.risks
alt.security
alt.security.index
bit.listserv.security
comp.security.announce
misc.security
sub.security

sura.security
de.comp.security
sb.security
comp.security.misc
alt.security.ripem
alt.security.keydist
alt.security.pgp
uwo.comp.security
comp.security.unix
alt.privacy
comp.society.privacy
comp.privacy
alt.privacy.anon-server
alt.privacy.clipper
alt.os.multics
alt.cellular
bit.listserv.virus-1
comp.virus
alt.dcom.telecom
comp.dcom.telecom
alt.hackers
alt.hackers.malicious
alt.hackers.cough.cough.cough
alt.cyberpunk
alt.2600
alt.society.cu-digest

If you can get to the IRC (Internet Relay Chat), look for the hacker discussion groups and join in or just listen. New groups pop up all the time and have their own forums on numerous large BBSs.

NET HANGOUTS FOR HACKERS

#hack   IRC channel with hacking discussions
#warez   IRC channel with software piracy discussions
#phreak   IRC channel with phone fraud discussions

NETWORK ARCHIVES

LOD Communications, a volumunous collection of BBS messages

from the great hacker BBSs of the past.

E-mail lodcom@mindvox.phantom.com for info.

LOD Communications
603 W. 13th #1A-278
Austin, Texas 78701

ftp.netsys.com
The official *Phrack* ftp site. /pub/phrack

ftp.eff.org

The CuD ftp site with hundreds of underground publications online. /pub/cud
The Hacker Chronicles. PC-compatible CD-ROM with thousands of underground files.

P-80 Systems
304-744-2253 (Data)

Forbidden Subjects. A PC-compatible CD-ROM with thousands of underground files.

Profit Press
824 E. Ft. Lowell Rd.
Tucson, Arizona 85719

SECURITY RELATED ELECTRONIC MAILING LISTS

Computer Emergency Response Team. A periodic mailing of security related problems affecting Internet users.
E-mail cert@cert.org and ask to be put on the list.

The Firewalls. The best mailing list going for issues dealing with securing systems through the implementation of system firewalls. E mail majordomo@greatcircle.com and in the body of the message write "SUBSCRIBE FIREWALLS."

The BugTraq. Serious security-related discussions pinpointing actual bugs, their invocations, and workarounds. E-mail bugtraq@crimelab.com and ask to be put on the list.

Getting Wired

Getting on the 'net is easy, and then it's just a matter of learning how to get around. Services are available for as little as $10 per month. Try these network service providers:

PSI
510 Huntmar Park Drive
Herndon, Virginia 22070
800-82PSI82
703-620-6651

Delphi
800-695-4005
For a free trial and test run on the Internet:
Dial by modem 1-800-365-4636, Press return once or twice.
At username enter JOINDELPHI.
At password enter NTW41

Complete details are given at registration.

Tyrell Corp.
8300 NE Underground Drive
Kansas City, Missouri 64161
800-989-7351
816-459-7584

For a great start on the 'net, get a copy of *The Internet Guide for New Users*, by Daniel Dern, published by McGraw Hill. 800-822-8158.

A series of books and pamphlets on the Internet are available from:

Meckler
11 Ferry Lane West
Westport, Connecticut 06880
203-226-6967

Artillery House
Artillery Row
London
United Kingdom
SW1P 1RT
011-44-71-976-0405

REPORTING COMPUTER CRIMES

If you are the victim of any kind of computer crime or other violation in Cyberspace, report it. Make sure your documentation is as complete as possible, and make sure you speak to people who also speak computerese. If there is any question about whom to report it to, call your local police department, your state police, or the FBI and ask for help. While most computer crimes do invite investigation, jurisdiction is sometimes confusing, so you may have to stick with it until you find the right group.

Computer Emergency Response Team, Coordination Center
Software Engineering Institute
Carnegie Mellon University
Pittsburgh, Pennsylvania 15213
412-268-7090
E-mail cert@cert.org

This federally-funded organization promotes security reactively and proactively. As a centralized repository for technical problems and system-wide breaches or attacks, especially on the Internet, they can generate a national response in minutes.

Federal Bureau of Investigation
National Computer Crime Squad
J. Edgar Hoover Building
10th and Pennsylvania Ave.
Washington, D.C., 20535.

For interstate crimes and those concerning federal interest computers, international incidents, and computer crimes in general. If in doubt, call them, and they'll point you in the right direction. Contact your local bureau office; their number is in the phone book.

U.S. Secret Service
Electronic Crimes Branch
1800 G St. Room 900
Washington, D.C. 20223
202-435-5850

For computer and communications crimes involving federal interest computers, presidential threats, counterfeiting, and general computer intrusions. Does not investigate classified security breaches. Coordinates with the FBI for jurisdiction and often the two agencies share cases.

For any computer crimes involving your communications equipment, or which were allegedly committed over the telephone lines, contact your local telephone company, regional Bell operating company, cellular carriers, long distance carrier or other service provider and make a formal complaint. If you don't know the number, call the operator and ask to be directed to the appropriate department. If you don't get satisfaction, be persistent. The security, fraud, or investigations unit should be able to help you.

Please, please, *please* report computer crimes.

You'll help the next guy if you do.

Footnotes

Introduction

1. Submitted testimony, Subcommittee on Technology and Competitiveness, Committee on Science, Space and Technology, U.S. House of Representatives. June 27, 1991.
2. *Computers at Risk: Safe Computing in the Information Age.* National Academy Press, 1991. p. 7.

Chapter 1

1. David Halberstam, *The Next Century*, Avon Books, 1992, p. 131.
2. *St. Petersburg Times*, September 6, 1992.
3. Steven Emerson, *The New York Times*, April 7, 1993.
4. Conversations with FBI Special Agent Jim Kallstrom, June 6, 1993.
5. *Time* Magazine, July 5, 1993, p. 24.
6. David Long, *Anatomy of Terrorism*, Free Press, 1990, p. 5.
7. *Ibid.*, p. 6.
8. Emerson, *The New York Times*.
9. "Terrorism in the USA," House Task Force on Terrorism and Unconventional Warfare report, January 25, 1991.

10. *Time* Magazine, July 5, 1993, p. 25.

11. Long, p. 7.

12. *Ibid.*, p. 11.

13. *New York Post*, July 2, 1992, page 1.

14. House Task Force on Terrorism and Unconventional Warfare, July 1, 1992.

15. *Ibid.*

16. *Ibid.*

17. "Narco Terrorism and the Syrian Connection," House Task Force on Terrorism and Unconventional Warfare report, August 23, 1991.

18. Long, p. 123.

19. *Ibid.*, p. 124.

20. Nixon, p. 25.

21. Count de Maranches and A. Andelman, *The Fourth World War*, Morrow, 1992, p. 266.

22. *Ibid.*, p. 24.

23. Lester Thurow, *Head to Head: The Coming Economic Battle Among Japan, Europe and America.* William Morrow and Co., 1992, p. 21.

24. *Wall Street Journal*, Sept. 24, 1993, p. R27.

25. *Ibid.*, p. 122.

26. Thurow, p. 23.

27. Peter Drucker, *Post Capitalist Society*, Harper Business, 1993, p. 96.

28. *Ibid.*, p. 4.

29. Nixon, p. 124.

30. Drucker, p. 8.

31. Shintaro Ishihara, *The Japan That Can Say No*, Simon and Schuster, 1991, p. 50.

32. Thurow, p. 31.

33. *Ibid.*, p. 31.

34. Nixon, p. 124.

35. Ronald Kessler, *Spy Vs. Spy*, Simon and Schuster, 1988, p. 12.

36. Nixon, p. 93.

37. Nixon, p. 94.

38. Nixon, p. 94.

39. John P. Mello, Jr., "Espionage! Are the Spooks Targeting Your Business?" *ISP News*, Volume 3 Number 5, September/October 1992.

Chapter 2

1. Quoted by David Ahl in a 1982 interview.
2. "Artificial Life Gets More Vivacious," *Wall Street Journal*, Dec. 23, 1992.
3. Douglas Hofstadter, *Godel, Escher, Bach*, Vintage Press, 1980, p. 26.
4. R. Buckminster Fuller, *Synergetics*, Macmillan Publishing, 1975, p. 3.
5. Winn Schwartau, *Terminal Compromise*, Inter. Pact Press, 1991.
6. Hudson Briefing Paper, February, 1992, Hudson Institute, Herman Kahn Center.
7. Joel Kurtzman, "The Death of Money," Simon and Schuster, 1993, p. 11.
8. *Ibid.*, p. 51.
9. *Ibid.*, p. 65.
10. *Ibid.*, p. 26.
11. *Ibid.*, p. 183.

Chapter 3

1. Daniel Boorstein, *The Discovers*, Random House, 1983, p. 500.
2. Bruce Sterling, *The Hacker Crackdown*, Bantam, 1992, p. 7.
3. *Ibid.*, p. 8.
4. *Wall Street Journal*, Dec. 23, 1992, p. B6.
5. Thomas P. Hughes, *American Genesis*, Viking, 1989, p. 450.
6. Charles A. Reich, *The Greening of America*, Bantam, 1971, p. 92.
7. Hughes, p. 452.
8. David Aheff, *Game Over*, Random House, 1993.
9. "Law and Disorder," *Virus Bulletin*, April 1993.
10. Kurtzman, p. 107.
11. *Ibid.*, p. 113.

Chapter 5

1. Leonard Lee, *The Day the Phones Stopped*, Donald I. Fine, Inc., 1991.

2. Tom Forester & Perry Morrison, "Computer Ethics", Basil Blackwell, Ltd. U.K., 1990.

3. Forester & Morrison p. 74.

4. Forester & Morrison p. 74.

5. Forester & Morrison p. 74.

6. Lee, p. 11.

7. Lee, p. 111.

8. Lee, p. 114.

9. Lucy Reilly, *Washington Technology News*, August 27, 1992.

10. Lee p. 96.

11. Reilly, *Washington Technology News*.

12. Forester & Morrison p. 78.

13. Hofstadter, p. 17.

14. Lee, p. 109.

15. Lee, p. 261.

16. National Computer Security Association.

17. Company prospectus, September 1992.

18. *Ibid.*

19. James Daly, *Computerworld*, March 1, 1993.

20. Mark Ludwig, *The Little Black Book of Computer Viruses*, American Eagle Publications.

21. *Ibid.*

22. *Ibid.* back cover.

23. Private Interview

24. *The New York Times*, January 5, 1994, C1.

25. "In House Hackers," *Wall Street Journal*, August 27, 1992.

26. Kurtzman, p. 181.

27. Kurtzman, p. 187.

28. Hansell, "Cash Machines Get Greedy," *The New York Times*, Feb 18, 1994.

29. Lee, p. 115.

30. Lee, p. 47.

Chapter 6

1. Private conversation with company officials.

2. Dave Powell, "Plugging the Leaks in Data Networks," *Networking Management*, May 1992.

3. Timothy Haight, "Network Security," *Network Computing*, July 1991. (From a diagram supplied by Enigma Logic, Concord, CA.)

4. Gary Anthes, *Computer World*, November 30, 1992.

5. Mark Kellner, *Federal Computer Week*, October 22, 1990.

6. Kevin Power, *Government Computer News*, August 3, 1992.

7. Terry Quindlen, *Government Computer News*, November 25, 1991.

8. *Hactic*, issue 16-17, 1992.

9. *Ibid.*

10. *Ibid.*, Quindlen.

11. Peter Lewis, "A Rise in Internet Break-Ins Sets off a Security Alarm," *The New York Times*, February 5, 1994; John Burgess, "Break-Ins Hit Huge Network of Computers," *The Washington Post*, February 4, 1994.

12. *Security Insider Report*, November 1992.

13. *2600 The Hacker Quarterly*, Summer 1992, Devil's Advocate.

14. *New York Times*, July 9, 1992.

15. Mike Alexander, *Computerworld*, May 14, 1990.

16. Presidential National Security Decision Directive-42.

17. *Monitoring Times*, July 1993

18. Radio Shack, Executive Offices Memorandum from Bernard S. Appel, November 11, 1987.

19. *The New York Times*, June 9, 1991.

20. *Monitoring Times*, September 1992.

23. *Radio Electronics*, October, 1986.

24. *Satellite Dealer*, June 1986.

25. *Ibid.*

26. *Ibid.*

27. *Ibid.*

28. *The State of Security in Cyberspace*, Stanford Research Institute, 1992.

Chapter 7

1. *ISP News*, October 1992.

2. *"Now! It Can Be Told,"* September 30, 1991.

3. Wim van Eck, "Electromagnetic Radiation from Video Display Units: An Eavesdropping Risk?" PTT Dr. Neher Laboratories, Leidschendam, Netherlands, April 16, 1985.

4. *Ibid.*

5. BBC Television, "High Tech Spies," produced by John Penycate.

6. Author interview with NSA-approved Tempest engineers, June 1991.

7. Author interviews with Bob Carp, November and December 1992.

8. "Beyond van Eck Phreaking," *Consumertronics*, 1988.

9. "CRT Spying: A Threat to Corporate Security?" *PC Week.*

10. Author interview with Don Delaney, November and December 1992.

11. Private conversations, May 1991.

12. "Eavesdropping on the Electromagnetic Emanations of Digital Equipment: The Laws of Canada, England and the United States," Christopher Seline, June 7, 1990. Privately distributed document.

13. Private conversations with NSA officials, November 1992, Washington, D.C.

14. David Johnston, "Tailed Cars and Tapped Telephones: How U.S. Drew Net on Spy Suspects," *The New York Times*, February 24, 1994.

Chapter 8

1. Lee Dembart, "Hide and Peek," *Reason*, November 1993.

2. NCSA White Paper on Encryption Export Control Policy in the United States, January 10, 1994.

3. Michael Weiner, "Efficient DES Key Search," Bell Northern Research, August 20, 1993.

4. NCSA Security Conference, June 10, 1993, Washington, D.C.

5. Edmund Andrews, "U.S. Plans to Push Computer Coding Police Can Read." *The New York Times*, February 5, 1994.

Chapter 10

1. Warren Getler, "Drug Warriors," *World Monitor*, October 1992, p. 38.

2. *Ibid.*, p. 39.

3. Thomas B. N. Ricks, "Nonlethal Arms: New Class of Weapons Could Incapacitate Foe Yet Limit Casualties—Military Sees Role for Lasers, Electromagnetic Pulses, Other High-Tech Tricks—Sticky Roads, Stalled Tanks," *Wall Street Journal*, January 4, 1993.

4. Neil Munro, "Microwave Weapon Stuns Iraqis," *Defense News*, April 15, 1992.

5. Ricks, *Wall Street Journal.*

6. "Space and Electronic Warfare, A Navy Policy Paper on a New Warfare Area," by LCDR M. S. Loescher, from the Office of Chief of Naval Operations.

7. Private conversations.

8. Lee, p. 56.

9. *Ibid.*, p. 179.

10. *Ibid.*, p. 182.

11. *EMC Technology*, February 1991.

12. E.R. Van Keuren, et al., *Utilization of High Power Microwave Sources in Electronic Sabotage and Terrorism*, Maxwell Labs, 1992.

13. E.R. Van Keuren, et al., *Implications of the High Power Microwave Weapon Threat in Electronic System Design*, Maxwell Labs, 1992.

14. Van Keuren, *Utilization*.

15. E.R. Van Keuren, "Electronic Terrorism and Sabotage: An Historical Perspective," draft paper, 1992.

16. James W. Rawles, "High Technology Terrorism," *Defense Electronics*, January 1990.

17. Private conversations with FAA contractors and suppliers.

18. Sharon Begley, et al., Newsweek, July 26, 1993. "Mystery Stories at 10,000 Feet."

19. *Ibid.*, Begley

20. Brochure from EMC.

Note: "Los Alamos Explosive RF Weapon Technology Development," by James W. Toeus, "A High Intensity Single Pulse Microwave Source for Defense Applications," by Michael Fazio, "Microwave Hardening Technology," by Drs. Robert Smith and Lamar Allen, and "Evaluation of a Miniaturized Coaxial Spark Gap," by Sergey Krimchanskey and Robert Garver were sources for much of Mr. Van Heuren's work.

Chapter 11

1. Conversation with Rop Gonggrijp, April 1992, Amsterdam, Netherlands.

2. Sterling, p. 68–70.

3. Indictment, U.S. District Court, Southern District of New York, received, July 9, 1992.

4. Court Exhibit #3, U.S. vs. Lee, received from U.S. Attorney, December 11, 1992.

5. "The Mad Hacker's Tea Party," *Now! It Can Be Told,* September 30, 1991.

6. Sterling, p. 313.

Chapter 12

1. A Paramount film, released in 1992.

2. Comments at the Computer Professionals for Social Responsibility Conference, June 7, 1993.

3. Jane Meinhardt, "Huge Credit Card Record Theft Uncovered," *St. Petersburg Times*, June 27, 1992.

4. William Carley, "In House Hackers," *Wall Street Journal*, August 27, 1992.

5. *Ibid.*, Forester & Morrison, p. 14.

6. *Ibid.*, Carley.

7. *Ibid.*, Carley.

8. *Information Week*, May 11, 1992.

9. Forester & Morrison page 9.

10. *Ibid.*, Carley.

11. Tim Rioche, "Two Charged With Computer Fraud in Credit Scam," *St. Petersburg Times*, January 26, 1993.

12. James Daly, "Notorious Hacker Charged with Stealing Fed Secrets," *Computerworld*, December 14, 1992.

13. "Computer Maker Blamed for Breakdown," *St. Petersburg Times*, April 30, 1993.

14. *Federal Computer Week*, January 13, 1992.

15. James Smith, "SSA Employees Accused of Selling Personal Data," *Government Computer News*, January 6, 1992.

16. *St. Petersburg Times*, November 13, 1992.

17. Mike Rothmiller and Ivan G. Goldman, *The L.A. Secret Police: Inside the LAPD Elite Spy Network*, Simon and Schuster, 1992, p. 166.

18. Anthony Kimery, "Big Brother Wants to Look Into Your Bank Account," WIRED, December 1993.

19. Jeffrey Rothfeder, *Privacy For Sale*, Simon and Schuster, 1992, p. 124.

20. *Ibid.*, p. 202.

21. *Security Insider Report*, May 1993.

22. *Information Week*, August 9, 1993.

23. Mark Barroso, "The Missing Files of Harry Lee Coe III," *Creative Loafing*, September 9, 1993.

24. John P. McPartlin, "GAO: FBI Breach Is An Inside Job," *Information Week*, August 9, 1993.

25. Rothfeder, p. 137.

26. Rothmiller and Goldman, p. 21.

27. *Ibid.*, p. 21

28. *Ibid.*, p. 112.

29. *Ibid.*, p. 79.

30. *Ibid.*, p. 111.

31. Rothfeder, p. 52.

32. *Ibid.*, p. 54.

33. Forester & Morrison, p. 9.

34. Forester & Morrison, p. 52.

35. Rothfeder, p. 123.

36. *Ibid.*, p. 175.

37. *Ibid.*, p. 112.

38. *Ibid.*, p. 80.

39. *Ibid.*, p. 95.

40. *St. Petersburg Times*, September 26, 1993.

41. "A Spy In the House of Hate," *Chic*, November 1993.

42. Rothfeder, p. 91.

43. Alvin and Heidi Toffler, *War and Anti-War*, Little, Brown and Co., 1993.

44. Rob Kelly, "Borland Releases Spy Case Details," *Information Week*, March 15, 1993.

45. Kevin Kelly, "There's Another Side to the Lopez Saga," *Business Week*, August 23, 1993.

46. Elizabeth Heichler, "Airline Hacking," *Computerworld*, January 18, 1993.

47. *Ibid.*

48. William Conley, "Global Spy Networks Eavesdrop on Projects of Petroleum Firms," *Wall Street Journal*, January 6, 1994.

Chapter 13

1. Closed door Congressional session. *Time*, July 19, 1993.

2. Winn Schwartau, "Fighting Terminal Terrorism," *Computerworld*, January 17, 1991.

3. John Gantz, "Meta-Virus Set to Unleash Plague on Windows 3.0 Users," *Infoworld*, April 1, 1991.

4. "Iraqi Virus Hoax," *Security Insider Report*, April, 1992.

6. "Now It Can Be Told," September 30, 1991.

7. Space and Electronic Warfare, Policy Paper developed by the Office of the Chief of Naval Operations, June 1992, p. 2.

8. *Ibid.*

9. RFP No: DAAL01-93-R-2900, Closing Date: 28 SEPTEMBER 92, U.S. Army LABCOM, Fort Monmouth, NY 07703-5601.

10. Toffler, p. 150.

Chapter 14

1. Judi Hassen, "Access to Medical Files Reform Issue," *USA Today*, July 27, 1993.

2. Editorial, "Full Disclosure," Summer 1992.
3. Telephonic Info promotional literature.
4. Mitch Betts, *Computerworld*, August 9, 1993.
5. *Computerworld*, August 9, 1993.
6. Private communications, September 20, 1993. (In early 1994, he won the first round of lawsuits.)

Chapter 15

1. Mello.
2. U.S. Dept. of State publication 10017, November 1992.
3. Hughes, p. 9.
4. Speech to the National Press Club, April 3, 1990.
5. *Washington Times*, February 9, 1992.
6. Peter Schweizer, *Friendly Spies*, Atlantic Monthly Press, 1993
7. *Ibid.*, p. 34.
8. *Ibid.*, p. 259.
9. *Ibid.*, p. 123.
10. Private interviews, September 1993.
11. Bill Gurtz, "French Spooks Scare Firms," *Washington Times*, February 9, 1992.
12. Schweizer, p. 96.
13. *Ibid.*, p. 97.
14. *Ibid.*, p. 98.
15. *Ibid.*, p. 110.
16. *Ibid.*, p. 290.
17. *Ibid.*, p. 5.
18. *Ibid.*, p. 17.
19. *Ibid.*, p. 158.
20. *Ibid.*, p. 161.
21. *Ibid.*, p. 163.
22. *Nashville Tennessean*, October 9, 1993, page E1.
23. Kurtzman, p. 107.
24. Kurtzman p. 107.
25. "Cold War Treachery Revealed," *Time*, July 5, 1993.
26. Schweizer, p. 256.

Chapter 16

1. "Space and Electronic Warfare," policy paper, Office of the Chief of Naval Operations, June 1992.
2. Count de Maranches, p. 204.

Chapter 17

1. Thurow, p. 257.

Chapter 18

1. Halberstam, p. 74.
2. Private letter to Samuel Kercheval from Monticello, July 12, 1816. Also inscribed on the wall of the Jefferson Memorial, Washington, D.C.
3. Drucker, p. 183.
4. Interview at the National Computer Security Association Conference, Washington, D.C., June 10, 1993.
5. Richard Heffernan and Dan Swartwood, "Trends in Competitive Intelligence," *Security Management*, January 1993, p. 70.
6. *U.S. News & World Report*, February 15, 1992.
7. Robert Steele, "ACCESS: Theory and Practice of Intelligence in the Age of Information," Proceedings of the Second International Symposium: National Security and National Competitiveness: Open Source Solutions. Sept. 17, 1993.
8. "Search and Seizure, the Supreme Court and the Police," video produced and sponsored by the National Endowment for the Humanities.
9. Speech at Second International Symposium: National Security and National Competitiveness: Open Source Solutions, Sept. 17, 1993.
10. *Wall Street Journal*, Letter to the Editor, January 24, 1993.
11. "Tomorrow Will Be Worse," Speech given at ISSS Expo, November 15, 1993.
12. Hughes, p. 452.

Index